Ronald R. Plew
Ryan K. Stephens

SAMS
Teach Yourself
SQL

in 24 Hours

SECOND EDITION

SAMS

201 West 103rd St., Indianapolis, Indiana, 46290 USA

Sams Teach Yourself SQL in 24 Hours, Second Edition

Copyright © 2000 by Sams Publishing

International Standard Book Number: 0-672-31899-7

Library of Congress Catalog Card Number: 99-068988

Printed in the United States of America

First Printing: March, 2000

03   02   01   5   4

Trademarks

Warning and Disclaimer

ASSOCIATE PUBLISHER
Michael Stephens

ACQUISITIONS EDITOR
Angela Kozlowski

DEVELOPMENT EDITOR
Tiffany Taylor

MANAGING EDITOR
Charlotte Clapp

PROJECT EDITOR
Christina Smith

COPY EDITOR
Pat Kinyon

INDEXER
Deborah Hittel

PROOFREADERS
Bob LaRoche
Tony Reitz

TECHNICAL EDITORS
Jason R. Wright
Dallas Releford

TEAM COORDINATOR
Pamalee Nelson

MEDIA DEVELOPER
Jason Haines

INTERIOR DESIGNER
Gary Adair

COVER DESIGNER
Aren Howell

COPYWRITER
Eric Borgert

PRODUCTION
Darin Crone
Steve Geiselman

Contents at a Glance

Contents

Dedication

This book is dedicated to my family: my wife, Linda; my mother, Betty; my children, Leslie, Nancy, Angela, and Wendy; my grandchildren, Andy, Ryan, Holly, Morgan, Schyler, Heather, Gavin, and Ragan; and my sons-in law, Jason and Dallas. Thanks for being patient with me during this busy time. Love all of you.

—Poppy

This book is dedicated to my son Daniel Thomas Stephens and to my nephews and nieces, Brandon, Jacob, Mariah, Harley, Tiffany, and little Tim.

—Ryan

Acknowledgments

Thanks to all the people in our lives that have been patient during our work on this project; mostly to our wives, Tina and Linda. Thanks also to the editorial staff at Sams for all of their hard work to make this edition better than the last. It has been a pleasure to work with each of you.

—Ryan and Ron

About the Authors

RONALD R. PLEW is vice president and CIO for Perpetual Technologies, Inc., in Indianapolis, Indiana. Ron is a Certified Oracle Professional, and his duties include Oracle database consulting and training. Ron is an adjunct professor at Indiana University-Purdue University in Indianapolis and Indiana University at Kokomo, where he teaches SQL and various database courses. He holds a Bachelor of Science degree in Business Management/Administration from Indiana Institute of Technology, Fort Wayne, Indiana. Ron also serves in the Indiana Army National Guard, where he is the programmer/analyst for the 433rd Personnel Detachment. Ron's hobbies include golf, chess, and collecting Indianapolis 500 racing memorabilia. He shares ownership of Plew's Indy 500 Museum with his brothers, Mark and Dennis; his sister, Arleen; and mother, Betty. Ron lives in Indianapolis with his wife Linda. Ron and Linda have four children and eight grandchildren with the ninth due in August, 2000.

RYAN STEPHENS is president and CEO for Perpetual Technologies, Inc., an Oracle training and consulting firm in Indianapolis, Indiana that is partnered with Oracle Corporation. He has specialized in Oracle databases and SQL for about 10 years, working as an Oracle programmer/analyst and Oracle Database Administrator. Ryan is a Certified Oracle Professional and is also an adjunct professor at Indiana University-Purdue University in Indianapolis and Indiana University at Kokomo, where he teaches SQL, PL/SQL, UNIX, Oracle Designer, Oracle Forms, and Oracle database administration. Ryan resides in Indianapolis with his wife Tina and his their Daniel.

Tell Us What You Think!

As the reader of this book, *you* are our most important critic and commentator. We value your opinion and want to know what we're doing right, what we could do better, what areas you'd like to see us publish in, and any other words of wisdom you're willing to pass our way.

As an Associate Publisher for Sams Publishing, I welcome your comments. You can email or write me directly to let me know what you did or didn't like about this book—as well as what we can do to make our books stronger.

Please note that I cannot help you with technical problems related to the topic of this book, and that due to the high volume of mail I receive, I might not be able to reply to every message.

When you write, please be sure to include this book's title and authors as well as your name and phone or fax number. I will carefully review your comments and share them with the authors and editors who worked on the book.

Email: feedback@samspublishing.com

Mail: Michael Stephens
         Associate Publisher
         Sams Publishing
         201 West 103rd Street
         Indianapolis, IN 46290 USA

Introduction

Who Should Read This Book?

Welcome to the world of relational databases and SQL! This book is written for those self-motivated individuals out there who would like to get an edge on relational database technology by learning the Structured Query Language—SQL. This book was written primarily for those with very little or no relative experience with relational database management systems using SQL. This book may also apply to those who have some experience with relational databases but need to learn how to navigate within the database, issue queries against the database, build database structures, manipulate data in the database, and more. This book was not geared toward individuals with significant relational database experience who have been using SQL on a regular basis.

What This Book Intends to Accomplish

This book was written for individuals with little or no experience using SQL or those who have used a relational database, but their tasks have been very limited within the realm of SQL. Keeping this thought in mind, it should be noted up front that this book is strictly a learning mechanism, and one in which we present the material from ground zero and provide examples and exercises with which to begin to apply the material covered. This book is not a reference and should not be relied on as a reference.

What We Added to This Edition

This edition contains the same content and format as the first edition. We have been through the entire book, searching for the little things that could be improved to produce a better edition. We have also added concepts and commands from the new SQL standard, SQL3, to bring this book up to date, making it more complete and applicable to today's SQL user.

What You Need

You may be wondering, what do I need to make this book work for me? Theoretically, you should be able to pick up this book, study the material for the current hour, study the examples, and either write out the exercises or run them on a relational database server. However, it would be to your benefit to have access to a relational database system to which to apply the material in each lesson. The relational database to which you have access is not a major factor, because SQL is the standard language for all relational databases. Some database systems that you can use include Oracle, Sybase, Informix, Microsoft SQL Server, Microsoft Access, and dBase.

Conventions Used in This Book

For the most part, we have tried to keep conventions in this book as simple as possible.

Many new terms are identified and are printed in italics.

In the listings, all code that you type in (Input) appears in **`boldface monospace`**. Output appears in standard `monospace`.

SQL code and keywords have been placed in uppercase for your convenience and general consistency. For example:

```
SELECT * FROM PRODUCTS_TBL;
```

```
PROD_ID    PROD_DESC                        COST
---------- -------------------------------- ----
11235      WITCHES COSTUME                  29.99
222        PLASTIC PUMPKIN 18 INCH          7.75
13         FALSE PARAFFIN TEETH             1.1
90         LIGHTED LANTERNS                 14.5
15         ASSORTED COSTUMES                10
9          CANDY CORN                       1.35
6          PUMPKIN CANDY                    1.45
87         PLASTIC SPIDERS                  1.05
119        ASSORTED MASKS                   4.95
```

```
9 rows selected.
```

The following special design features enhance the text:

There are syntax boxes to draw your attention to the syntax of the commands discussed during each hour.

```
SELECT [ ALL | * | DISTINCT COLUMN1, COLUMN2 ]
FROM TABLE [ , TABLE2 ];
```

Notes are provided to expand on the material covered in each hour of the book.

Warnings are provided to warn the reader about "disasters" that could occur and certain precautions that should be taken.

Tips are also given to supplement the material covered during appropriate hours of study.

ANSI SQL and Vendor Implementations

One thing that is difficult about writing a book like this on standard SQL is that although there is an ANSI standard for SQL, each database vendor has its own implementation of SQL. With each implementation come variations from the actual standard, enhancements to the standard, and even missing elements from the standard.

The expected question is, "Because there is an ANSI standard for SQL, what is so difficult about teaching standard SQL?" The answer to this question begins with the statement that ANSI SQL is just that, a standard. ANSI SQL is not an actual language. To teach you SQL, we had to come up with examples and exercises that involve using one or more implementations of SQL. Because each vendor has its own implementation with its own specifications for the language of SQL, these variations, if not handled properly in this book, could actually cause confusion concerning the syntax of various SQL commands. Therefore, we have tried to stay as close to the ANSI standard as possible, foremost discussing the ANSI standard and then showing examples from different implementations that are very close, if not the same, as the exact syntax that ANSI prescribes.

We have, however, accompanied examples of variations among implementations with notes for reminders and tips on what to watch out for. Just remember this—each implementation differs slightly from other implementations. The most important thing is that you understand the underlying concepts of SQL and its commands. Although slight variations do exist, SQL is basically the same across the board and is very portable from database to database, regardless of the particular implementation.

Understanding the Examples and Exercises

We have chosen to use Oracle for most of the examples in this book; however, we have also shown examples from Sybase, Microsoft SQL Server, and dBase. Oracle was used the most for various reasons, including Oracle's compliance with ANSI SQL, and the fact that Oracle is one of the most popular relational database products today.

As stated, there are some differences in the exact syntax among implementations of SQL. For example, if you attempt to execute some examples in this book, you may have to make minor modifications to fit the exact syntax of the implementation that you are using. We have tried to keep all of the examples compliant with the standard; however, we have intentionally shown you some examples that are not exactly compliant. The basic structure for all of the commands is the same. To learn SQL, you have to start with an implementation using practical examples. You should be able to emulate the database and examples used in this book without very much difficulty. Any adjustments that you may have to make to the examples in this book to fit your implementation exactly will only help you to better understand the syntax and features of your implementation.

The Sams Web site, www.samspublishing.com, contains all the source code from the chapters in this book, as well as the code needed to create the sample tables and insert data into the sample tables used in the book (also found in Appendixes D and E).

Good luck!

PART I

A SQL Concepts Overview

Hour

HOUR 1

Welcome to the World of SQL

Welcome to the world of SQL and the vast, growing database technologies of today's businesses all over the world. By reading this book, you have begun accepting the knowledge that will soon be required for survival in today's world of relational databases and data management. Unfortunately, because it is first necessary to provide the background of SQL and cover some preliminary concepts that you need to know, the majority of this hour is text in paragraph format. Bear with the book; this will be exciting, and the "boring stuff" in this hour definitely pays off.

The highlights of this hour include

- An introduction to and brief history of SQL
- An introduction to database management systems
- An overview of some basic terms and concepts
- An introduction to the database used in this book

SQL Definition and History

NEW TERM Every business has data, which requires some organized method or mechanism for maintaining the data. This mechanism is referred to as a *database management system* (*DBMS*). Database management systems have been around for years, many of which started out as flat-file systems on a mainframe. With today's technologies, the accepted use of database management systems has begun to flow in other directions, driven by the demands of growing businesses, increased volumes of corporate data, and of course, Internet technologies.

The modern wave of information management is primarily carried out through the use of a *relational database management system* (*RDBMS*), derived from the traditional DBMS. Relational databases and client/server technologies are typical combinations used by current businesses to successfully manage their data and stay competitive in their appropriate markets. The next few sections discuss the relational database and client/server technology to provide you with a stronger foundation of knowledge for the standard relational database language—SQL.

What Is SQL?

SQL, Structured Query Language, is the standard language used to communicate with a relational database. The prototype was originally developed by IBM using Dr. E.F. Codd's paper ("A Relational Model of Data for Large Shared Data Banks") as a model. In 1979, not long after IBM's prototype, the first SQL product, ORACLE, was released by Relational Software, Incorporated (it was later renamed Oracle Corporation). It is, today, one of the distinguished leaders in relational database technologies. SQL is pronounced either of two ways: as the letters S-Q-L, or as "sequel"; both pronunciations are acceptable.

If you travel to a foreign country, you may be required to know that country's language to get around. For example, you may have trouble ordering from a menu via your native tongue if the waiter speaks only his country's language. Look at a database as a foreign land in which you seek information. SQL is the language you use to express your needs to the database. Just as you would order a meal from a menu in another country, you can request specific information from within a database in the form of a query using SQL.

What Is ANSI SQL?

The American National Standards Institute (ANSI) is an organization that approves certain standards in many different industries. SQL has been deemed the standard language in relational database communication, originally approved in 1986 based on IBM's implementation. In 1987, the ANSI SQL standard was accepted as the international standard by the International Standards Organization (ISO). The standard was revised again in 1992 and was called SQL/92. The newest standard is now called SQL3 or is sometimes referred to as SQL/99.

The New Standard: SQL3

SQL3 has five interrelated documents and other documents may be added in the near future. The five interrelated parts are as follows:

- *Part 1—SQL/Framework*—Specifies the general requirements for conformance and defines the fundamental concepts of SQL.
- *Part 2—SQL/Foundation*—Defines the syntax and operations of SQL.
- *Part 3—SQL/Call-Level Interface*—Defines the interface for application programming to SQL.
- *Part 4—SQL/Persistent Stored Modules*—Defines the control structures that then define SQL routines. Part 4 also defines the modules that contain SQL routines.
- *Part 5—SQL/Host Language Bindings*—Defines how to embed SQL statements in application programs that are written in a standard programming language.

The new ANSI standard (SQL3) has two levels of minimal conference that a DBMS may claim: Core SQL Support and Enhanced SQL Support.

NEW TERM   *ANSI* stands for *American National Standards Institute*, an organization that is responsible for devising standards for various products and concepts.

With any standard come numerous, obvious advantages, as well as some disadvantages. Foremost, a standard steers vendors in the appropriate industry direction for development; in the case of SQL, providing a basic skeleton of necessary fundamentals which, as an end result, allows consistency between various implementations and better serves increased portability (not only for database programs, but databases in general and individuals who manage databases).

Some may argue that a standard is not so good, limiting the flexibility and possible capabilities of a particular implementation. However, most vendors who comply with the standard have added product-specific enhancements to standard SQL to fill in these gaps.

A standard is good, considering the advantages and disadvantages. The expected standard demands features that should be available in any complete SQL implementation and outlines basic concepts that not only force consistency between all competitive SQL implementations, but increase the value of a SQL programmer or relational database user in today's database market.

NEW TERM   A *SQL implementation* is a particular vendor's SQL product.

What Is a Database?

In very simple terms, a *database* is a collection of data. Some like to think of a database as an organized mechanism that has the capability of storing information, through which a user can retrieve stored information in an effective and efficient manner.

People use databases every day without realizing it. A phone book is a database. The data contained consists of individuals' names, addresses, and telephone numbers. The listings are alphabetized or indexed, which allows the user to reference a particular local resident with ease. Ultimately, this data is stored in a database somewhere on a computer. After all, each page of a phone book is not manually typed each year a new edition is released.

The database has to be maintained. As people move to different cities or states, entries may have to be added or removed from the phone book. Likewise, entries will have to be modified for people changing names, addresses, or telephone numbers, and so on. Figure 1.1 illustrates a simple database.

FIGURE 1.1
The database.

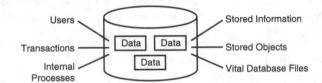

An Introduction to the Relational Database

NEW TERM   A *relational database* is a database divided into logical units called *tables*, where tables are related to one another within the database. A relational database allows data to be broken down into logical, smaller, more manageable units, allowing for easier maintenance and providing more optimal database performance according to the level of organization. In Figure 1.2, you can see that tables are related to one another through a common key in a relational database.

FIGURE 1.2
The relational database.

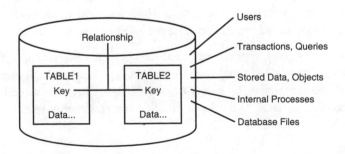

Again, tables are related in a relational database, allowing adequate data to be retrieved in a single query (although the desired data may exist in more than one table). By having common *keys*, or *fields*, among relational database tables, data from multiple tables can be joined to form one large result set. As you venture deeper into this book, you see more of a relational database's advantages, including overall performance and easy data access.

NEW TERM A *relational database* is a database composed of related objects, primarily tables. A *table* is the most basic means of storage for data in a database.

An Introduction to Client/Server Technology

In the past, the computer industry was predominately ruled by mainframe computers; large, powerful systems capable of high storage capacity and high data processing capabilities. Users communicated with the mainframe through dumb terminals—terminals that did not think on their own, but relied solely on the mainframe's CPU, storage, and memory. Each terminal had a data line attached to the mainframe. The mainframe environment definitely served its purpose, and does today in many businesses, but a greater technology was soon to be introduced: the client/server model.

NEW TERM In the *client/server system*, the main computer, called the *server*, is accessible from a network—typically a local area network (LAN) or a wide area network (WAN). The server is normally accessed by personal computers (PCs) or by other servers, instead of dumb terminals. Each PC, called a *client*, is provided access to the network, allowing communication between the client and the server, thus explaining the name client/server. The main difference between client/server and mainframe environments is that the user's PC in a client/server environment is capable of thinking on its own, capable of running its own processes using its own CPU and memory, but readily accessible to a server computer through a network. In most cases, a client/server system is much more flexible for today's overall business needs and is much preferred.

Relational database systems reside on both mainframes and on client/server platforms, Although a client/server system is preferred, the continued use of mainframes can certainly be justified according to a company's needs. A high percentage of companies have recently been leaving their mainframe systems behind and moving their data to a client/server system, motivated by the urge to stay current with new technologies, provide more flexibility to better suit their business needs, and make old systems Year 2000-compliant.

The switch to a client/server system has proven beneficial for some companies, while others have failed in the client/server implementation and have, as a result, wasted millions of dollars, causing some to return to their mainframes; others still hesitate to make a change. The lack of appropriate expertise—a result of new technology combined with a lack of training—is the main reason for failed implementations. Nevertheless, an understanding of the client/server model is imperative with the rising (and sometimes unreasonable) demands placed on today's businesses as well as the development of Internet technologies and network computing. Figure 1.3 illustrates the concept of client/server technology.

FIGURE 1.3
The client/server model.

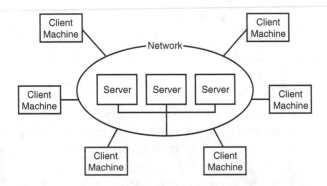

Some Popular Relational Database Vendors

Some of the most predominant database vendors include Oracle, Microsoft, Informix, Sybase, and IBM. Although there are many more, this list includes names that you may have recognized on the bookshelf, in the newspaper, magazines, the stock market, or on the World Wide Web.

Differences Between Implementations

As each individual in this world is unique in both features and nature, so is each vendor-specific implementation of SQL. A database server is a product, like any other product on the market, manufactured by a widespread number of vendors. It is to the benefit of the vendor to ensure that its implementation is compliant with the current ANSI standard for portability and user convenience. For instance, if a company is migrating from one database server to another, it would be rather discouraging for the database users to have to learn another language to maintain functionality with the new system.

With each vendor's SQL implementation, however, you find that there are enhancements that serve the purpose for each database server. These enhancements, or *extensions*, are additional commands and options that are simply a bonus to the standard SQL package and available with a specific implementation.

SQL Sessions

NEW TERM An *SQL session* is an occurrence of a user interacting with a relational database through the use of SQL commands. When a user initially connects to the database, a session is established. Within the scope of an SQL session, valid SQL commands can be entered to query the database, manipulate data in the database, and define database structures, such as tables.

CONNECT

When a user connects to a database, the SQL session is initialized. The CONNECT command is used to establish a database connection. With the CONNECT command, you can either invoke a connection or change connections to the database. For example, if you are connected as USER1, you can use the CONNECT command to connect to the database as USER2. When this happens, the SQL session for USER1 is implicitly disconnected.

SYNTAX

```
CONNECT user@database
```

When you attempt to connect to a database, you are automatically prompted for a password that corresponds with your current username.

DISCONNECT

When a user disconnects from a database, the SQL session is terminated. The DISCON-NECT command is used to disconnect a user from the database. When you disconnect from the database, you may still appear to be in the tool that allows you to communicate with the database, but you have lost your connection. When you use EXIT to leave the database, your SQL session is terminated and the tool that you are using to access the database is normally closed.

SYNTAX

```
CONNECT
```

Types of SQL Commands

The following sections discuss the basic categories of commands used in SQL to perform various functions. These functions include building database objects, manipulating objects, populating database tables with data, updating existing data in tables, deleting data, performing database queries, controlling database access, and overall database administration.

The main categories are

- DDL (Data Definition Language)
- DML(Data Manipulation Language)

- DQL (Data Query Language)
- DCL (Data Control Language)
- Data administration commands
- Transactional control commands

Defining Database Structures (DDL)

 Data Definition Language, DDL, is the part of SQL that allows a database user to create and restructure database objects, such as the creation or the deletion of a table.

The main DDL commands discussed during following hours include the following:

```
CREATE TABLE

ALTER TABLE

DROP TABLE

CREATE INDEX

ALTER INDEX

DROP INDEX
```

These commands are discussed in detail during Hour 3, "Managing Database Objects," and Hour 17, "Improving Database Performance."

Manipulating Data (DML)

NEW TERM *Data Manipulation Language, DML,* is the part of SQL used to manipulate data within objects of a relational database.

There are three basic DML commands:

```
INSERT

UPDATE

DELETE
```

These commands are discussed in detail during Hour 5, "Manipulating Data."

Selecting Data (DQL)

Though comprised of only one command, Data Query Language (DQL) is the most concentrated focus of SQL for a relational database user. The command is as follows:

```
SELECT
```

This command, accompanied by many options and clauses, is used to compose queries against a relational database. Queries, from simple to complex, from vague to specific, can be easily created. The SELECT command is discussed in exhilarating detail during Hours 7 through 16.

NEW TERM A *query* is an inquiry to the database for information.

Data Control Language (DCL)

Data control commands in SQL allow you to control access to data within the database. These DCL commands are normally used to create objects related to user access and also control the distribution of privileges among users. Some data control commands are as follows:

```
ALTER PASSWORD

GRANT

REVOKE

CREATE SYNONYM
```

You find that these commands are often grouped with other commands and may appear in a number of different chapters.

Data Administration Commands

Data administration commands allow the user to perform audits and perform analyses on operations within the database. They can also be used to help analyze system performance. Two general data administration commands are as follows:

```
START AUDIT

STOP AUDIT
```

NEW TERM Do not get data administration confused with database administration. *Database administration* is the overall administration of a database, which envelops the use of all levels of commands.

Transactional Control Commands

In addition to the previously introduced categories of commands, there are commands that allow the user to manage database transactions.

- COMMIT   Used to save database transactions
- ROLLBACK   Used to undo database transactions
- SAVEPOINT   Creates points within groups of transactions in which to ROLLBACK
- SET TRANSACTION   Places a name on a transaction

Transactional commands are discussed extensively during Hour 6, "Managing Database Transactions."

An Introduction to the Database Used in This Book

Before continuing with your journey through SQL fundamentals, the next step is introducing the tables and data that you use throughout the course of instruction for the next 23 one-hour lessons. The next two sections provide an overview of the specific tables (the database) being used, their relationship to one another, their structure, and examples of the data contained.

Diagram of the Tables in This Book

Figure 1.4 reveals the relationship between the tables that you use for examples, quiz questions, and exercises in this book. Each table is identified by the table name as well as each residing field in the table. Follow the mapping lines to compare the specific tables' relationship through a common field, in most cases referred to as the primary key (discussed in Hour 3, "Managing Database Objects").

Table-Naming Standards

Table-naming standards, as well as any standard within a business, is critical to maintain control. After studying the tables and data in the previous sections, you probably noticed that each table's suffix is _TBL. This is a naming standard selected for use, such as what's been used at various client sites. The _TBL simply tells you that the object is a table; there are many different types of objects in a relational database. For example, you will see that the suffix _INX is used to identify indexes on tables in later hours. Naming standards exist almost exclusively for overall organization and assist immensely in the administration of any relational database. Remember, the use of a suffix is not mandatory when naming database objects.

Figure 1.4

Table relationships for this book.

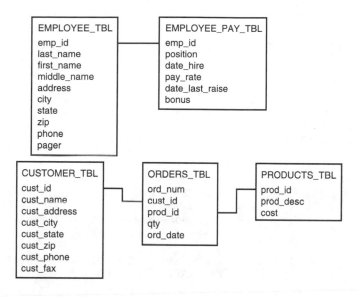

You should not only adhere to the object naming syntax of any SQL implementation, but also follow local business rules and make names descriptive and related to the data groupings for the company.

A Look at the Data

This section offers a picture of the data contained in each one of the tables used in this book. Take a few minutes and study the data, the variations, and the relationships between the tables and the data itself. Notice that some fields may not require data, which is specified when each table is created in the database.

EMPLOYEE_TBL

EMP_ID	LAST_NAM	FIRST_NAM	ADDRESS	CITY	ST	ZIP	PHONE
311549902	STEPHENS	TINA	D RR 3 BOX 17A	GREENWOOD	IN	47890	3178784465
442346889	PLEW	LINDA	C 3301 BEACON	INDIANAPOLIS	IN	46224	3172978990
213764555	GLASS	BRANDON	S 1710 MAIN ST	WHITELAND	IN	47885	3178984321
313782439	GLASS	JACOB	3789 RIVER BLVD	INDIANAPOLIS	IN	45734	3175457676
220984332	WALLACE	MARIAH	7889 KEYSTONE	INDIANAPOLIS	IN	46741	3173325986
443679012	SPURGEON	TIFFANY	5 GEORGE COURT	INDIANAPOLIS	IN	46234	3175679007

```
EMPLOYEE_PAY_TBL

EMP_ID      POSITION         DATE_HIRE    PAY_RATE DATE_LAST     SALARY    BONUS
---------   ---------------  -----------  -------- ------------- --------- ------
311549902   MARKETING        23-MAY-89             01-MAY-99     4000
442346889   TEAM LEADER      17-JUN-90    14.75    01-JUN-99
213764555   SALES MANAGER    14-AUG-94             01-AUG-99     3000      2000
313782439   SALESMAN         28-JUN-97                           2000      1000
220984332   SHIPPER          22-JUL-96             11 01-JUL-99
443679012   SHIPPER          14-JAN-91             15 01-JAN-99
```

```
CUSTOMER_TBL

CUST_ID  CUST_NAME        ADDRESS       CUST_CITY      ST ZIP    CUST_PHONE    CUST_FAX
-------  ---------------  ------------  ------------   -- -----  ------------  --------
232      LESLIE GLEASON   798 HARDAW    INDIANAPOLIS   IN 47856  3175457690
                          AY DR

109      NANCY BUNKER     APT A 4556    BROAD RIPPLE   IN 47950  3174262323
                          WATERWAY

345      ANGELA DOBKO     RR3 BOX 76    LEBANON        IN 49967  7658970090

090      WENDY WOLF       3345 GATEW    INDIANAPOLIS   IN 46224  3172913421
                          AY DR

12       MARYS GIFT SHOP  435 MAIN S    DANVILLE       IL 47978  3178567221   3178523434
                          T

432      SCOTTYS MARKET   RR2 BOX 17    BROWNSBURG     IN 45687  3178529835   3178529836
                          3

333      JASONS AND DALL  LAFAYETTE     INDIANAPOLIS   IN 46222  3172978886   3172978887
         AS GOODIES       SQ MALL

21       MORGANS CANDIES  5657 W        INDIANAPOLIS   IN 46234  3172714398
         AND TREATS       TENTH ST

43       SCHYLERS NOVELT  17 MAPLE      LEBANON        IN 48990  3174346758
         IES              ST

287      GAVINS PLACE     9880 ROCKV    INDIANAPOLIS   IN 46244  3172719991   3172719992
                          ILLE RD

288      HOLLYS GAMEARAM  567 US 31     WHITELAND      IN 49980  3178879023

590      HEATHERS FEATHE  4090 N SHA    INDIANAPOLIS   IN 43278  3175456768
         RS AND THINGS    DELAND AVE

610      RAGANS HOBBIES   451 GREEN     PLAINFIELD     IN 46818  3178393441   3178399090
```

1

```
560      ANDYS CANDIES    RR 1        NASHVILLE     IN 48756 8123239871
                          BOX 34

221      RYANS STUFF      2337 S      INDIANAPOLIS IN 47834 3175634402
                          SHELBY ST
```

ORDERS_TBL

ORD_NUM	CUST_ID	PROD_ID	QTY	ORD_DATE
56A901	232	11235	1	22-OCT-99
56A917	12	907	100	30-SEP-99
32A132	43	222	25	10-OCT-99
16C17	090	222	2	17-OCT-99
18D778	287	90	10	17-OCT-99
23E934	432	13	20	15-OCT-99

PRODUCTS_TBL

PROD_ID	PROD_DESC	COST
11235	WITCHES COSTUME	29.99
222	PLASTIC PUMPKIN 18 INCH	7.75
13	FALSE PARAFFIN TEETH	1.10
90	LIGHTED LANTERNS	14.50
15	ASSORTED COSTUMES	10.00
9	CANDY CORN	1.35
6	PUMPKIN CANDY	1.45
87	PLASTIC SPIDERS	1.05
119	ASSORTED MASKS	4.95

A Closer Look at What Composes a Table

The storage and maintenance of valuable data is the reason for any database's existence. You have just viewed the data that is used to explain SQL concepts in this book. The following sections take a closer look at the elements within a table. Remember, a table is the most common and simplest form of data storage in a relational database.

A Field

NEW TERM Every table is broken up into smaller entities called fields. The fields in the PRODUCTS_TBL table consist of PROD_ID, PROD_DESC, and COST. These fields categorize the specific information that is maintained in a given table. A *field* is a column in a table that is designed to maintain specific information about every record in the table.

A Record, or Row, of Data

NEW TERM   A *record*, also called a *row* of data, is each individual entry that exists in a table. Looking at the last table, `PRODUCTS_TBL`, consider the following first record in that table:

```
<C1>11235      WITCHES COSTUME                  29.99
```

The record is obviously composed of a product identification, product description, and unit cost. For every distinct product, there should be a corresponding record in the `PRODUCTS_TBL` table. A record is a horizontal entity in a table.

NEW TERM   A *row of data* is an entire record in a relational database table.

A Column

NEW TERM   A *column* is a vertical entity in a table that contains all information associated with a specific field in a table. For example, a column in the `PRODUCTS_TBL` having to do with the product description would consist of the following:

```
WITCHES COSTUME
PLASTIC PUMPKIN 18 INCH
FALSE PARAFFIN TEETH
LIGHTED LANTERNS
ASSORTED COSTUMES
CANDY CORN
PUMPKIN CANDY
PLASTIC SPIDERS
ASSORTED MASKS
```

This column is based on the field `PROD_DESC`, the product description. A column pulls information about a certain field from every record within a table.

The Primary Key

A *primary key* is a column that makes each row of data in the table unique in a relational database. The primary key in the `PRODUCTS_TBL` table is `PROD_ID`, which is typically initialized during the table creation process. The nature of the primary key is to ensure that all product identifications are unique, so that each record in the `PRODUCTS_TBL` table has its own `PROD_ID`. Primary keys alleviate the possibility of a duplicate record in a table and are used in other ways, which you read about in Hour 3.

A NULL Value

NEW TERM   `NULL` is the term used to represent a missing value. A `NULL` value in a table is a value in a field that appears to be blank. A field with a `NULL` value is a field with no value. It is very important to understand that a `NULL` value is different than a zero value or a field that contains spaces. A field with a `NULL` value is one that has been left blank during record creation. Notice that in the EMPLOYEE_TBL table, not every employee has a middle initial. Those records for employees who do not have an entry for middle initial signify a NULL value.

Additional table elements are discussed in detail during the next two hours.

Summary

You have been introduced to the standard language of SQL and have been given a brief history and thumbnail of how the standard has evolved over the last several years. Database systems and current technologies were also discussed, including the relational database and client/server systems, both of which are vital to your understanding of SQL. The main SQL language components and the fact that there are numerous players in the relational database market, and likewise, many different flavors of SQL, were discussed. Despite ANSI SQL variations, most vendors do comply, to some extent, with the current standard, rendering consistency across the board and forcing the development of SQL applications that are portable.

The database that will be used during your course of study was also introduced. The database, as you have seen it so far, has consisted of a few tables, which are related to one another, and the data that each table contains at this point (at the end of Hour 1). You should have acquired some overall background knowledge of the fundamentals of SQL and should understand the concept of a relational database. After a few refreshers in the Workshop for this hour, you should feel very confident about continuing to the next hour.

Q&A

Q If I learn SQL, will I be able to use any of the implementations that use SQL?

A Yes, you will be able to communicate with a database whose implementation is ANSI SQL-compliant. If an implementation is not completely compliant, you should be able to pick it up quickly with some adjustments.

Q In a client/server environment, is the personal computer the client or the server?

A The personal computer is known as the client, although a server can also serve as a client.

Q Do I have to use _TBL for each table I create?

A Certainly not. The use of _TBL is a standard chosen for use to name and easily identify the tables in your database. You could spell out _TBL as TABLE, or may want to avoid using a suffix. For example, EMPLOYEETBL could simply be EMPLOYEE.

Q What happens when I am inserting a new record into a table and am missing, for example, a new employee's phone number—and the column for the phone number entry is NOT NULL?

A One of two things will happen. Because the column was specified as NOT NULL (something has to be entered), and because you do not have the necessary information, you could delay inserting the record until you have the phone number. Another option is to change the column from NOT NULL to NULL, thereby allowing you to update the phone number later when the information is received. One other option would be to insert a default fake value, such as 1111111111, and then change it later after receiving the correct information. Changing the column definitions is discussed in Hour 3.

Workshop

The following workshop is composed of a series of quiz questions and practical exercises. The quiz questions are designed to test your overall understanding of the current material. The practical exercises are intended to afford you the opportunity to apply the concepts discussed during the current hour, as well as build upon the knowledge acquired in previous hours of study. Please take time to complete the quiz questions and exercises before continuing. Refer to Appendix C, "Answers to Quizzes and Exercises," for answers.

Quiz

1. What does the acronym SQL stand for?
2. What are the six main categories of SQL commands?
3. What are the four transactional control commands?
4. What is the main difference between client/server technologies and the mainframe?
5. If a field is defined as NULL, does that mean that something has to be entered into that field?

Exercises

1. Identify the categories in which the following SQL commands fall:

```
CREATE TABLE
DELETE
SELECT
INSERT
ALTER TABLE
UPDATE
```

PART II
Building Your Database

Hour

HOUR 2

Defining Data Structures

In this second hour, you learn more about the data you viewed at the end of Hour 1. You learn the characteristics of the data itself and how such data is stored in a relational database. There are several data types, as you'll soon discover.

The highlights of this hour include

- A look at the underlying data of a table
- An introduction to the basic data types
- Instruction on the use of various data types
- Examples depicting differences between data types

What Is Data?

Data is a collection of information stored in a database as one of several different data types. Data includes names, numbers, dollar amounts, text, graphics, decimals, figures, calculations, summarization, and just about anything else you can possibly imagine. Data can be stored in uppercase, lowercase, or mixed case. Data can be manipulated or changed; most data does not remain static for its lifetime.

NEW TERM   *Data types* are used to provide rules for data for particular columns. A data type
           deals with the way values are stored in a column as far as the length allocated for
a column and whether values such as alphanumeric, numeric, and date and time data are
allowed.

The data is the purpose of any database and must be protected. The protector of the
data is normally the database administrator (DBA), although it is every database user's
responsibility to ensure that measures are taken to protect data. Data security is discussed
in-depth in Hour 18, "Managing Database Users," and Hour 19, "Managing Database
Security."

Basic Data Types

The following sections discuss the basic data types supported by ANSI SQL. Data types
are characteristics of the data itself, whose attributes are placed on fields within a table.
For example, you can specify that a field must contain numeric values, disallowing the
entering of alphanumeric strings. After all, you would not want to enter alphabetic characters in a field for a dollar amount.

> Every implementation of SQL seems to have its own specific data types.
> The use of implementation-specific data types is necessary to support the
> philosophy of each implementation on how to handle the storage of data.
> However, the basics are the same among all implementations.

The very basic data types, as with most other languages, are

- Character strings
- Numeric strings
- Date and time values

Fixed-Length Characters

NEW TERM   *Constant characters*, those strings that always have the same length, are stored
           using a fixed-length data type. The following is the standard for an SQL fixed-
length character:

CHARACTER(n)

n represents a number identifying the allocated, or maximum length, of the particular
field with this definition.

Some implementations of SQL use the CHAR data type to store fixed-length data. Alphanumeric data can be stored in this data type. An example of a constant length data type would be for a state abbreviation because all state abbreviations are two characters.

Spaces are normally used to fill extra spots when using a fixed-length data type; if a field's length was set to 10 and data entered filled only five places, the remaining five spaces are recorded as spaces. The padding of spaces ensures that each value in a field is a fixed length.

> Be careful not to use a fixed-length data type for fields that may contain varying-length values, such as an individual's name. If you use the fixed-length data type inappropriately, problems such as the waste of available space and the inability to make accurate comparisons between data will eventually be encountered.

Variable Characters

New Term SQL supports the use of *varying-length strings*, strings whose length is not constant for all data. The following is the standard for an SQL varying-length character:

CHARACTER VARYING(n)

n represents a number identifying the allocated, or maximum length, of the particular field with this definition.

Common data types for variable-length character values are the VARCHAR and VARCHAR2 data types. VARCHAR is the ANSI standard, which Microsoft SQL Server uses; VARCHAR2 is used by Oracle and should be used in Oracle, because VARCHAR's usage in the future may change. The data stored can be alphanumeric.

Remember that fixed-length data types typically pad spaces to fill in allocated places not used by the field. The varying-length data type does not work this way. For instance, if the allocated length of a varying-length field is 10, and a string of five characters is entered, the total length of that particular value is only 5. Spaces are not used to fill unused places in a column.

> Always use the varying-length data type for non-constant character strings to save database space.

Numeric Values

Numeric values are stored in fields that are defined as some type of number, typically referred to as NUMBER, INTEGER, REAL, DECIMAL, and so on.

The following are the standards for SQL numeric values:

```
BIT(n)

BIT VARYING(n)

DECIMAL(p,s)

INTEGER

SMALLINT

FLOAT(p)

REAL(s)

DOUBLE PRECISION(P)
```

p represents a number identifying the allocated, or maximum length, of the particular field for each appropriate definition.

s is a number to the right of the decimal point, such as 34.ss.

A common numeric data type in SQL implementations is NUMBER, which accommodates the direction for numeric values provided by ANSI. Numeric values can be stored as zero, positive, negative, fixed, and floating-point numbers. The following is an example using NUMBER:

```
NUMBER(5)
```

This example restricts the maximum value entered in a particular field to 99999.

Decimal Values

Decimal values are numeric values that include the use of a decimal point. The standard for a decimal in SQL follows, where the p is the precision and the s is the decimal's scale:

```
DECIMAL(p,s)
```

2

New Term The *precision* is the total length of the numeric value. In a numeric defined DECIMAL(4,2), the precision is 4, which is the total length allocated for a numeric value.

New Term The *scale* is the number of digits to the right of the decimal point. The scale is 2 in the previous DECIMAL(4,2) example.

34.33 inserted into a DECIMAL(3,1) is typically rounded to 34.3.

If a numeric value was defined as the following data type, the maximum value allowed would be 99.99:

DECIMAL(4,2)

New Term The precision is 4, which represents the total length allocated for an associated value. The scale is 2, which represents the number of *places*, or *bytes*, reserved to the right side of the decimal point. The decimal point itself does not count as a character.

Allowed values for a column defined as DECIMAL(4,2) include the following:

    12

    12.4

    12.44

    12.449

The last numeric value, 12.449, is rounded off to 12.45 upon input into the column.

Integers

New Term An *integer* is a numeric value that does not contain a decimal, only whole numbers (both positive and negative).

Valid integers include the following:

    1

    0

    -1

    99

    -99

    199

Floating-Point Decimals

NEW TERM   *Floating-point decimals* are decimal values whose precision and scale are vari-
           able lengths and virtually without limit. Any precision and scale is acceptable.
The REAL data type designates a column with single-precision, floating-point numbers.
The DOUBLE PRECISION data type designates a column that contains double-precision,
floating-point numbers. To be considered a single-precision floating point, the precision
must be between 1 and 21 inclusive. To be considered a double-precision floating point,
the precision must be between 22 and 53 inclusive. The following are examples of the
FLOAT data type:

    FLOAT

    FLOAT(15)

    FLOAT(50)

Dates and Time

Date and time data types are quite obviously used to keep track of information concerning dates and time. Standard SQL supports what are called DATETIME data types, which
include the following specific data types:

    DATE

    TIME

    INTERVAL

    TIMESTAMP

The elements of a DATETIME data type consist of the following:

    YEAR

    MONTH

    DAY

    HOUR

    MINUTE

    SECOND

> The SECOND element can also be broken down to fractions of a second. The range is from 00.000 to 61.999, although some implementations of SQL may not support this range.

Be aware that each implementation of SQL may have its own customized data type for dates and times. The previous data types and elements are standards to which each SQL vendor should adhere, but be advised that most implementations have their own data type for date values, varying in both appearance and the way date information is actually stored internally.

A length is not normally specified for a date data type. Later in this hour, you learn more about dates, how date information is stored in some implementations, how to manipulate dates and times using conversion functions, and study practical examples of how dates and time are used in the real world.

Literal Strings

NEW TERM   A *literal string* is a series of characters, such as a name or a phone number, that is explicitly specified by a user or program. Literal strings consist of data with the same attributes as the previously discussed data types, but the value of the string is known; the value of a column itself is usually unknown, because there is typically a different value for a column associated with each row of data in a table.

You do not actually specify data types with literal strings—you simply specify the string. Some examples of literal strings follow:

    'Hello'

    45000

    "45000"

    3.14

    'November 1, 1997'

The alphanumeric strings are enclosed by single quotation marks, whereas the number value 45000 is not. Also notice that the second numeric value of 45000 is enclosed by quotation marks. Generally speaking, character strings require quotation marks, whereas numeric strings don't. You see later how literal strings are used with database queries.

NULL Data Types

As you should know from Hour 1, "Welcome to the World of SQL," a NULL value is a missing value or a column in a row of data that has not been assigned a value. NULL values are used in nearly all parts of SQL, including the creation of tables, search conditions for queries, and even in literal strings.

The following are two methods for referencing a NULL value:

- NULL (the keyword NULL itself)
- ' ' (single quotation marks with nothing in between)

The following does not represent a NULL value, but a literal string containing the characters N-U-L-L:

```
'NULL'
```

BOOLEAN Values

A BOOLEAN value is a value of either TRUE, FALSE, or NULL. BOOLEAN values are used to make data comparisons. For example, when criteria are specified for a query, each condition evaluates to either a TRUE, FALSE, or NULL. If the BOOLEAN value of TRUE is returned by all conditions in a query, data is returned. If a BOOLEAN value of FALSE or NULL is returned, data may not be returned.

Consider the following example:

```
WHERE NAME = 'SMITH'
```

This line might be a condition found in a query. The condition is evaluated for every row of data in the table that is being queried. If the value of NAME is SMITH for a row of data in the table, the condition returns the value TRUE, thereby returning the data associated with that record.

User-Defined Types

 A *user-defined type* is a data type that is defined by the user. User-defined types allow users to customize their own data types based on existing data types. The CREATE TYPE statement is used to create a user-defined type.

For example, you can create a type as follows:

```
CREATE TYPE PERSON AS OBJECT
(NAME        VARCHAR2(30),
 SSN     VARCHAR2(9));
```

You can reference your user-defined type as follows:

```
CREATE TABLE EMP_PAY
(EMPLOYEE    PERSON,
 SALARY      NUMBER(10,2),
 HIRE_DATE       DATE);
```

Notice that the data type referenced for the first column EMPLOYEE is PERSON. PERSON is the user-defined type you created in the first example.

Domains

NEW TERM   A *domain* is a set of valid data types that can be used. A domain is associated with a data type, so that only certain data is accepted. After a domain is created, you can add constraints to the domain. The domain is used like the user-defined type.

You can create a domain as follows:

```
CREATE DOMAIN MONEY_D AS NUMBER(8,2);
```

You can add constraints to your domain as follows:

```
ALTER DOMAIN MONEY_D
ADD CONSTRAINT MONEY_CON1
CHECK (VALUE > 5);
```

You can reference the domain as follows:

```
CREATE TABLE EMP_PAY
(EMP_ID        NUMBER(9),
 EMP_NAME      VARCHAR2(30),
 PAY_RATE      MONEY_D);
```

> Note that some of the data types mentioned during this hour may not be available by name in the implementation of SQL that you are using. Data types are often named differently among implementations of SQL, but the concept behind each data type remains. Most, if not all, data types are supported by most relational databases.

Summary

There are several data types available with SQL. If you have programmed in other languages, you probably recognize many of the data types mentioned. Data types allow different types of data to be stored in the database, ranging from simple characters to decimal points to date and time. The concept of data types is the same in all languages, whether programming in a third-generation language such as C and passing variables or using a relational database implementation and coding in SQL. Of course, each implementation has its own names for standard data types, but they basically work the same.

Care must be taken in planning for both the near and distant future when deciding on data types, lengths, scales, and precisions in which to store your data. Business rules and how you want the end user to access the data are other factors in deciding on specific data types. You should know the nature of the data itself and how data in the database is related to assign proper data types.

Q&A

Q How is it that I can enter numbers such as a person's Social Security number in fields defined as character fields?

A Numeric values are still alphanumeric, which are allowed in character data types. Typically, the only data stored as numeric values are values used in computations. However, it may be helpful for some to define all numeric fields with a numeric data type to help control the data entered in that field.

Q I still do not understand the difference between constant-length and varying-length data types. Can you explain?

A Say you have an individual's last name defined as a constant data type with a length of 20 bytes. Suppose the individual's name is Smith. When the data is inserted into the table, 20 bytes are taken, 5 for the name and 15 for the extra spaces (remember that this is a constant-length data type). If you use a varying-length data type with a length of 20 and inserted Smith, only 5 bytes of space are taken.

Workshop

The following workshop is composed of a series of quiz questions and practical exercises. The quiz questions are designed to test your overall understanding of the current material. The practical exercises are intended to afford you the opportunity to apply the concepts discussed during the current hour, as well as build upon the knowledge acquired in previous hours of study. Please take time to complete the quiz questions and exercises before continuing. You may refer to Appendix C, "Answers to Quizzes and Exercises," for answers.

Quiz

1. True or false: An individual's Social Security number can be any of the following data types: constant-length character, varying-length character, numeric.

2. True or false: The scale of a numeric value is the total length allowed for values.

3. Do all implementations use the same data types?

4. What are the precision and scale of the following?

   ```
   DECIMAL(4,2)
   DECIMAL(10,2)
   DECIMAL(14,1)
   ```

5. Which numbers could be inserted into a column whose data type is DECIMAL(4,1)?

   a. 16.2

   b. 116.2

   c. 16.21

   d. 1116.2

   e. 1116.21

Exercises

1. Take the following column titles, assign them to a data type, and decide on the proper length.

   a. ssn

   b. state

   c. city

   d. phone_number

   e. zip

   f. last_name

   g. first_name

   h. middle_name

   i. salary

   j. hourly_pay_rate

   k. date_hired

2. Take the same column titles and decide whether they should be NULL or NOT NULL, realizing that in some cases where a column would normally be NOT NULL, the column could be NULL or vice-versa, depending on the application.

    a. ssn

    b. state

    c. city

    d. phone_number

    e. zip

    f. last_name

    g. first_name

    h. middle_name

    i. salary

    j. hourly_pay_rate

    k. date_hired

HOUR 3

Managing Database Objects

NEW TERM In this hour, you learn about database objects: what they are, how they act, how they are stored, and how they relate to one another. Database objects are the underlying backbone of the relational database. These *objects* are logical units within the database that are used to store information, and are referred to as the *back-end database*. The majority of the instruction during this hour revolves around the table, but keep in mind that there are other database objects, many of which are discussed in later hours of study.

The highlights of this hour include

- An introduction to database objects
- An introduction to the schema
- An introduction to the table
- A discussion of the nature and attributes of tables
- Examples for the creation and manipulation of tables
- A discussion of table storage options
- Concepts on referential integrity and data consistency

What Are Database Objects?

A *database object* is any defined object in a database that is used to store or reference data. Some examples of database objects include tables, views, clusters, sequences, indexes, and synonyms. The table is this hour's focus, because it is the simplest form of data storage in a relational database.

What Is a Schema?

NEW TERM A *schema* is a collection of database objects (as far as this hour is concerned—tables) associated with one particular database username. This username is called the *schema owner*, or the owner of the related group of objects. You may have one or multiple schemas in a database. Basically, any user who creates an object has just created his or her own schema. A schema can consist of a single table and has no limits to the number of objects that it may contain, unless restricted by a specific database implementation.

Say you have been issued a database username and password by the database administrator. Your username is USER1. Suppose you log on to the database and then create a table called EMPLOYEE_TBL. Your table's actual name is USER1.EMPLOYEE_TBL. The schema name for that table is USER1, which is also the owner of that table. You have just created the first table of a schema.

The good thing about schemas is that when you access a table that you own (in your own schema), you do not have to refer to the schema name. For instance, you could refer to your table as either one of the following:

```
EMPLOYEE_TBL
USER1.EMPLOYEE_TBL
```

The first option is preferred because it requires fewer keystrokes. If another user were to query one of your tables, the user would have to specify the schema, as follows:

```
USER1.EMPLOYEE_TBL
```

In Hour 20, "Creating and Using Views and Synonyms," you learn about the distribution of permissions so that other users can access your tables. You also learn about synonyms, which allow you to give a table another name so you do not have to specify the schema name when accessing a table. Figure 3.1 illustrates two schemas in a relational database.

There are, in Figure 3.1, two user accounts in the database that own tables: USER1 and USER2. Each user account has its own schema. Some examples for how the two users can access their own tables and tables owned by the other user follow:

USER1 accesses own `table1`:	TABLE1
USER1 accesses own test:	TEST
USER1 accesses USER2's `table10`:	`USER2.TABLE10`
USER1 accesses USER2's test:	`USER2.TEST`

Both users have a table called TEST. Tables can have the same names in a database as long as they belong to different schemas. If you look at it this way, table names are always unique in a database, because the schema owner is actually part of the table name. For instance, USER1.TEST is different than USER2.TEST. If you do not specify a schema with the table name when accessing tables in a database, the database server looks for a table that you own by default. That is, if USER1 tries to access TEST, the database server looks for a USER1-owned table named TEST before it looks for other objects owned by USER1, such as synonyms to tables in another schema. Hour 21, "Working with the System Catalog," helps you fully understand how synonyms work.

FIGURE 3.1

Schemas in a database.

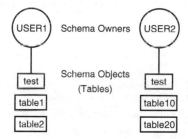

DATABASE

Every database server has rules concerning how you can name objects and elements of objects, such as field names. You must check your particular implementation for the exact naming conventions or rules.

A Table: The Primary Storage for Data

The table is the primary storage object for data in a relational database. A table consists of row(s) and column(s), both of which hold the data. A table takes up physical space in a database and can be permanent or temporary.

Fields and Columns

A field, also called a column in a relational database, is part of a table that is assigned a specific data type; a field should be named to correspond with the type of data that will be entered into that column. Columns can be specified as NULL or NOT NULL, meaning that if a column is NOT NULL, something must be entered. If a column is specified as NULL, nothing has to be entered.

Every database table must consist of at least one column. Columns are those elements within a table that hold specific types of data, such as a person's name or address. For example, a valid column in a customer table may be the customer's name.

Generally, a name must be one continuous string. An object name must typically be one continuous string and can be limited to the number of characters used according to each implementation of SQL. It is typical to use underscores with names to provide separations between characters. For example, a column for the customer's name can be named CUSTOMER_NAME instead of CUSTOMERNAME.

> Be sure to check your implementation for rules when naming objects and other database elements.

Rows

A row is a record of data in a database table. For example, a row of data in a customer table might consist of a particular customer's identification number, name, address, phone number, fax number, and so on. A row is comprised of fields that contain data from one record in a table. A table can contain as little as one row of data and up to as many as millions of rows of data or records.

The CREATE TABLE Statement

The CREATE TABLE statement is obviously used to create a table. Although the very act of creating a table is quite simple, much time and effort should be put into planning table structures before the actual execution of the CREATE TABLE statement.

Some elementary questions need to be answered when creating a table:

- What type of data will be entered into the table?
- What will be the table's name?
- What column(s) will compose the primary key?
- What names shall be given to the columns (fields)?

- What data type will be assigned to each column?
- What will be the allocated length for each column?
- Which columns in a table require data?

After these questions are answered, the actual CREATE TABLE statement is simple.

The basic syntax to create a table is as follows:

SYNTAX

```
CREATE TABLE TABLE_NAME
( FIELD1   DATA TYPE   [ NOT NULL ],
  FIELD2   DATA TYPE   [ NOT NULL ],
  FIELD3   DATA TYPE   [ NOT NULL ],
  FIELD4   DATA TYPE   [ NOT NULL ],
  FIELD5   DATA TYPE   [ NOT NULL ] );
```

In this hour's examples, you use the popular data types CHAR (constant-length character), VARCHAR (variable-length character), NUMBER (numeric values, decimal and non-decimal), and DATE (date and time values).

3

Create a table called EMPLOYEE_TBL in the following example:

INPUT

```
CREATE TABLE EMPLOYEE_TBL
(EMP_ID         CHAR(9)         NOT NULL,
 EMP_NAME       VARCHAR2(40)    NOT NULL,
 EMP_ST_ADDR    VARCHAR2(20)    NOT NULL,
 EMP_CITY       VARCHAR2(15)    NOT NULL,
 EMP_ST         CHAR(2)         NOT NULL,
 EMP_ZIP        NUMBER(5)       NOT NULL,
 EMP_PHONE      NUMBER(10)      NULL,
 EMP_PAGER      NUMBER(10)      NULL);
```

Eight different columns make up this table. Notice the use of the underscore character to break the column names up into what appears to be separate words (EMPLOYEE ID is stored as EMP_ID). Each column has been assigned a specific data type and length, and by using the NULL/NOT NULL constraint, you have specified which columns require values for every row of data in the table. The EMP_PHONE is defined as NULL, meaning that NULL values are allowed in this column because there may be individuals without a telephone number. The information concerning each column is separated by a comma, with parentheses surrounding all columns (a left parenthesis before the first column and a right parenthesis following the information on the last column).

A semicolon is the last character in the previous statement. Most SQL implementations have some character that terminates a statement or submits a statement to the database server. Oracle uses the semicolon. Transact-SQL uses the GO statement. This book uses the semicolon.

Each record, or row of data, in this table would consist of the following:

```
EMP_ID, EMP_NAME, EMP_ST_ADDR, EMP_CITY, EMP_ST, EMP_ZIP, EMP_PHONE, EMP_PAGER
```

In this table, each field is a column. The column EMP_ID could consist of one employee's identification number or many employees' identification numbers, depending on the requirements of a database query or transactions. The column is a vertical entity in a table, whereas a row of data is a horizontal entity.

> NULL is the default value for a column; therefore, it does not have to be entered in the CREATE TABLE statement.

STORAGE Clause

Some form of a STORAGE clause is available in many relational database implementations of SQL. The STORAGE clause in a CREATE TABLE statement is used for initial table sizing and is usually done at table creation. The syntax of a STORAGE clause as used in one implementation is shown in the following example:

```
CREATE TABLE EMPLOYEE_TBL
(EMP_ID         CHAR(9)        NOT NULL,
 EMP_NAME       VARCHAR(40)    NOT NULL,
 EMP_ST_ADDR    VARCHAR(20)    NOT NULL,
 EMP_CITY       VARCHAR(15)    NOT NULL,
 EMP_ST         CHAR(2)        NOT NULL,
 EMP_ZIP        NUMBER(5)      NOT NULL,
 EMP_PHONE      NUMBER(10)     NULL,
 EMP_PAGER      NUMBER(10)     NULL)
STORAGE
    (INITIAL    3K
     NEXT       2K );
```

In some implementations, there are several options available in the STORAGE clause. INITIAL allocates a set amount of space in bytes, kilobytes, and so on, for the initial amount of space to be used by a table. The NEXT part of the STORAGE identifies the amount of additional space that should be allocated to the table if it should grow beyond the space allocated for the initial allocation. You find that there are other options available with the STORAGE clause, and remember that these options vary from implementation to implementation. If the STORAGE clause is omitted from most major implementations, there are default storage parameters invoked, which may not be the best for the application.

Notice the neatness of the CREATE TABLE statement. This is for ease of reading and error resolution. Indentation has been used to help.

The STORAGE clause differs between relational database implementations of SQL. The previous example used Oracle's STORAGE clause, which was added to the CREATE TABLE statement. Remember that the ANSI standard for SQL is just that, a standard. The standard is not a language itself, but guidelines on how vendors should develop their SQL implementation. You also find that data types differ between implementations. Most issues concerning the actual storage and processing of data are implementation-specific.

Naming Conventions

When selecting names for objects, specifically tables and columns, the name should reflect the data that is to be stored. For example, the name for a table pertaining to employee information could be named EMPLOYEE_TBL. Names for columns should follow the same logic. When storing an employee's phone number, an obvious name for that column would be PHONE_NUMBER.

3

Check your particular implementation for name length limits and characters that are allowed; they could differ from implementation to implementation.

The ALTER TABLE Command

A table can be modified through the use of the ALTER TABLE command after that table's creation. You can add column(s), drop column(s), change column definitions, add and drop constraints, and, in some implementations, modify table STORAGE values. The standard syntax for the ALTER TABLE command follows:

```
ALTER TABLE TABLE_NAME [MODIFY] [COLUMN COLUMN_NAME][DATATYPE|NULL NOT NULL]
[RESTRICT|CASCADE]
                      [DROP]    [CONSTRAINT CONSTRAINT_NAME]
                      [ADD]     [COLUMN] COLUMN DEFINITION
```

SYNTAX

Modifying Elements of a Table

NEW TERM   The *attributes* of a column refer to the rules and behavior of data in a column. You can modify the attributes of a column with the ALTER TABLE command. The word attributes here refers to the following:

- The data type of a column
- The length, precision, or scale of a column
- Whether the column can contain NULL values

The following example uses the `ALTER TABLE` command on `EMPLOYEE_TBL` to modify the attributes of the column `EMP_ID`:

INPUT   `ALTER TABLE EMPLOYEE_TBL MODIFY (EMP_ID VARCHAR2(10));`

OUTPUT   `Table altered.`

The column was already defined as data type `VARCHAR2` (a varying-length character), but you increased the maximum length from `9` to `10`.

Adding Mandatory Columns to a Table

One of the basic rules for adding columns to an existing table is that the column you are adding cannot be defined as `NOT NULL` if data currently exists in the table. `NOT NULL` means that a column must contain some value for every row of data in the table, so if you are adding a column defined as `NOT NULL`, you are contradicting the `NOT NULL` constraint right off the bat if the preexisting rows of data in the table do not have values for the new column.

There is, however, a way to add a mandatory column to a table:

1. Add the column and define it as `NULL` (the column does not have to contain a value).

2. Insert a value into the new column for every row of data in the table.

3. After ensuring that the column contains a value for every row of data in the table, you can alter the table to change the column's attribute to `NOT NULL`.

Modifying Columns

There are many things to take into consideration when modifying existing columns of a table.

Common rules for modifying columns:

- The length of a column can be increased to the maximum length of the given data type.

- The length of a column can be decreased only if the largest value for that column in the table is less than or equal to the new length of the column.

- The number of digits for a number data type can always be increased.

- The number of digits for a number data type can be decreased only if the value with the most number of digits for that column is less than or equal to the new number of digits specified for the column.

- The number of decimal places for a number data type can either be increased or decreased.
- The data type of a column can normally be changed.

Some implementations may actually restrict you from using certain ALTER TABLE options. For example, you may not be allowed to drop columns from a table. To do this, you would have to drop the table itself, and then rebuild the table with the desired columns. You could run into problems by dropping a column in one table that is dependent on a column in another table, or a column that is referenced by a column in another table. Be sure to refer to your specific implementation documentation.

Creating a Table from an Existing Table

A copy of an existing table can be created using a combination of the CREATE TABLE statement and the SELECT statement. The new table has the same column definitions. All columns or specific columns can be selected. New columns that are created via functions or a combination of columns automatically assume the size necessary to hold the data. The basic syntax for creating a table from another table is as follows:

```
CREATE TABLE NEW_TABLE_NAME AS
SELECT [ *|COLUMN1, COLUMN2 ]
FROM TABLE_NAME
[ WHERE ]
```

Notice some new keywords in the syntax, particularly the SELECT keyword. SELECT is a database query, and is discussed in more detail later. However, it is important to know that you can create a table based on the results from a query.

First, do a simple query to view the data in the PRODUCTS_TBL table.

INPUT   SELECT * FROM PRODUCTS_TBL;

OUTPUT

PROD_ID	PROD_DESC	COST
11235	WITCHES COSTUME	29.99
222	PLASTIC PUMPKIN 18 INCH	7.75
13	FALSE PARAFFIN TEETH	1.1
90	LIGHTED LANTERNS	14.5
15	ASSORTED COSTUMES	10
9	CANDY CORN	1.35
6	PUMPKIN CANDY	1.45
87	PLASTIC SPIDERS	1.05
119	ASSORTED MASKS	4.95

SELECT * selects data from all fields in the given table. The * represents a complete row of data, or record, in the table.

Next, create a table called PRODUCTS_TMP based on the previous query:

```
CREATE TABLE PRODUCTS_TMP AS
SELECT * FROM PRODUCTS_TBL;
```

OUTPUT Table created.

Now, if you run a query on the PRODUCTS_TMP table, your results appear the same as if you had selected data from the original table.

```
SELECT *
FROM PRODUCTS_TMP;
```

OUTPUT

```
PROD_ID    PROD_DESC                           COST
---------- ----------------------------------- ------
11235      WITCHES COSTUME                     29.99
222        PLASTIC PUMPKIN 18 INCH             7.75
13         FALSE PARAFFIN TEETH                1.1
90         LIGHTED LANTERNS                    14.5
15         ASSORTED COSTUMES                   10
9          CANDY CORN                          1.35
6          PUMPKIN CANDY                       1.45
87         PLASTIC SPIDERS                     1.05
119        ASSORTED MASKS                      4.95
```

When creating a table from an existing table, the new table takes on the same STORAGE attributes as the original table.

Dropping Tables

Dropping a table is actually one of the easiest things to do. When the RESTRICT option is used and the table is referenced by a view or constraint, the DROP statement returns an error. When the CASCADE option is used, the drop succeeds and all referencing views and constraints are dropped. The syntax to drop a table follows:

```
DROP TABLE TABLE_NAME [ RESTRICT|CASCADE ]
```

In the following example, you drop the table that you just created:

```
DROP TABLE PRODUCTS_USER1.TMP;
```

OUTPUT Table dropped.

> Whenever dropping a table, be sure to specify the schema name or owner
> of the table before submitting your command. You could drop the incorrect
> table. If you have access to multiple user accounts, ensure that you are con-
> nected to the database through the correct user account before dropping
> tables.

Integrity Constraints

Integrity constraints are used to ensure accuracy and consistency of data in a relational
database. Data integrity is handled in a relational database through the concept of referential integrity. There are many types of integrity constraints that play a role in referential
integrity (RI).

Primary Key Constraints

NEW TERM *Primary key* is the term used to identify one or more columns in a table that
make a row of data unique. Although the primary key typically consists of one
column in a table, more than one column can comprise the primary key. For example,
either the employee's Social Security number or an assigned employee identification
number is the logical primary key for an employee table. The objective is for every
record to have a unique primary key or value for the employee's identification number.
Because there is probably no need to have more than one record for each employee in
an employee table, the employee identification number makes a logical primary key.
The primary key is assigned at table creation.

The following example identifies the EMP_ID column as the PRIMARY KEY for the
EMPLOYEES table:

```
CREATE TABLE EMPLOYEE_TBL
(EMP_ID          CHAR(9)          NOT NULL PRIMARY KEY,
EMP_NAME         VARCHAR2(40)     NOT NULL,
EMP_ST_ADDR      VARCHAR2(20)     NOT NULL,
EMP_CITY         VARCHAR2(15)     NOT NULL,
EMP_ST           CHAR(2)          NOT NULL,
EMP_ZIP          NUMBER(5)        NOT NULL,
```

```
EMP_PHONE      NUMBER(10)     NULL,
EMP_PAGER      NUMBER(10)     NULL);
```

This method of defining a primary key is accomplished during table creation. The primary key in this case is an implied constraint. You can also specify a primary key explicitly as a constraint when setting up a table, as follows:

```
CREATE TABLE EMPLOYEE_TBL
(EMP_ID         CHAR(9)         NOT NULL,
EMP_NAME       VARCHAR2(40)    NOT NULL,
EMP_ST_ADDR    VARCHAR2(20)    NOT NULL,
EMP_CITY       VARCHAR2(15)    NOT NULL,
EMP_ST         CHAR(2)         NOT NULL,
EMP_ZIP        NUMBER(5)       NOT NULL,
EMP_PHONE      NUMBER(10)      NULL,
EMP_PAGER      NUMBER(10)      NULL,
PRIMARY KEY (EMP_ID));
```

The primary key constraint in this example is defined after the column comma list in the CREATE TABLE statement.

A primary key that consists of more than one column can be defined by either of the following methods:

```
CREATE TABLE PRODUCTS
(PROD_ID        VARCHAR2(10)    NOT NULL,
 VEND_ID        VARCHAR2(10)    NOT NULL,
 PRODUCT        VARCHAR2(30)    NOT NULL,
 COST                 NUMBER(8,2)     NOT NULL,
PRIMARY KEY (PROD_ID, VEND_ID));

ALTER TABLE PRODUCTS
ADD CONSTRAINT PRODUCTS_PK PRIMARY KEY (PROD_ID, VEND_ID);
```

Unique Constraints

NEW TERM   A *unique column constraint* in a table is similar to a primary key in that the value in that column for every row of data in the table must have a unique value. While a primary key constraint is placed on one column, you can place a unique constraint on another column even though it is not actually for use as the primary key.

Study the following example:

```
CREATE TABLE EMPLOYEE_TBL
(EMP_ID         CHAR(9)         NOT NULL     PRIMARY KEY,
EMP_NAME       VARCHAR2(40)    NOT NULL,
EMP_ST_ADDR    VARCHAR2(20)    NOT NULL,
EMP_CITY       VARCHAR2(15)    NOT NULL,
EMP_ST         CHAR(2)         NOT NULL,
EMP_ZIP        NUMBER(5)       NOT NULL,
EMP_PHONE      NUMBER(10)      NULL         UNIQUE,
EMP_PAGER      NUMBER(10)      NULL);
```

The primary key in this example is EMP_ID, meaning that the employee identification number is the column that is used to ensure that every record in the table is unique. The primary key is a column that is normally referenced in queries, particularly to join tables. The column EMP_PHONE has been designated as a UNIQUE value, meaning that no two employees can have the same telephone number. There is not a lot of difference between the two, except that the primary key is used to provide an order to data in a table and, in the same respect, join related tables.

Foreign Key Constraints

NEW TERM A *foreign key* is a column in a child table that references a primary key in the parent table. A *foreign key constraint* is the main mechanism used to enforce referential integrity between tables in a relational database. A column defined as a foreign key is used to reference a column defined as a primary key in another table.

Study the creation of the foreign key in the following example:

```
CREATE TABLE EMPLOYEE_PAY_TBL
(EMP_ID              CHAR(9)         NOT NULL,
POSITION             VARCHAR2(15)    NOT NULL,
DATE_HIRE            DATE            NULL,
PAY_RATE             NUMBER(4,2)     NOT NULL,
DATE_LAST_RAISE      DATE            NULL,
CONSTRAINT EMP_ID_FK FOREIGN KEY (EMP_ID) REFERENCES EMPLOYEE_TBL (EMP_ID));
```

The EMP_ID column in this example has been designated as the foreign key for the EMPLOYEE_PAY_TBL table. This foreign key, as you can see, references the EMP_ID column in the EMPLOYEE_TBL table. This foreign key ensures that for every EMP_ID in the EMPLOYEE_PAY_TBL, there is a corresponding EMP_ID in the EMPLOYEE_TBL. This is called a *parent/child relationship*. The parent table is the EMPLOYEE_TBL table, and the child table is the EMPLOYEE_PAY_TBL table. Study Figure 3.2 for a better understanding of the parent table/child table relationship.

FIGURE 3.2
The parent/child table relationship.

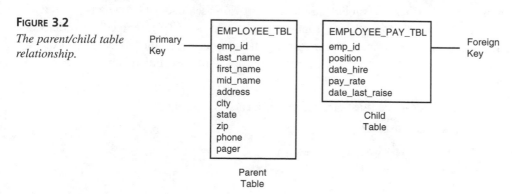

In this figure, the EMP_ID column in the child table references the EMP_ID column in the parent table. In order for a value to be inserted for EMP_ID in the child table, there must first exist a value for EMP_ID in the parent table. Likewise, for a value to be removed for EMP_ID in the parent table, all corresponding values for EMP_ID must first be removed from the child table. This is how referential integrity works.

A foreign key can be added to a table using the ALTER TABLE command, as shown in the following example:

```
ALTER TABLE EMPLOYEE_PAY_TBL
ADD CONSTRAINT ID_FK FOREIGN KEY (EMP_ID)
REFERENCES EMPLOYEE_TBL (EMP_ID);
```

The options available with the ALTER TABLE command differ among different implementations of SQL, particularly when dealing with constraints.In addition, the actual use and definitions of constraints also vary, but the concept of referential integrity should be the same with all relational databases.

NOT NULL Constraints

Previous examples use the keywords NULL and NOT NULL listed on the same line as each column and after the data type. NOT NULL is a constraint that you can place on a table's column. This constraint disallows the entrance of NULL values into a column; in other words, data is required in a NOT NULL column for each row of data in the table. NULL is generally the default for a column if NOT NULL is not specified, allowing NULL values in a column.

Using Check (CHK) Constraints

Check constraints can be utilized to check the validity of data entered into particular table columns. Check constraints are used to provide back-end database edits, although edits are commonly found in the front-end application as well. General edits restrict values that can be entered into columns or objects, whether within the database itself or on a front-end application. The check constraint is a way of providing another protective layer for the data.

The following example illustrates the use of a check constraint:

```
CREATE TABLE EMPLOYEE_TBL
(EMP_ID        CHAR(9)        NOT NULL,
 EMP_NAME      VARCHAR2(40)   NOT NULL,
 EMP_ST_ADDR   VARCHAR2(20)   NOT NULL,
```

```
EMP_CITY        VARCHAR2(15)   NOT NULL,
EMP_ST          CHAR(2)        NOT NULL,
EMP_ZIP         NUMBER(5)      NOT NULL,
EMP_PHONE       NUMBER(10)     NULL,
EMP_PAGER       NUMBER(10)     NULL),
PRIMARY KEY (EMP_ID),
CONSTRAINT CHK_EMP_ZIP CHECK ( EMP_ZIP = '46234' );
```

The check constraint in this table has been placed on the EMP_ZIP column, ensuring that all employees entered into this table have a ZIP code of '46234'. Perhaps that is a little restricting. Nevertheless, you can see how it works.

If you wanted to use a check constraint to verify that the ZIP code is within a list of values, your constraint definition could look like the following:

```
CONSTRAINT CHK_EMP_ZIP CHECK ( EMP_ZIP in ('46234','46227','46745') );
```

If there is a minimum pay rate that can be designated for an employee, you could have a constraint that looks like the following:

```
CREATE TABLE EMPLOYEE_PAY_TBL
(EMP_ID             CHAR(9)        NOT NULL,
POSITION           VARCHAR2(15)   NOT NULL,
DATE_HIRE          DATE           NULL,
PAY_RATE           NUMBER(4,2)    NOT NULL,
DATE_LAST_RAISE    DATE           NULL,
CONSTRAINT  EMP_ID_FK FOREIGN KEY (EMP_ID) REFERENCES EMPLOYEE_TBL (EMP_ID),
CONSTRAINT CHK_PAY CHECK ( PAY_RATE > 12.50 ) );
```

In this example, any employee entered in this table must be paid more than $12.50 an hour. You can use just about any condition in a check constraint, as you can with an SQL query. You learn more about these conditions in later hours.

Dropping Constraints

Any constraint that you have defined can be dropped using the ALTER TABLE command with the DROP CONSTRAINT option. For example, to drop the primary key constraint in the EMPLOYEES table, you can use the following command:

INPUT   `ALTER TABLE EMPLOYEES DROP CONSTRAINT EMPLOYEES_PK;`

OUTPUT   `Table altered.`

Some implementations may provide shortcuts for dropping certain constraints. For example, to drop the primary key constraint for a table in Oracle, you can use the following command:

INPUT   `ALTER TABLE EMPLOYEES DROP PRIMARY KEY;`

OUTPUT   `Table altered.`

 Some implementations allow you to disable constraints. Instead of permanently dropping a constraint from the database, you may want to temporarily disable the constraint, and then enable it later.

Summary

You have learned a little about database objects in general, but have specifically learned about the table. The table is the simplest form of data storage in a relational database. Tables contain groups of logical information, such as employee, customer, or product information. A table is composed of various columns, with each column having attributes; those attributes mainly consist of data types and constraints, such as NOT NULL values, primary keys, foreign keys, and unique values.

You learned the CREATE TABLE command and options, such as storage parameters, that may be available with this command. You have also learned how to modify the structure of existing tables using the ALTER TABLE command. Although the process of managing database tables may not be the most basic process in SQL, it is our philosophy that if you first learn the structure and nature of tables, you more easily grasp the concept of accessing the tables, whether through data manipulation operations or database queries. In later hours, you learn about the management of other objects in SQL, such as indexes on tables and views.

Q&A

Q When I name a table that I am creating, is it necessary to use a suffix such as _TBL?

A Absolutely not. You do not have to use anything. For example, a table to hold employee information could be named similar to the following, or anything else that would refer to what type of data is to be stored in that particular table:

EMPLOYEE

EMP_TBL

EMPLOYEE_TBL

EMPLOYEE_TABLE

WORKER

Q Why is it so important to use the schema name when dropping a table?

A Here's a true story about a new DBA that dropped a table: A programmer had created a table under his schema with the same name as a production table. That particular programmer left the company. The programmer's database account was being deleted from the database, but the DROP USER statement returned an error due to the fact that outstanding objects were owned by the programmer. After some investigation it was determined that the programmer's table was not needed, so a DROP TABLE statement was issued.

It worked like a charm—but the problem was that the DBA was logged in as the production schema when the DROP TABLE statement was issued. The DBA should have specified a schema name, or owner, for the table to be dropped. Yes, the wrong table in the wrong schema was dropped. It took approximately eight hours to restore the production database.

Workshop

The following workshop is composed of a series of quiz questions and practical exercises. The quiz questions are designed to test your overall understanding of the current material. The practical exercises are intended to afford you the opportunity to apply the concepts discussed during the current hour, as well as build upon the knowledge acquired in previous hours of study. Please take time to complete the quiz questions and exercises before continuing. Refer to Appendix C, "Answers to Quizzes and Exercises," for answers.

Quiz

1. Will the following CREATE TABLE statement work? If not, what needs to be done to correct the problem(s)?

```
CREATE TABLE EMPLOYEE_TABLE AS:
   ( SSN              NUMBER(9)      NOT NULL,
     LAST_NAME        VARCHAR2(20)   NOT NULL,
     FIRST_NAME       VARCHAR2(20)   NOT NULL,
     MIDDLE_NAME      VARCHAR2(20)   NOT NULL,
     ST ADDRESS       VARCHAR2(30)   NOT NULL,
     CITY             CHAR(20)       NOT NULL,
     STATE            CHAR2)         NOT NULL,
     ZIP              NUMBER(4)      NOT NULL,
     DATE HIRED       DATE)
     STORAGE
         (INITIAL       3K,
          NEXT        1K);
```

2. Can you drop a column from a table?

3. What happens if you do not include the STORAGE clause in the CREATE TABLE statement?

Exercises

1. Go to Appendix D, "Create Table Statements for Book Examples," to get the DDL for the tables used in this book and create the tables.

HOUR 4

The Normalization Process

In this hour, you learn the process of taking a raw database and breaking it into logical units called tables. This process is referred to as normalization.

The advantages and disadvantages of both normalization and denormalization of a database are discussed, as well as data integrity versus performance issues that pertain to normalization.

The highlights of this hour include

- What normalization is
- Benefits of normalization
- Advantages of denormalization
- Normalization techniques
- Guidelines of normalization
- The three normal forms
- Database design

Normalizing a Database

 Normalization is a process of reducing redundancies of data in a database. In addition to data, names, object names, and forms are also normalized in a database.

The Raw Database

A database that is not normalized may include data that is contained in one or more different tables for no apparent reason. This could be bad for security reasons, disk space usage, speed of queries, efficiency of database updates, and, maybe most importantly, data integrity. A database before normalization is one that has not been broken down logically into smaller, more manageable tables. Figure 4.1 illustrates the database used for this book before it was normalized.

FIGURE 4.1
The raw database.

```
COMPANY_DATABASE

emp_id              cust_id
last_name           cust_name
first_name          cust_address
middle_name         cust_city
address             cust_state
city                cust_zip
state               cust_phone
zip                 cust_fax
phone               ord_num
pager               qty
position            ord_date
date_hire           prod_id
pay_rate            prod_desc
bonus               cost
date_last_raise
```

Logical Database Design

NEW TERM Any database should be designed with the end user in mind. Logical database design, also referred to as the *logical model*, is the process of arranging data into logical, organized groups of objects that can easily be maintained. The logical design of a database should reduce data repetition or go so far as to completely eliminate it. After all, why store the same data twice? Naming conventions used in a database should also be standard and logical.

What Are the End User's Needs?

NEW TERM The needs of the end user should be one of the top considerations when designing a database. Remember that the end user is the person who ultimately uses the database. There should be ease of use through the user's *front-end tool* (a program that allows a user access to a database), but this, along with optimal performance, cannot be achieved if the user's needs are not taken into consideration.

Some user-related design considerations include the following:

- What data should be stored in the database?
- How will the user access the database?
- What privileges does the user require?
- How should the data be grouped in the database?
- What data is the most commonly accessed?
- How is all data related in the database?
- What measures should be taken to ensure accurate data?

Data Redundancy

Data should not be redundant, which means that the duplication of data should be kept to a minimum for several reasons. For example, it is unnecessary to store an employee's home address in more than one table. With duplicate data, unnecessary space is used. Confusion is always a threat when, for instance, an address for an employee in one table does not match the address of the same employee in another table. Which table is correct? Do you have documentation to verify the employee's current address? As if data management is not difficult enough, redundancy of data could prove to be a disaster.

The Normal Forms

The next sections discuss the normal forms, an integral concept involved in the process of database normalization.

 Normal form is a way of measuring the levels, or depth, to which a database has been normalized. A database's level of normalization is determined by the normal form.

The following are the three most common normal forms in the normalization process:

- The first normal form
- The second normal form
- The third normal form

Of the three normal forms, each subsequent normal form depends on normalization steps taken in the previous normal form. For example, to normalize a database using the second normal form, the database must first be in the first normal form.

The First Normal Form

The objective of the first normal form is to divide the base data into logical units called tables. When each table has been designed, a primary key is assigned to most or all tables. Examine Figure 4.2, which illustrates how the raw database, shown in the previous figure, has been redeveloped using the first normal form.

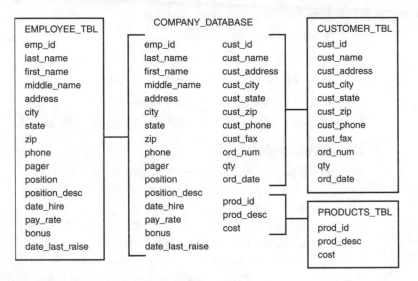

that to achieve the first normal form, data had to be broken into logical units, each having a primary key and ensuring that there are no repeated groups in any of the tables. Instead of one large table, there are now smaller, more manageable tables: EMPLOYEE_TBL, CUS-TOMER_TBL, and PRODUCTS_TBL. The primary keys are normally the first columns listed in a table, in this case: EMP_ID, CUST_ID, and PROD_ID.

The Second Normal Form

The objective of the second normal form is to take data that is only partly dependent on the primary key and enter that data into another table. Figure 4.3 illustrates the second normal form.

According to the figure, the second normal form is derived from the first normal form by further breaking two tables down into more specific units.

EMPLOYEE_TBL split into two tables called EMPLOYEE_TBL and EMPLOYEE_PAY_TBL. Personal employee information is dependent on the primary key (EMP_ID), so that information remained in the EMPLOYEE_TBL (EMP_ID, LAST_NAME, FIRST_NAME, MIDDLE_NAME,

ADDRESS, CITY, STATE, ZIP, PHONE, and PAGER). On the other hand, the information that is only partly dependent on the EMP_ID (each individual employee) is used to populate EMPLOYEE_PAY_TBL (EMP_ID, POSITION, POSITION_DESC, DATE_HIRE, PAY_RATE, DATE_LAST_RAISE). Notice that both tables contain the column EMP_ID. This is the primary key of each table and is used to match corresponding data between the two tables.

FIGURE 4.3

The second normal form.

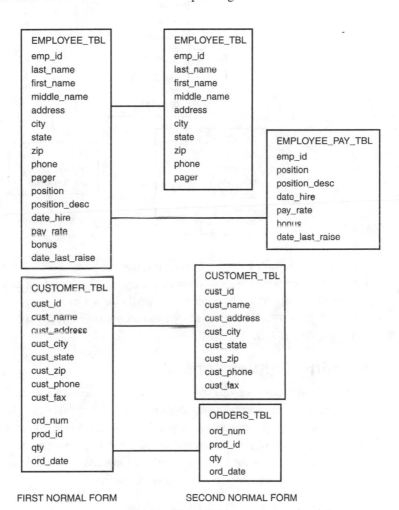

FIRST NORMAL FORM   SECOND NORMAL FORM

CUSTOMER_TBL split into two tables called CUSTOMER_TBL and ORDERS_TBL. What took place is similar to what occurred in the EMPLOYEE_TBL. Columns that were partly dependent on the primary key were directed to another table. The order information for a customer is dependent on each CUST_ID, but does not directly depend on the general customer information in the original table.

The Third Normal Form

The third normal form's objective is to remove data in a table that is not dependent on the primary key. Figure 4.4 illustrates the third normal form.

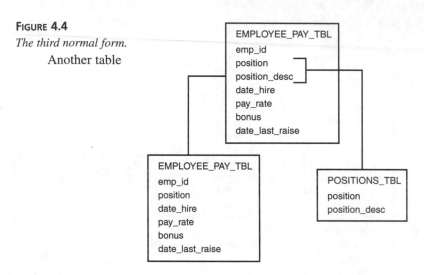

FIGURE 4.4

The third normal form.

Another table

was created to display the use of the third normal form. EMPLOYEE_PAY_TBL is split into two tables, one table containing the actual employee pay information and the other containing the position descriptions, which really do not need to reside in EMPLOYEE_PAY_TBL. The POSITION_DESC column is totally independent of the primary key, EMP_ID.

Naming Conventions

Naming conventions are one of the foremost considerations when you're normalizing a database. You want to give your tables names that are descriptive of the type of information they contain. A company-wide naming convention should be set, providing guidance in the naming of not only tables within the database, but users, filenames, and other related objects. Designing and enforcing naming conventions is one of a company's first steps toward a successful database implementation.

Benefits of Normalization

Normalization provides numerous benefits to a database. Some of the major benefits include the following:

- Greater overall database organization
- Reduction of redundant data

- Data consistency within the database
- A much more flexible database design
- A better handle on database security

Organization is brought about by the normalization process, making everyone's job easier, from the user who accesses tables to the database administrator (DBA) who is responsible for the overall management of every object in the database. Data redundancy is reduced, which simplifies data structures and conserves disk space. Because duplicate data is minimized, the possibility of inconsistent data is greatly reduced. For example, in one table an individual's name could read STEVE SMITH, whereas the name of the same individual reads STEPHEN R. SMITH in another table. Because the database has been normalized and broken into smaller tables, you are provided with more flexibility as far as modifying existing structures. It is much easier to modify a small table with little data than to modify one big table that holds all the vital data in the database. Lastly, security is also provided in the sense that the DBA can grant access to limited tables to certain users. Security is easier to control when normalization has occurred.

NEW TERM   *Data integrity* is the assurance of consistent and accurate data within a database.

Referential Integrity

Referential integrity simply means that the values of one column in a table depend on the values of a column in another table. For instance, in order for a customer to have a record in the ORDERS_TBL table, there must first be a record for that customer in the CUSTOMER_TBL table. Integrity constraints can also control values by restricting a range of values for a column. The integrity constraint should be created at the table's creation. Referential integrity is typically controlled through the use of primary and foreign keys.

In a table, a *foreign key*, normally a single field, directly references a primary key in another table to enforce referential integrity. In the preceding paragraph, the CUST_ID in ORDERS_TBL is a foreign key that references CUST_ID in CUSTOMER_TBL.

Drawbacks of Normalization

Although most successful databases are normalized to some degree, there is one substantial drawback of a normalized database: reduced database performance. The acceptance of reduced performance requires the knowledge that when a query or transaction request is sent to the database, there are factors involved, such as CPU usage, memory usage, and input/output (I/O). To make a long story short, a normalized database requires much more CPU, memory, and I/O to process transactions and database queries than does a denormalized database. A normalized database must locate the requested tables and then join the data from the tables to either get the requested information or to process the desired data. A more in-depth discussion concerning database performance occurs in Hour 18, "Managing Database Users."

Denormalizing a Database

NEW TERM   *Denormalization* is the process of taking a normalized database and modifying table structures to allow controlled redundancy for increased database performance. Attempting to improve performance is the only reason to ever denormalize a database. A denormalized database is not the same as a database that has not been normalized. *Denormalizing* a database is the process of taking the level of normalization within the database down a notch or two. Remember, normalization can actually slow performance with its frequently occurring table join operations. (Table joins are discussed during Hour 13, "Joining Tables in Queries.") Denormalization may involve recombining separate tables or creating duplicate data within tables to reduce the number of tables that need to be joined to retrieve the requested data, which results in less I/O and CPU time.

There are costs to denormalization, however. Data redundancy is increased in a denormalized database, which can improve performance but requires more extraneous efforts to keep track of related data. Application coding renders more complications, because the data has been spread across various tables and may be more difficult to locate. In addition, referential integrity is more of a chore; related data has been divided among a number of tables. There is a happy medium in both normalization and denormalization, but both require a thorough knowledge of the actual data and the specific business requirements of the pertinent company.

Summary

A difficult decision has to be made concerning database design—to normalize or not to normalize, that is the question. You will always want to normalize a database to some degree. How much do you normalize a database without destroying performance? The real decision relies on the application itself. How large is the database? What is its purpose? What types of users are going to access the data?

This hour covered the three most common normal forms, the concepts behind the normalization process, and the integrity of data. The normalization process involves many steps, most of which are optional but vital to the functionality and performance of your database. Regardless of how deep you decide to normalize, there will most always be a trade-off, either between simple maintenance and questionable performance or complicated maintenance and better performance. In the end, the individual (or team of individuals) designing the database must decide, and that person or team is responsible.

Q&A

Q Why should I be so concerned with the end user's needs when designing the database?

A The end users are the real data experts who use the database, and, in that respect, they should be the focus of any database design effort. The database designer only helps organize the data.

Q It seems to me that normalization is more advantageous than denormalization. Do you agree?

A It can be more advantageous. However, denormalization, to a point, could be more advantageous. Remember, there are many factors that help determine which way to go. You will probably normalize your database to reduce repetition in the database, but may turn around and denormalize to a certain extent to improve performance.

Workshop

The following workshop is composed of a series of quiz questions and practical exercises. The quiz questions are designed to test your overall understanding of the current material. The practical exercises are intended to afford you the opportunity to apply the concepts discussed during the current hour, as well as build upon the knowledge acquired in previous hours of study. Please take time to complete the quiz questions and exercises before continuing. Refer to Appendix C, "Answers to Quizzes and Exercises," for answers.

Quiz

1. True or false: Normalization is the process of grouping data into logical related groups.

2. True or false: Having no duplicate or redundant data in a database, and having everything in the database normalized, is always the best way to go.

3. True or false: If data is in the third normal form, it is automatically in the first and second normal forms.

4. What is a major advantage of a denormalized database versus a normalized database?

5. What are some major disadvantages of denormalization?

Exercises

1. You are developing a new database for a small company. Take the following data and normalize it. Keep in mind that there would be many more items for a small company than you are given here.

   Employees:

   Angela Smith, secretary, 317-545-6789, RR 1 Box 73, Greensburg, Indiana, 47890, $9.50 hour, date started January 22, 1996, SSN is 323149669.

   Jack Lee Nelson, salesman, 3334 N Main St, Brownsburg, IN, 45687, 317-852-9901, salary of $35,000.00 year, SSN is 312567342, date started 10/28/95.

   Customers:

   Robert's Games and Things, 5612 Lafayette Rd, Indianapolis, IN, 46224, 317-291-7888, customer ID is 432A.

   Reed's Dairy Bar, 4556 W 10th St, Indianapolis, IN, 46245, 317-271-9823, customer ID is 117A.

   Customer Orders:

   Customer ID is 117A, date of last order is December 20, 1999, product ordered was napkins and the product ID is 661.

HOUR 5

Manipulating Data

In this hour, you learn the part of SQL known as Data Manipulation Language—DML. DML is the part of SQL that is used to make changes to data and tables in a relational database.

This hour's highlights include

- An overview of data manipulation language
- Instruction on how to manipulate data in tables
- Concepts behind table population of data
- How to delete data from tables
- How to change or modify data in tables

Overview of Data Manipulation

Data Manipulation Language (DML) is the part of SQL that allows a database user to actually propagate changes among data in a relational database. With DML, the user can populate tables with new data, update existing data in tables, and delete data from tables. Simple database queries can also be performed within a DML command.

There are three basic DML commands in SQL:

    INSERT

    UPDATE

    DELETE

The SELECT command, which can be used with DML commands, is discussed in more detail in Hour 7, "Introduction to the Database Query."

Populating Tables with New Data

NEW TERM *Populating* a table with data is simply the process of entering new data into a table, whether through a manual process using individual commands or through batch processes using programs or other related software.

Many factors can affect what data and how much data can be put into a table when populating tables with data. Some major factors include existing table constraints, the physical table size, column data types, the length of columns, and other integrity constraints, such as primary and foreign keys. The following sections help you learn the basics of inserting new data into a table, in addition to offering some Dos and Don'ts.

> Do not forget that SQL statements can be in upper- or lowercase. The data, depending on how it is stored in the database, is not case-sensitive. These examples use both lower- and uppercases just to show that it does not affect the outcome.

Inserting Data into a Table

Use the INSERT statement to insert new data into a table. There are a few options with the INSERT statement; look at the following basic syntax to begin:

SYNTAX
```
insert into schema.table_name
VALUES ('value1', 'value2', [ NULL ] );
```

Using this INSERT statement syntax, you must include every column in the specified table in the VALUES list. Notice that each value in this list is separated by a comma. The values inserted into the table must be enclosed by quotation marks for character and date data types. Quotation marks are not required for numeric data types or NULL values using the NULL keyword. A value should be present for each column in the table.

In the following example, you insert a new record into the PRODUCTS_TBL table.

Table structure:

```
products_tbl

COLUMN Name                       Null?      DATA Type
-------------------------------   --------   -------------
PROD_ID                           NOT NULL   VARCHAR2(10)
PROD_DESC                         NOT NULL   VARCHAR2(25)
COST                              NOT NULL   NUMBER(6,2)
```

Sample INSERT statement:

```
INSERT INTO PRODUCTS_TBL
VALUES ('7725','LEATHER GLOVES',24.99);
```

```
1 row created.
```

In this example, you insert three values into a table with three columns. The inserted values are in the same order as the columns listed in the table. The first two values are inserted using quotation marks, because the data types of the corresponding columns are of character type. The third value's associated column, COST, is a numeric data type and does not require quotation marks, although they can be used.

The schema name, or table owner, has not been specified as part of the table name, as it was shown in the syntax. The schema name is not required if you are connected to the database as the user who owns the table.

5

Inserting Data into Limited Columns of a Table

There is a way you can insert data into a table's limited columns. For instance, suppose you want to insert all values for an employee except a pager number. You must, in this case, specify a column list as well as a VALUES list in your INSERT statement.

```
INSERT INTO EMPLOYEE_TBL
(EMP_ID, LAST_NAME, FIRST_NAME, MIDDLE_NAME, ADDRESS, CITY, STATE, ZIP,
PHONE)
VALUES
('123456789', 'SMITH', 'JOHN', 'JAY', '12 BEACON CT',
'INDIANAPOLIS', 'IN', '46222', '3172996868');
```

```
1 row created.
```

SYNTAX

The syntax for inserting values into a limited number of columns in a table is as follows:

```
INSERT INTO SCHEMA TABLE_NAME ('COLUMN1', 'COLUMN2')
VALUES ('VALUE1', 'VALUE2');
```

You use ORDERS_TBL and insert values into only specified columns in the following example.

Table structure:

ORDERS_TBL

```
COLUMN NAME                        Null?      DATA TYPE
--------------------------------   --------   -----------
ORD_NUM                            NOT NULL   VARCHAR2(10)
CUST_ID                            NOT NULL   VARCHAR2(10)
PROD_ID                            NOT NULL   VARCHAR2(10)
QTY                                NOT NULL   NUMBER(4)
ORD_DATE                                      DATE
```

Sample INSERT statement:

```
insert into orders_tbl (ord_num,cust_id,prod_id,qty)
values ('23A16','109','7725',2);
```

```
1 row created.
```

You have specified a column list enclosed by parentheses after the table name in the INSERT statement. You have listed all columns into which you want to insert data. ORD_DATE is the only excluded column. You can see, if you look at the table definition, that ORD_DATE does not require data for every record in the table. You know that ORD_DATE does not require data because NOT NULL is not specified in the table definition. NOT NULL tells us that NULL values are not allowed in the column. Furthermore, the list of values must appear in the order in which you want to insert them according to the column list.

The column list in the INSERT statement does not have to reflect the same order of columns as in the definition of the associated table, but the list of values must be in the order of the associated columns in the column list.

Inserting Data from Another Table

You can insert data into a table based on the results of a query from another table using a combination of the INSERT statement and the SELECT statement. Briefly, a *query* is an inquiry to the database that expects data to be returned. See Hour 7 for more information on queries. A query is a question that the user asks the database, and the data returned is the answer. In the case of combining the INSERT statement with the SELECT statement, you are able to insert the data retrieved from a query into a table.

The syntax for inserting data from another table is

SYNTAX

```
insert into schema.table_name [('column1', 'column2')]
select [*|('column1', 'column2')]
from table_name
[where condition(s)];
```

You see three new keywords in this syntax, which are covered here briefly. These keywords are SELECT, FROM, and WHERE. SELECT is the main command used to initiate a query in SQL. FROM is a clause in the query that specifies the names of tables in which the target data should be found. The WHERE clause, also part of the query, is used to place conditions on the query itself. An example condition may state: WHERE NAME = 'SMITH'. These three keywords are covered extensively during Hour 7 and Hour 8, "Using Operators to Categorize Data."

NEW TERM   A *condition* is a way of placing criteria on data affected by a SQL statement.

The following example uses a simple query to view all data in the PRODUCTS_TBL table. SELECT * tells the database server that you want information on all columns of the table. Because there is no WHERE clause, you want to see all records in the table as well.

INPUT   `select * from products_tbl;`

OUTPUT

```
PROD_ID    PROD_DESC                      COST
---------  ---------------------------    -----
11235      WITCHES COSTUME                29.99
222        PLASTIC PUMPKIN 18 INCH         7.75
13         FALSE PARAFFIN TEETH            1.1
90         LIGHTED LANTERNS               14.5
15         ASSORTED COSTUMES              10
9          CANDY CORN                      1.35
6          PUMPKIN CANDY                   1.45
87         PLASTIC SPIDERS                 1.05
119        ASSORTED MASKS                  4.95
1234       KEY CHAIN                       5.95
2345       OAK BOOKSHELF                  59.99

11 rows selected.
```

Now, insert values into the PRODUCTS_TMP table based on the preceding query. You can see that 11 rows are created in the temporary table.

5

INPUT

```
INSERT INTO PRODUCTS_TMP
SELECT * FROM PRODUCTS_TBL;
```

OUTPUT

```
11 rows created.
```

The following query shows all data in the PRODUCTS_TMP table that you just inserted:

INPUT

```
SELECT * FROM PRODUCTS_TMP;
```

OUTPUT

```
PROD_ID    PROD_DESC                         COST
---------- --------------------------------- -----
11235      WITCHES COSTUME                   29.99
222        PLASTIC PUMPKIN 18 INCH           7.75
13         FALSE PARAFFIN TEETH              1.1
90         LIGHTED LANTERNS                  14.5
15         ASSORTED COSTUMES                 10
9          CANDY CORN                        1.35
6          PUMPKIN CANDY                     1.45
87         PLASTIC SPIDERS                   1.05
119        ASSORTED MASKS                    4.95
1234       KEY CHAIN                         5.95
2345       OAK BOOKSHELF                     59.99

11 rows selected.
```

Inserting NULL Values

Inserting a NULL value into a column of a table is a simple matter. You might want to insert a NULL value into a column if the value of the column in question is unknown. For instance, not every person carries a pager, so it would be inaccurate to enter an erroneous pager number—not to mention, you would not be budgeting space. A NULL value can be inserted into a column of a table using the keyword NULL.

The syntax for inserting a NULL value follows:

SYNTAX

```
insert into schema.table_name values
('column1', NULL, 'column3');
```

The NULL keyword should be used in the associated column that exists in the table. That column will not have data in it for that row if you enter NULL. In the syntax, a NULL value is being entered in the place of COLUMN2.

Study the two following examples:

```
INSERT INTO ORDERS_TBL (ORD_NUM,CUST_ID,PROD_ID,QTY,ORD_DATE)
VALUES ('23A16','109','7725',2,NULL);
```

```
1 row created.
```

In the first example, all columns in which to insert values are listed, which also happen to be every column in the ORDERS_TBL table. You insert a NULL value for the ORD_DATE column, meaning that you either do not know the order date, or there is no order date at this time.

INPUT
```
INSERT INTO ORDERS_TBL
VALUES ('23A16','109','7725',2, '');
```

OUTPUT
```
1 row created.
```

There are two differences from the first statement in the second example, but the results are the same. First, there is not a column list. Remember that a column list is not required if you are inserting data into all columns of a table. Second, instead of inserting the value NULL into the ORD_DATE column, you insert ' ' (two single quotation marks together), which also symbolizes a NULL value (because there is nothing between them) .

Updating Existing Data

Pre-existing data in a table can be modified using the UPDATE command. The UPDATE command does not add new records to a table, nor does it remove records—it simply updates existing data. The update is generally used to update one table at a time in a database, but can be used to update multiple columns of a table at the same time. An individual row of data in a table can be updated, or numerous rows of data can be updated in a single statement, depending on what's needed.

Updating the Value of a Single Column

The most simple form of the UPDATE statement is its use to update a single column in a table. Either a single row of data or numerous records can be updated when updating a single column in a table.

The syntax for updating a single column follows:

SYNTAX
```
update table_name
set column_name = 'value'
[where condition];
```

The following example updates the QTY column in the ORDERS table to the new value 1 for the ORD_NUM 23A16, which you have specified using the WHERE clause.

INPUT
```
UPDATE ORDERS_TBL
SET QTY = 1
WHERE ORD_NUM = '23A16';
```

OUTPUT
```
1 row updated.
```

5

The following example is identical to the previous example, except for the absence of the WHERE clause:

TYPE
```
UPDATE ORDERS_TBL
SET QTY = 1;
```

OUTPUT
```
11 rows updated.
```

Notice that in this example, 11 rows of data were updated. You set the QTY to 1, which updated the quantity column in the ORDERS_TBL table for all rows of data. Is this really what you wanted to do? Perhaps in some cases, but rarely will you issue an UPDATE statement without a WHERE clause.

> Extreme caution must be used when using the UPDATE statement without a WHERE clause. The target column is updated for all rows of data in the table if conditions are not designated using the WHERE clause.

Updating Multiple Columns in One or More Records

Next, you see how to update multiple columns with a single UPDATE statement. Study the following syntax:

SYNTAX
```
update table_name
set column1 = 'value',
   [column2 = 'value',]
   [column3 = 'value']
[where condition];
```

Notice the use of the SET in this syntax—there is only one SET, but multiple columns. Each column is separated by a comma. You should start to see a trend in SQL. The comma is usually used to separate different types of arguments in SQL statements.

INPUT
```
UPDATE ORDERS_TBL
SET QTY = 1,
    CUST_ID = '221'
WHERE ORD_NUM = '23A16';
```

OUTPUT
```
1 row updated.
```

A comma is used to separate the two columns being updated. Again, the WHERE clause is optional, but usually necessary.

The SET keyword is used only once for each UPDATE statement. If more than one column is to be updated, a comma is used to separate the columns to be updated.

Deleting Data from Tables

The DELETE command is used to remove entire rows of data from a table. The DELETE command is not used to remove values from specific columns; a full record, including all columns, is removed. The DELETE statement must be used with caution—it works all too well. The next section discusses methods for deleting data from tables.

To delete a single record or selected records from a table, the DELETE statement must be used with the following syntax:

```
delete from schema.table_name
[where condition];
```

TYPE
```
DELETE FROM ORDERS_TBL
WHERE ORD_NUM = '23A16';
```

OUTPUT   1 row deleted.

Notice the use of the WHERE clause. The WHERE clause is an essential part of the DELETE statement if you are attempting to remove selected rows of data from a table. You rarely issue a DELETE statement without the use of the WHERE clause. If you do, your results are similar to the following example:

```
DELETE FROM ORDERS_TBL;
```

11 rows deleted.

If the WHERE clause is omitted from the DELETE statement, all rows of data are deleted from the table. As a general rule, always use a WHERE clause with the DELETE statement.

The temporary table that was populated from the original table earlier in this hour can be very useful for testing the DELETE and UPDATE commands before issuing them against the original table.

5

Summary

You have learned the three basic commands in Data Manipulation Language (DML): the INSERT, UPDATE, and DELETE statements. As you have seen, data manipulation is a very powerful part of SQL, allowing the database user to populate tables with new data, update existing data, and delete data.

A very important lesson when updating or deleting data from tables in a database is sometimes learned when neglecting the use of the WHERE clause. Remember that the WHERE clause places conditions on an SQL statement—particularly in the case of UDPATE and DELETE operations, when specifying specific rows of data that will be affected during a transaction. All target table data rows are affected if the WHERE clause is not used, which could be disastrous to the database. Protect your data and be cautious during data manipulation operations.

Q&A

Q With all the warnings about DELETE and UPDATE, I'm a little afraid to use them. If I accidentally update all the records in a table because the WHERE clause was not used, can the changes be reversed?

A There is no reason to be afraid, because there is not much you can do to the database that cannot be corrected, although considerable time and work may be involved. The next hour discusses the concepts of transactional control, which allows data manipulation operations to either be finalized or undone.

Q Is the INSERT statement the only way to enter data into a table?

A No, just remember that the INSERT statement is ANSI standard. The various implementations have their tools to enter data into tables. For example, Oracle has a utility called SQL*Loader. Also, many of the various implementations have utilities called IMPORT that can be used to insert data. There are many good books on the market that will expand on these utilities.

Workshop

The following workshop is composed of a series of quiz questions and practical exercises. The quiz questions are designed to test your overall understanding of the current material. The practical exercises are intended to afford you the opportunity to apply the concepts discussed during the current hour, as well as build upon the knowledge acquired in previous hours of study. Please take time to complete the quiz questions and exercises before continuing. Refer to Appendix C, "Answers to Quizzes and Exercises," for answers.

Quiz

1. Use the EMPLOYEE_TBL with the following structure:

COLUMN	DATA TYPE	(NOT)NULL
LAST_NAME	VARCHAR2(20)	NOT NULL
FIRST_NAME	VARCHAR2(20)	NOT NULL
SSN	CHAR(9)	NOT NULL
PHONE	NUMBER(10)	NULL

LAST_NAME	FIRST_NAME	SSN	PHONE
SMITH	JOHN	312456788	3174549923
ROBERTS	LISA	232118857	3175452321
SMITH	SUE	443221989	3178398712
PIERCE	BILLY	310239856	3176763990

What would happen if the following statements were run:

a.
```
insert into employee_tbl
('JACKSON', 'STEVE', '313546078', '3178523443');
```

b.
```
insert into employee_tbl values
('JACKSON', 'STEVE', '313546078', '3178523443');
```

c.
```
insert into employee_tbl values
('MILLER', 'DANIEL', '230980012', NULL);
```

d.
```
insert into employee_tbl values
('TAYLOR', NULL, '445761212', '3179221331');
```

e.
```
delete from employee_tbl;
```

f.
```
delete from employee_tbl
where last_name = 'SMITH';
```

g.
```
delete from employee_tbl
where last_name = 'SMITH'
and first_name = 'JOHN';
```

5

h.

```
update employee_tbl
set last_name = 'CONRAD';
```

i.

```
update employee_tbl
set last_name = 'CONRAD'
where last_name = 'SMITH';
```

j.

```
update employee_tbl
set last_name = 'CONRAD',
first_name = 'LARRY';
```

k.

```
update employee_tbl
set last_name = 'CONRAD'
first_name = 'LARRY'
where ssn = '313546078';
```

Exercises

1. Go to Appendix E of this book, "INSERT Statements for Data in Book Examples." Run the INSERT statements to populate the tables that you created in Exercise 1 of Hour 3. When this has been accomplished, you should be able to better follow the examples and exercise questions in this book.

2. Using the EMPLOYEE_TBL with the following structure:

COLUMN	DATA TYPE	(NOT)NULL
LAST_NAME	VARCHAR2(20)	NOT NULL
FIRST_NAME	VARCHAR2(20)	NOT NULL
SSN	CHAR(9)	NOT NULL
PHONE	NUMBER(10)	NULL

LAST_NAME	FIRST_NAME	SSN	PHONE
SMITH	JOHN	312456788	3174549923
ROBERTS	LISA	232118857	3175452321
SMITH	SUE	443221989	3178398712
PIERCE	BILLY	310239856	3176763990

Write DML to accomplish the following:

a. Correct Billy Pierce's SSN to read 310239857.

b. Add Ben Moore, PHONE is 317-5649880, ssn is 313456789.

c. John Smith quit; remove his record.

Hour 6

Managing Database Transactions

In this hour, you learn the concepts behind the management of database transactions.

The highlights of this hour include

- The definition of a transaction
- The commands used to control transactions
- The syntax and examples of transaction commands
- When to use transactional commands
- The consequences of poor transactional control

What Is a Transaction?

NEW TERM A *transaction* is a unit of work that is performed against a database. Transactions are units or sequences of work accomplished in a logical order, whether in a manual fashion by a user or automatically by some sort of a database program. In a relational database using SQL, transactions are accomplished using the DML commands that were discussed during Hour 5, "Manipulating Data" (INSERT, UPDATE, and DELETE). A transaction is the propagation of one or more changes to the database. For instance, you are performing a transaction if you performed an UPDATE statement on a table to change an individual's name.

A transaction can either be one DML statement or a group of statements. When managing groups of transactions, each designated group of transactions must be successful as one entity or none of them will be successful.

The following list describes the nature of transactions:

- All transactions have a beginning and an end.
- A transaction can be saved or undone.
- If a transaction fails in the middle, no part of the transaction can be saved to the database.

To start or execute transactions is implementation-specific. You must check your particular implementation for how to begin transactions. There is no explicit start or begin transaction in the ANSI standard.

What Is Transactional Control?

NEW TERM *Transactional control* is the ability to manage various transactions that may occur within a relational database management system. When you speak of transactions, you are referring to the INSERT, UPDATE, and DELETE commands, which were covered during the last hour.

When a transaction is executed and completes successfully, the target table is not immediately changed, although it may appear so according to the output. When a transaction successfully completes, there are transactional control commands that are used to finalize the transaction, either saving the changes made by the transaction to the database or reversing the changes made by the transaction.

There are three commands used to control transactions:

- COMMIT
- ROLLBACK
- SAVEPOINT

Each of these is discussed in detail in the following sections.

Transactional control commands are only used with the DML commands
INSERT, UPDATE, and DELETE. For example, you do not issue a COMMIT statement
after creating a table. When the table is created, it is automatically committed
to the database. Likewise, you cannot issue a ROLLBACK to replenish a table
that was just dropped.

When a transaction has completed, the transactional information is stored either in an
allocated area or in a temporary rollback area in the database. All changes are held in this
temporary rollback area until a transactional control command is issued. When a transactional control command is issued, changes are either made to the database or discarded;
then, the temporary rollback area is emptied. Figure 6.1 illustrates how changes are
applied to a relational database.

FIGURE 6.1
Rollback area.

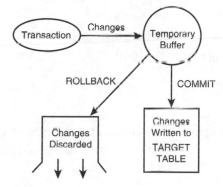

The COMMIT Command

The COMMIT command is the transactional command used to save changes invoked by a
transaction to the database. The COMMIT command saves all transactions to the database
since the last COMMIT or ROLLBACK command.

The syntax for this command is

```
COMMIT [ WORK ];
```

The keyword COMMIT is the only mandatory part of the syntax, along with the character
or command used to terminate a statement according to each implementation. WORK is a
keyword that is completely optional; its only purpose is to make the command more
user-friendly.

SYNTAX

6

In the following example, you begin by selecting all data from the PRODUCT_TMP table:

```
SELECT * FROM PRODUCTS_TMP;
```

```
PROD_ID    PROD_DESC                      COST
.........  ....................          ......
11235      WITCHES COSTUME               29.99
222        PLASTIC PUMPKIN 18 INCH        7.75
13         FALSE PARAFFIN TEETH           1.1
90         LIGHTED LANTERNS              14.5
15         ASSORTED COSTUMES             10
9          CANDY CORN                     1.35
6          PUMPKIN CANDY                  1.45
87         PLASTIC SPIDERS                1.05
119        ASSORTED MASKS                 4.95
1234       KEY CHAIN                      5.95
2345       OAK BOOKSHELF                 59.99

11 rows selected.
```

Next, you delete all records from the table where the product cost is less than $14.00.

```
DELETE FROM PRODUCTS_TMP
WHERE COST < 14;
```

OUTPUT   8 rows deleted.

A COMMIT statement is issued to save the changes to the database, completing the transaction.

INPUT   `COMMIT;`

OUTPUT   Commit complete.

Frequent COMMITs in large loads or unloads of the database are highly recommended; however, too many COMMITs cause the job running to take a lot of extra time to complete. Remember that all changes are sent to the temporary rollback area first. If this temporary rollback area runs out of space and cannot store information about changes made to the database, the database will probably halt, disallowing further transactional activity.

In some implementations, transactions are committed without issuing the COMMIT command—instead, merely signing out of the database causes a commit to occur.

The ROLLBACK Command

The ROLLBACK command is the transactional control command used to undo transactions that have not already been saved to the database. The ROLLBACK command can only be used to undo transactions since the last COMMIT or ROLLBACK command was issued.

The syntax for the ROLLBACK command is as follows:

SYNTAX

```
rollback [ work ];
```

Once again, as in the COMMIT statement, the WORK keyword is an optional part of the ROLLBACK syntax.

In the following example, you begin by selecting all records from the PRODUCTS_TMP table since the previous deletion of 14 records:

INPUT
```
SELECT * FROM PRODUCTS_TMP;
```

OUTPUT
```
PROD_ID    PROD_DESC                          COST
.......... ................................. ......
11235      WITCHES COSTUME                   29.99
90         LIGHTED LANTERNS                  14.5
2345       OAK BOOKSHELF                     59.99

3 rows selected.
```

Next, you update the table, changing the product cost to $39.99 for the product identification number 11235:

INPUT
```
UPDATE PRODUCTS_TMP
SET COST = 39.99
WHERE PROD_ID = '11235';
```

OUTPUT
```
1 row updated.
```

If you perform a quick query on the table, the change appears to have occurred:

INPUT
```
SELECT * FROM PRODUCTS_TMP;
```

OUTPUT
```
PROD_ID    PROD_DESC                          COST
.......... ................................. ......
11235      WITCHES COSTUME                   39.99
90         LIGHTED LANTERNS                  14.5
2345       OAK BOOKSHELF                     59.99

3 rows selected.
```

6

Now, issue the ROLLBACK statement to undo the last change:

INPUT   `ROLLBACK;`

OUTPUT   `Rollback complete.`

Finally, verify that the change was not committed to the database:

INPUT   `SELECT * FROM PRODUCTS_TMP;`

OUTPUT

```
PROD_ID     PROD_DESC                         COST
---------   -------------------------------   ------
11235       WITCHES COSTUME                   29.99
90          LIGHTED LANTERNS                  14.5
2345        OAK BOOKSHELF                     59.99
```

3 rows selected

The SAVEPOINT Command

A SAVEPOINT is a point in a transaction when you can roll the transaction back to a certain point without rolling back the entire transaction.

The syntax for the SAVEPOINT command is

SAVEPOINT SAVEPOINT_NAME

This command serves only in the creation of a SAVEPOINT among transactional statements. The ROLLBACK command is used to undo a group of transactions. The SAVEPOINT is a way of managing transactions by breaking large numbers of transactions into smaller, more manageable groups.

> The SAVEPOINT name must be unique to the associated group of transactions. However, the SAVEPOINT can have the same name as a table or other object. Refer to specific implementation documentation for more details on naming conventions.

The ROLLBACK TO SAVEPOINT Command

The syntax for rolling back to a SAVEPOINT is as follows:

ROLLBACK TO SAVEPOINT_NAME;

In this example, you plan to delete the remaining three records from the PRODUCTS_TMP table. You want to create a SAVEPOINT before each delete, so that you can ROLLBACK to any SAVEPOINT at any time to return the appropriate data to its original state:

INPUT
```
SAVEPOINT SP1;
```

OUTPUT
```
Savepoint created.
```

INPUT
```
DELETE FROM PRODUCTS_TMP WHERE PROD_ID = '11235';
```

OUTPUT
```
1 row deleted.
```

INPUT
```
SAVEPOINT SP2;
```

OUTPUT
```
Savepoint created.
```

INPUT
```
DELETE FROM PRODUCTS_TMP WHERE PROD_ID = '90';
```

OUTPUT
```
1 row deleted.
```

INPUT
```
SAVEPOINT SP3;
```

OUTPUT
```
Savepoint created.
```

INPUT
```
DELETE FROM PRODUCTS_TMP WHERE PROD_ID = '2345';
```

OUTPUT
```
1 row deleted.
```

Now that the three deletions have taken place, say you have changed your mind and decided to ROLLBACK to the SAVEPOINT that you identified as SP2. Because SP2 was created after the first deletion, the last two deletions are undone:

6

INPUT
```
ROLLBACK TO SP2;
```

OUTPUT
```
Rollback complete.
```

Notice that only the first deletion took place since you rolled back to SP2:

INPUT

```
SELECT * FROM PRODUCTS_TMP;
```

OUTPUT

```
PROD_ID      PROD_DESC                          COST
.........    ..............................     .....
90           LIGHTED LANTERNS                   14.5
2345         OAK BOOKSHELF                      59.99
```

```
2 rows selected.
```

Remember, the ROLLBACK command by itself will roll back to the last COMMIT or
ROLLBACK. You have not yet issued a COMMIT, so all deletions are undone, as in the
following example:

INPUT

```
ROLLBACK;
```

OUTPUT

```
Rollback complete.
```

INPUT

```
SELECT * FROM PRODUCTS_TMP;
```

OUTPUT

```
PROD_ID      PROD_DESC                          COST
.........    ..............................     ......
11235        WITCHES COSTUME                    29.99
90           LIGHTED LANTERNS                   14.5
2345         OAK BOOKSHELF                      59.99
```

```
3 rows selected.
```

The RELEASE SAVEPOINT Command

The RELEASE SAVEPOINT command is used to remove a SAVEPOINT that you have
created. Once a SAVEPOINT has been released, you can no longer use the ROLLBACK
command to undo transactions performed since the SAVEPOINT.

```
RELEASE SAVEPOINT SAVEPOINT_NAME;
```

SYNTAX

The SET TRANSACTION Command

The SET TRANSACTION command can be used to initiate a database transaction. This
command is used to specify characteristics for the transaction that follows. For example,
you can specify a transaction to be read only, or read write. For example,

```
SET TRANSACTION READ WRITE;
SET TRANSACTION READ ONLY;
```

There are other characteristics that can be set for a transaction which are out of the scope of
this book. For more information, see the documentation for your implementation of SQL.

Transactional Control and Database Performance

Poor transactional control can hurt database performance and even bring the database to a halt. Repeatedly poor database performance may be due to a lack of transactional control during large inserts, updates, or deletes. Not only are large batch processes, such as these, demanding on the CPU and memory themselves, but the temporary storage for rollback information continues to grow until either a COMMIT or ROLLBACK command is issued.

When a COMMIT is issued, rollback transactional information is written to the target table and the rollback information in temporary storage is cleared. When a ROLLBACK is issued, no changes are made to the database and the rollback information in the temporary storage is cleared. If neither a COMMIT or ROLLBACK is issued, the temporary storage for rollback information continues to grow until there is no more space left, thus forcing the database to stop all processes until space is freed.

Summary

During this hour, you learned the preliminary concepts of transactional management through the use of three transactional control commands: COMMIT, ROLLBACK, and SAVEPOINT. COMMIT is used to save a transaction to the database. ROLLBACK is used to undo a transaction that was performed. SAVEPOINT is used to break a transaction or transactions into groups, allowing you to roll back to specific logical points in transaction processing.

Remember that you should frequently use the COMMIT and ROLLBACK commands when running large transactional jobs to keep space free in the database. Also keep in mind that these transactional commands are used only with the three DML commands (INSERT, UPDATE, and DELETE).

Q&A

Q **Is it necessary to issue a commit after every INSERT statement?**

A No, not necessarily. If you were inserting a few hundred thousand rows into a table, a COMMIT would be recommended every 5,000–10,000, depending on the size of the temporary rollback area. Remember that the database stops when the rollback area fills up.

Q **How does the ROLLBACK command undo a transaction?**

A The ROLLBACK command clears all changes from the rollback area.

6

Q **If I issue a transaction and 99 percent of the transaction completes but the
other 1 percent errs, will I be able to redo only the error part?**

A No, the entire transaction must succeed; otherwise, data integrity is compromised.

Q **A transaction is permanent after I issue a COMMIT, but can't I change data with
an update?**

A *Permanent* used in this matter means that it is now a part of the database. The
UPDATE statement can always be used to make corrections to the database.

Workshop

The following workshop is composed of a series of quiz questions and practical exercises.
The quiz questions are designed to test your overall understanding of the current material.
The practical exercises are intended to afford you the opportunity to apply the concepts
discussed during the current hour, as well as build upon the knowledge acquired in previous hours of study. Please take time to complete the quiz questions and exercises before
continuing. Refer to Appendix C, "Answers to Quizzes and Exercises," for answers.

Quiz

1. True or false: If you have committed several transactions, have several more
   transactions that have not been committed, and issue a ROLLBACK command, all
   your transactions for the same session are undone.

2. True or false: A SAVEPOINT actually saves transactions after a specified amount
   of transactions have executed.

3. Briefly describe the purpose of each one of the following commands: COMMIT,
   ROLLBACK, and SAVEPOINT.

Exercises

1. Take the following transactions and create SAVEPOINTs after every three
   transactions. Then, COMMIT the transactions.

   ```
   transaction1;
   transaction2;
   transaction3;
   transaction4;
   transaction5;
   transaction6;
   transaction7;
   transaction8;
   transaction9;
   transaction10;
   transaction11;
   transaction12;
   ```

PART III

Getting Effective Results from Queries

Hour

Hour 7

Introduction to the Database Query

In this seventh hour, you learn about database queries, which involve the use of the SELECT statement. The SELECT statement is probably the most frequently used of all SQL commands after a database's establishment.

The highlights of this hour include

- What a database query is
- How to use the SELECT statement
- Adding conditions to queries using the WHERE clause
- Using column aliases
- Selecting data from another user's table

What Is a Query?

NEW TERM   A *query* is an inquiry into the database using the SELECT statement. A query is used to extract data from the database in a readable format according to the user's request. For instance, if you have an employee table, you might issue a SQL statement that returns the employee who is paid the most. This request to the database for usable employee information is a typical query that can be performed in a relational database.

Introduction to the SELECT Statement

The SELECT statement, the command that represents Data Query Language (DQL) in SQL, is the statement used to construct database queries. The SELECT statement is not a standalone statement, which means that clauses are required. In addition to the required clauses, there are optional clauses that increase the overall functionality of the SELECT statement. The SELECT statement is by far one of the most powerful statements in SQL. The FROM clause is the mandatory clause and must always be used in conjunction with the SELECT statement.

 There are four keywords, or *clauses*, that are valuable parts of a SELECT statement. These keywords are as follows:

- SELECT
- FROM
- WHERE
- ORDER BY

Each of these keywords is covered in detail during the following sections.

The SELECT Statement

The SELECT statement is used in conjunction with the FROM clause to extract data from the database in an organized, readable format. The SELECT part of the query is for selecting the data you want to see according to the columns in which they are stored in a table.

The syntax for a simple SELECT statement is as follows:

```
SELECT [ * | ALL | DISTINCT COLUMN1, COLUMN2 ]
FROM TABLE1 [ , TABLE2 ];
```

The SELECT keyword in a query is followed by a list of columns that you want displayed as part of the query output. The FROM keyword is followed by a list of one or more tables from which you want to select data. The asterisk (*) is used to denote that all columns in a table should be displayed as part of the output. Check your particular implementation for its usage. The ALL option is used to display all values for a column, including duplicates. The DISTINCT option is used to eliminate duplicate rows. The default between DISTINCT and ALL is ALL, which does not have to be specified. Notice that the columns following the SELECT are separated by commas, as is the table list following the FROM.

Commas are used to separate arguments in a list in SQL statements. Some common lists include lists of columns in a query, lists of tables to be selected from in a query, values to be inserted into a table, and values grouped as a condition in a query's WHERE clause.

NEW TERM   *Arguments* are values that are either required or optional to the syntax of a SQL statement or command.

Explore the basic capabilities of the SELECT statement by studying the following examples. First, perform a simple query from the PRODUCTS_TBL table:

INPUT
```
SELECT * FROM PRODUCTS_TBL;
```

OUTPUT
```
PROD_ID     PROD_DESC                      COST
---------   ----------------------------   ------
11235       WITCHES COSTUME                29.99
222         PLASTIC PUMPKIN 18 INCH        7.75
13          FALSE PARAFFIN TEETH           1.1
90          LIGHTED LANTERNS               14.5
15          ASSORTED COSTUMES              10
9           CANDY CORN                     1.35
6           PUMPKIN CANDY                  1.45
87          PLASTIC SPIDERS                1.05
119         ASSORTED MASKS                 4.95
1234        KEY CHAIN                      5.95
2345        OAK BOOKSHELF                  59.99

11 rows selected.
```

The asterisk represents all columns in the table, which, as you can see, are displayed in the form PROD_ID, PROD_DESC, and COST. Each column in the output is displayed in the order that it appears in the table. There are 11 records in this table, identified by the feedback 11 rows selected. This feedback differs among implementations; for example, another feedback for the same query would be 11 rows affected.

Now select data from another table, CANDY_TBL. Create this table in the image of the PRODUCTS_TBL table for the following examples. List the column name after the SELECT keyword to display only one column in the table:

INPUT
```
SELECT PROD_DESC FROM CANDY_TBL;
```

OUTPUT
```
PROD_DESC
-----------------
CANDY CORN
CANDY CORN
HERSHEYS KISS
SMARTIES

4 rows selected.
```

7

Four records exist in the CANDY_TBL table. You have used the ALL option in the next statement to show you that the ALL is optional and redundant. There is never a need to specify ALL; it is a default option.

INPUT
```
SELECT ALL PROD_DESC
FROM CANDY_TBL;
```

OUTPUT
```
PROD_DESC
------------------
CANDY CORN
CANDY CORN
HERSHEYS KISS
SMARTIES

4 rows selected.
```

The DISTINCT option is used in the following statement to suppress the display of duplicate records. Notice that the value CANDY CORN is only printed once in this example.

INPUT
```
SELECT DISTINCT PROD_DESC
FROM CANDY_TBL;
```

OUTPUT
```
PROD_DESC
------------------
CANDY CORN
HERSHEYS KISS
SMARTIES

3 rows selected.
```

DISTINCT and ALL can also be used with parentheses enclosing the associated column. The use of parentheses is often used in SQL—as well as many other languages—to improve readability.

INPUT
```
SELECT DISTINCT(PROD_DESC)
FROM CANDY_TBL;
```

OUTPUT
```
PROD_DESC
------------------
CANDY CORN
HERSHEYS KISS
SMARTIES

3 rows selected.
```

The FROM Clause

The FROM clause is always used in conjunction with the SELECT statement. It is a required element for any query. The FROM clause's purpose is to tell the database what table(s) to access to retrieve the desired data for the query. The FROM clause can contain one or more tables.

The syntax for the FROM clause is as follows:

```
FROM TABLE1 [ , TABLE2 ]
```

Using Conditions to Distinguish Data

NEW TERM   A *condition* is part of a query that is used to display selective information as specified by the user. The value of a condition is either TRUE or FALSE, thereby limiting the data received from the query. The WHERE clause is used to place conditions on a query by eliminating rows that would normally be returned by a query without conditions.

There can be more than one condition in the WHERE clause. If there is more than one condition, they are connected by the AND and OR operators, which are discussed during Hour 8, "Using Operators to Categorize Data." As you also learn during the next hour, there are several conditional operators that can be used to specify conditions in a query. This hour only deals with a single condition for each query.

NEW TERM   An *operator* is a character or keyword in SQL that is used to combine elements in a SQL statement.

The syntax for the WHERE clause is as follows:

```
SELECT [ ALL | * | DISTINCT COLUMN1, COLUMN2 ]
FROM TABLE1 [ , TABLE2 ]
WHERE [ CONDITION1 | EXPRESSION1 ]
[ AND CONDITION2 | EXPRESSION2 ]
```

The following is a simple SELECT without conditions specified by the WHERE clause:

INPUT
```
SELECT *
FROM PRODUCTS_TBL;
```

OUTPUT
```
PROD_ID     PROD_DESC                          COST
----------  --------------------------------   ------
11235       WITCHES COSTUME                    29.99
222         PLASTIC PUMPKIN 18 INCH             7.75
13          FALSE PARAFFIN TEETH                1.1
90          LIGHTED LANTERNS                   14.5
15          ASSORTED COSTUMES                  10
9           CANDY CORN                          1.35
6           PUMPKIN CANDY                       1.45
87          PLASTIC SPIDERS                     1.05
119         ASSORTED MASKS                      4.95
1234        KEY CHAIN                           5.95
2345        OAK BOOKSHELF                      59.99

11 rows selected.
```

7

Now add a condition for the same query.

INPUT

```
SELECT * FROM PRODUCTS_TBL
WHERE COST < 5;
```

OUTPUT

```
PROD_ID    PROD_DESC                        COST
.........  ..............................   .....
13         FALSE PARAFFIN TEETH             1.1
9          CANDY CORN                       1.35
6          PUMPKIN CANDY                    1.45
87         PLASTIC SPIDERS                  1.05
119        ASSORTED MASKS                   4.95

5 rows selected.
```

The only records displayed are those that cost less than $5.

In the following query, you want to display the product description and cost that matches the product identification 119.

INPUT

```
SELECT PROD_DESC, COST
FROM PRODUCTS_TBL
WHERE PROD_ID = '119';
```

OUTPUT

```
PROD_DESC                          COST
.................................  .....
ASSORTED MASKS                     4.95

1 row selected.
```

Sorting Your Output

You usually want your output to have some kind of order. Data can be sorted by using the ORDER BY clause. The ORDER BY clause arranges the results of a query in a listing format you specify. The default ordering of the ORDER BY clause is an *ascending order*; the sort displays in the order A–Z if it's sorting output names alphabetically. A *descending order* for alphabetical output would be displayed in the order Z–A. Ascending order for output for numeric values between 1 and 9 would be displayed 1–9; descending order is displayed as 9–1.

The syntax for the ORDER BY is as follows:

SYNTAX

```
SELECT [ ALL | * | DISTINCT COLUMN1, COLUMN2 ]
FROM TABLE1 [ , TABLE2 ]
WHERE [ CONDITION1 | EXPRESSION1 ]
[ AND CONDITION2 | EXPRESSION2 ]
ORDER BY COLUMN1|INTEGER [ ASC|DESC ]
```

Begin your exploration of the ORDER BY clause with an extension of one of the previous statements. Order by the product description in ascending order or alphabetical order.

Note the use of the ASC option. ASC can be specified after any column in the ORDER BY clause.

```
SELECT PROD_DESC, PROD_ID, COST
FROM PRODUCTS_TBL
WHERE COST < 20
ORDER BY PROD_DESC ASC;
```

OUTPUT

```
PROD_DESC                  PROD_ID           COST
-------------------------  ---------------   ------
ASSORTED COSTUMES          15                10
ASSORTED MASKS             119               4.95
CANDY CORN                 9                 1.35
FALSE PARAFFIN TEETH       13                1.1
LIGHTED LANTERNS           90                14.5
PLASTIC PUMPKIN 18 INCH    222               7.75
PLASTIC SPIDERS            87                1.05
PUMPKIN CANDY              6                 1.45

8 rows selected.
```

> Because ascending order for output is the default, ASC does not have to be specified.

You can use DESC, as in the following statement, if you want the same output to be sorted in reverse alphabetical order.

INPUT

```
SELECT PROD_DESC, PROD_ID, COST
FROM PRODUCTS_TBL
WHERE COST < 20
ORDER BY PROD_DESC DESC;
```

OUTPUT

```
PROD_DESC                  PROD_ID           COST
-------------------------  ---------------   ------
PUMPKIN CANDY              6                 1.45
PLASTIC SPIDERS            87                1.05
PLASTIC PUMPKIN 18 INCH    222               7.75
LIGHTED LANTERNS           90                14.5
FALSE PARAFFIN TEETH       13                1.1
CANDY CORN                 9                 1.35
ASSORTED MASKS             119               4.95
ASSORTED COSTUMES          15                10

8 rows selected.
```

7

There are shortcuts in SQL. A column listed in the ORDER BY clause can be abbreviated with an integer. The INTEGER is a substitution for the actual column name, identifying the position of the column after the SELECT keyword.

An example of using an integer as an identifier in the ORDER BY clause follows:

INPUT

```
SELECT PROD_DESC, PROD_ID, COST
FROM PRODUCTS_TBL
WHERE COST < 20
ORDER BY 1;
```

OUTPUT

```
PROD_DESC                   PROD_ID          COST
------------------------    ---------------  ------
ASSORTED COSTUMES           15               10
ASSORTED MASKS              119              4.95
CANDY CORN                  9                1.35
FALSE PARAFFIN TEETH        13               1.1
LIGHTED LANTERNS            90               14.5
PLASTIC PUMPKIN 18 INCH     222              7.75
PLASTIC SPIDERS             87               1.05
PUMPKIN CANDY               6                1.45

8 rows selected.
```

In this query, the integer 1 represents the column PROD_DESC. The integer 2 represents the PROD_ID column, 3 represents the COST column, and so on.

You can order by multiple columns in a query, using either the column name itself or the associated number of the column in the SELECT:

```
ORDER BY 1,2,3
```

Columns in an ORDER BY clause are not required to appear in the same order as the associated columns following the SELECT, as shown by the following example:

```
ORDER BY 1,3,2
```

Case Sensitivity

Case sensitivity is a very important concept to understand when coding with SQL. Typically, SQL commands and keywords are not case-sensitive, which allows you to enter your commands and keywords in either upper- or lowercase—whatever you prefer. The case may be mixed (both upper- and lowercase for a single word or statement). See Hour 5, "Manipulating Data," on case sensitivity.

Case sensitivity is, however, a factor when dealing with data in SQL. In most situations, data seems to be stored exclusively in uppercase in a relational database to provide data consistency.

For instance, your data would not be consistent if you arbitrarily entered your data using random case:

```
SMITH
```

```
Smith
```

```
smith
```

If the last name was stored as smith and you issued a query as follows, no rows would be returned.

```
SELECT *
FROM EMPLOYEE_TBL
WHERE LAST_NAME = 'SMITH';
```

You must use the same case in your query as the data is stored when referencing data in the database. When entering data, consult the rules set forth by your company for the appropriate case to be used.

Examples of Simple Queries

This section provides several examples of queries based on the concepts that have been discussed. The hour begins with the simplest query you can issue, and builds upon the initial query progressively. You use the EMPLOYEE_TBL table.

Selecting all records from a table and displaying all columns:

```
SELECT * FROM EMPLOYEE_TBL;
```

Selecting all records from a table and displaying a specified column:

```
SELECT EMP_ID
FROM EMPLOYEE_TBL;
```

Selecting all records from a table and displaying a specified column. You can enter code on one line or use a carriage return as desired:

```
SELECT EMP_ID FROM EMPLOYEE_TBL;
```

Selecting all records from a table and displaying multiple columns separated by commas:

```
SELECT EMP_ID, LAST_NAME
FROM EMPLOYEE_TBL;
```

Displaying data for a given condition:

```
SELECT EMP_ID, LAST_NAME
FROM EMPLOYEE_TBL
WHERE EMP_ID = '333333333';
```

Displaying data for a given condition and sorting the output:

```
SELECT EMP_ID, LAST_NAME
FROM EMPLOYEE_TBL
WHERE CITY = 'INDIANAPOLIS'
ORDER BY EMP_ID;
```

7

Displaying data for a given condition and sorting the output on multiple columns, one column sorted in reverse order:

```
SELECT EMP_ID, LAST_NAME
FROM EMPLOYEE_TBL
WHERE CITY = 'INDIANAPOLIS'
ORDER BY EMP_ID, LAST_NAME DESC;
```

Displaying data for a given condition and sorting the output using an integer in the place of the spelled-out column name:

```
SELECT EMP_ID, LAST_NAME
FROM EMPLOYEE_TBL
WHERE CITY = 'INDIANAPOLIS'
ORDER BY 1;
```

Displaying data for a given condition and sorting the output by multiple columns using integers, the order of the columns in the sort is different than their corresponding order after the SELECT keyword:

```
SELECT EMP_ID, LAST_NAME
FROM EMPLOYEE_TBL
WHERE CITY = 'INDIANAPOLIS'
ORDER BY 2, 1;
```

When selecting all rows of data from a large table, the results could render a substantial amount of data returned.

Counting the Records in a Table

A simple query can be issued on a table to get a quick count on the number of records in the table or on the number of values for a column in the table. A count is accomplished by the function COUNT. Although functions are not discussed until later in this book, this function should be introduced here because it is often a part of one of the simplest queries that you can create.

The syntax of the COUNT function is as follows:

```
SELECT COUNT(*)
FROM TABLE_NAME;
```

The COUNT function is used with parentheses, which are used to enclose the target column to count or the asterisk to count all rows of data in the table.

Counting the number of records in the PRODUCTS_TBL table:

```
SELECT COUNT(*) FROM PRODUCTS_TBL;
```

```
COUNT(*)
----------
         9
```

1 row selected.

Counting the number of values for PROD_ID in the PRODUCTS_TBL table:

```
SELECT COUNT(PROD_ID) FROM PRODUCTS_TBL;
```

```
COUNT(PROD_ID)
--------------
             9
```

1 row selected.

> Counting the number of values for a column is the same as counting the number of records in a table, if the column being counted is NOT NULL (a required column).

Selecting Data from Another User's Table

Permission must be granted to a user to access another user's table. If no permission has been granted, access is not allowed by users that do not own the table. You can select data from another user's table after access has been granted (the GRANT command is discussed in Hour 20, "Creating and Using Views and Synonyms") to select from another user's table. To access another user's table in a SELECT statement, you must precede the table name with the schema name or the username that owns the table, as in the following example:

```
SELECT EMP_ID
FROM SCHEMA.EMPLOYEE_TBL;
```

> If a synonym exists in the database for the table to which you desire access, you do not have to specify the schema name for the table. *Synonyms* are alternate names for tables, which are discussed in Hour 21, "Working with the System Catalog."

7

Column Aliases

Column aliases are used to rename a table's columns for the purpose of a particular query. The PRODUCTS_TBL illustrates the use of column aliases.

```
SELECT COLUMN_NAME ALIAS_NAME
FROM TABLE_NAME;
```

The following example displays the product description twice, giving the second column an alias named PRODUCT. Notice the column headers in the output.

INPUT
```
SELECT PROD_DESC,
       PROD_DESC PRODUCT
FROM PRODUCTS_TBL;
```

OUTPUT
```
PROD_DESC                     PRODUCT
----------------------------  ------------------------
WITCHES COSTUME               WITCHES COSTUME
PLASTIC PUMPKIN 18 INCH       PLASTIC PUMPKIN 18 INCH
FALSE PARAFFIN TEETH          FALSE PARAFFIN TEETH
LIGHTED LANTERNS              LIGHTED LANTERNS
ASSORTED COSTUMES             ASSORTED COSTUMES
CANDY CORN                    CANDY CORN
PUMPKIN CANDY                 PUMPKIN CANDY
PLASTIC SPIDERS               PLASTIC SPIDERS
ASSORTED MASKS                ASSORTED MASKS
1234                          KEY CHAIN
2345                          OAK BOOKSHELF

11 rows selected.
```

Column aliases can be used to customize names for column headers, and can also be used to reference a column with a shorter name in some SQL implementations.

When a column is renamed in a SELECT statement, the name is not a permanent change. The change is for that particular SELECT statement.

Summary

You have been introduced to the database query, a means for obtaining useful information from a relational database. The SELECT statement, which is known as the Data Query Language (DQL) command, is used to create queries in SQL. The FROM clause must be included with every SELECT statement. You have learned how to place a condition on a query using the WHERE clause and how to sort data using the ORDER BY clause. You have learned the fundamentals of writing queries, and, after a few exercises, you should be prepared to learn more about queries during the next hour.

Q&A

Q Why won't the SELECT clause work without the FROM clause?

A The SELECT clause merely tells the database what data you want to see. The FROM clause tells the database where to get the data.

Q When I use the ORDER BY clause and choose the option descending, what does that really do to the data?

A Say that you use the ORDER BY clause and have selected the last_name from the EMPLOYEE_TBL. If you used the descending option, the order would start with the letter Z and finish with the letter A. Now, let's say that you have used the ORDER BY clause and have selected the salary from the EMPLOYEE_PAY_TBL. If you used the descending option, the order would start with the largest salary down to the lowest salary.

Q What advantage is there to renaming columns?

A The new column name could fit the description of the returned data more closely for a particular report.

Workshop

The following workshop is composed of a series of quiz questions and practical exercises. The quiz questions are designed to test your overall understanding of the current material. The practical exercises are intended to afford you the opportunity to apply the concepts discussed during the current hour, as well as build upon the knowledge acquired in previous hours of study. Please take time to complete the quiz questions and exercises before continuing. Refer to Appendix C, "Answers to Quizzes and Exercises," for answers.

Quiz

1. Name the required parts for any SELECT statement.
2. In the WHERE clause, are single quotation marks required for all the data?
3. Under what part of the SQL language does the SELECT statement (database query) fall?
4. Can multiple conditions be used in the WHERE clause?

7

Exercises

1. Look over the following SELECT statements. Determine whether the syntax is correct. If the syntax is incorrect, what would correct it? A table called EMPLOYEE_TBL is used here.

   a.
   ```
   SELECT EMP_ID, LAST_NAME, FIRST_NAME,
   FROM EMPLOYEE_TBL;
   ```

   b.
   ```
   SELECT EMP_ID, LAST_NAME
   ORDER BY EMPLOYEE_TBL
   FROM EMPLOYEE_TBL;
   ```

   c.
   ```
   SELECT EMP_ID, LAST_NAME, FIRST_NAME
   FROM EMPLOYEE_TBL
   WHERE EMP_ID = '333333333'
   ORDER BY EMP_ID;
   ```

   d.
   ```
   SELECT EMP_ID SSN, LAST_NAME
   FROM EMPLOYEE_TBL
   WHERE EMP_ID = '333333333'
   ORDER BY 1;
   ```

   e.
   ```
   SELECT EMP_ID, LAST_NAME, FIRST_NAME
   FROM EMPLOYEE_TBL
   WHERE EMP_ID = '333333333'
   ORDER BY 3, 1, 2;
   ```

HOUR 8

Using Operators to Categorize Data

The highlights of this hour include

- What is an operator?
- An overview of operators in SQL
- How are operators used singularly?
- How are operators used in combinations?

What Is an Operator in SQL?

NEW TERM An operator is a reserved word or a character used primarily in an SQL statement's WHERE clause to perform operation(s), such as comparisons and arithmetic operations. *Operators* are used to specify conditions in an SQL statement and to serve as conjunctions for multiple conditions in a statement.

The operators discussed during this hour are

- Comparison operators
- Logical operators
- Operators used to negate conditions
- Arithmetic operators

Comparison Operators

Comparison operators are used to test single values in an SQL statement. The comparison operators discussed consist of =, <>, <, and >.

These operators are used to test

- Equality
- Non-equality
- Less-than values
- Greater-than values

Examples and the meanings of comparison operators are covered in the following sections.

Equality

The *equal operator* compares single values to one another in an SQL statement. The equal sign (=) symbolizes equality. When testing for equality, the compared values must match exactly or no data is returned. If two values are equal during a comparison for equality, the returned value for the comparison is TRUE; the returned value is FALSE if equality is not found. This Boolean value (TRUE/FALSE) is used to determine whether data is returned according to the condition.

The = operator can be used by itself or combined with other operators. An example and the meaning of the equality operator follows:

Example	Meaning
WHERE SALARY = '20000'	Salary equals 20000

The following query returns all rows of data where the PROD_ID is equal to 2345:

```
SELECT *
FROM PRODUCTS_TBL
WHERE PROD_ID = '2345';
```

8

OUTPUT

```
PROD_ID    PROD_DESC                        COST
---------- -------------------------------- ------
2345       OAK BOOKSHELF                    59.99
```

1 row selected.

Non-Equality

For every equality, there is a non-equality. In SQL, the operator used to measure non-equality is <> (the less-than sign combined with the greater-than sign). The condition returns TRUE if the condition finds non-equality; FALSE is returned if equality is found.

Another option comparable to <> is !=. Many of the major implementations have adopted != to represent not-equal. Check your particular implementation for the usage.

Example	*Meaning*
WHERE SALARY <> '20000'	Salary does not equal 20000

INPUT

```
SELECT *
FROM PRODUCTS_TBL
WHERE PROD_ID <> '2345';
```

OUTPUT

```
PROD_ID    PROD_DESC                        COST
---------- -------------------------------- ------
11235      WITCHES COSTUME                  29.99
222        PLASTIC PUMPKIN 18 INCH          7.75
13         FALSE PARAFFIN TEETH             1.1
90         LIGHTED LANTERNS                 14.5
15         ASSORTED COSTUMES                10
9          CANDY CORN                       1.35
6          PUMPKIN CANDY                    1.45
87         PLASTIC SPIDERS                  1.05
119        ASSORTED MASKS                   4.95
1234       KEY CHAIN                        5.95
2345       OAK BOOKSHELF                    59.99
```

11 rows selected.

Less-Than, Greater-Than

The symbols < (less-than) and > (greater-than) can be used by themselves, or in combination with each other or other operators.

Example	Meaning
WHERE SALARY < '20000'	Salary is less than 20000
WHERE SALARY > '20000'	Salary is greater than 20000

In the first example, anything less-than and not equal to 20000 returns TRUE. Any value of 20000 or more returns FALSE. Greater-than works the opposite of less-than.

INPUT
```
SELECT *
FROM PRODUCTS_TBL
WHERE COST > 20;
```

OUTPUT
```
PROD_ID     PROD_DESC                           COST
..........  ..................................  ......
11235       WITCHES COSTUME                     29.99
2345        OAK BOOKSHELF                       59.99

2 rows selected.
```

In the next example, notice that the value 24.99 was not included in the query's result set. The less-than operator is not inclusive.

INPUT
```
SELECT *
FROM PRODUCTS_TBL
WHERE COST < 24.99;
```

OUTPUT
```
PROD_ID     PROD_DESC                           COST
..........  ..................................  ......
222         PLASTIC PUMPKIN 18 INCH             7.75
13          FALSE PARAFFIN TEETH                1.1
90          LIGHTED LANTERNS                    14.5
15          ASSORTED COSTUMES                   10
9           CANDY CORN                          1.35
6           PUMPKIN CANDY                       1.45
87          PLASTIC SPIDERS                     1.05
119         ASSORTED MASKS                      4.95
1234        KEY CHAIN                           5.95

9 rows selected.
```

Combination Examples of Comparison Operators

The equal operator can be combined with the less-than and greater-than operators, as in the following examples):

Example	Meaning
WHERE SALARY <= '20000'	Salary less-than or equal-to
WHERE SALARY >= '20000'	Salary greater-than or equal-to

Less-than or equal-to 20000 includes 20000 and all values less than 20000. Any value in that range returns TRUE; any value greater than 20000 returns FALSE. Greater-than or equal-to also includes the value 20000 in this case and works the same as the less-than or equal-to.

INPUT
```
SELECT *
FROM PRODUCTS_TBL
WHERE COST <= 24.99;
```

OUTPUT
```
PROD_ID    PROD_DESC                          COST
.......... .................................. ......
222        PLASTIC PUMPKIN 18 INCH            7.75
13         FALSE PARAFFIN TEETH               1.1
90         LIGHTED LANTERNS                   14.5
15         ASSORTED COSTUMES                  10
9          CANDY CORN                         1.35
6          PUMPKIN CANDY                      1.45
87         PLASTIC SPIDERS                    1.05
119        ASSORTED MASKS                     4.95
1234       KEY CHAIN                          5.95

9 rows selected.
```

Logical Operators

NEW TERM *Logical operators* are those operators that use SQL keywords to make comparisons instead of symbols. The logical operators covered in the following subsections are

- IS NULL
- BETWEEN
- IN
- LIKE
- EXISTS
- UNIQUE
- ALL and ANY

IS NULL

The NULL operator is used to compare a value with a NULL value. For example, you might look for employees who do not have a pager by searching for NULL values in the PAGER column of the EMPLOYEE_TBL table.

The following example shows comparing a value to a NULL value:

Example	Meaning
WHERE SALARY IS NULL	Salary has no value

The following example does not find a NULL value:

Example	Meaning
WHERE SALARY = NULL	Salary has a value containing the letters N-U-L-L

```
SELECT EMP_ID, LAST_NAME, FIRST_NAME, PAGER
FROM EMPLOYEE_TBL
WHERE PAGER IS NULL;
```

```
EMP_ID     LAST_NAM FIRST_NA PAGER
---------- -------- -------- -----
311549902 STEPHENS TINA
442346889 PLEW     LINDA
220984332 WALLACE  MARIAH
443679012 SPURGEON TIFFANY

4 rows selected.
```

Understand that the literal word "null" is different than a NULL value. Examine the following example:

INPUT
```
SELECT EMP_ID, LAST_NAME, FIRST_NAME, PAGER
FROM EMPLOYEE_TBL
WHERE PAGER = NULL;
```

OUTPUT
```
no rows selected.
```

BETWEEN

The BETWEEN operator is used to search for values that are within a set of values, given the minimum value and the maximum value. The minimum and maximum values are included as part of the conditional set.

Example	Meaning
WHERE SALARY BETWEEN '20000' AND '30000'	The salary must fall between 20000 and 30000, including the values 20000 and 30000

INPUT
```
SELECT *
FROM PRODUCTS_TBL
WHERE COST BETWEEN 5.95 AND 14.5;
```

OUTPUT
```
PROD_ID     PROD_DESC                           COST
----------  ------------------------------      ------
222         PLASTIC PUMPKIN 18 INCH             7.75
90          LIGHTED LANTERNS                    14.5
15          ASSORTED COSTUMES                   10
1234        KEY CHAIN                           5.95

4 rows selected.
```

Notice that the values 5.95 and 14.5 are included in the output.

> BETWEEN is inclusive and therefore includes the minimum and maximum
> values in the query results.

IN

The IN operator is used to compare a value to a list of literal values that have been specified. For TRUE to be returned, the compared value must match at least one of the values in the list.

Examples	Meaning
WHERE SALARY IN ('20000', '30000', '40000')	The salary must match one of the values 20000, 30000, or 40000

INPUT
```
SELECT *
FROM PRODUCTS_TBL
WHERE PROD_ID IN ('13','9','87','119');
```

OUTPUT
```
PROD_ID     PROD_DESC                           COST
----------  ------------------------------      ------
119         ASSORTED MASKS                      4.95
87          PLASTIC SPIDERS                     1.05
9           CANDY CORN                          1.35
13          FALSE PARAFFIN TEETH                1.1

4 rows selected.
```

Using the IN operator can achieve the same results as using the OR operator and can return the results more quickly.

LIKE

The LIKE operator is used to compare a value to similar values using wildcard operators. There are two wildcards used in conjunction with the LIKE operator:

- The percent sign (%)
- The underscore (_)

The percent sign represents zero, one, or multiple characters. The underscore represents a single number or character. The symbols can be used in combinations.

Examples are

`WHERE SALARY LIKE '200%'`	Finds any values that start with 200
`WHERE SALARY LIKE '%200%'`	Finds any values that have 200 in any position
`WHERE SALARY LIKE '_00%'`	Finds any values that have 00 in the second and third positions
`WHERE SALARY LIKE '2_%_%'`	Finds any values that start with 2 and are at least 3 characters in length
`WHERE SALARY LIKE '%2'`	Finds any values that end with 2
`WHERE SALARY LIKE '_2%3'`	Finds any values that have a 2 in the second position and end with a 3
`WHERE SALARY LIKE '2___3'`	Finds any values in a five-digit number that start with 2 and end with 3

The following example shows all product descriptions that end with the letter *S*:

```
SELECT PROD_DESC
FROM PRODUCTS_TBL
WHERE PROD_DESC LIKE '%S';
```

```
PROD_DESC
------------------
LIGHTED LANTERNS
ASSORTED COSTUMES
PLASTIC SPIDERS
ASSORTED MASKS

4 rows selected.
```

The following example shows all product descriptions whose second character is the letter S:

INPUT
```
SELECT PROD_DESC
FROM PRODUCTS_TBL
WHERE PROD_DESC LIKE '_S%';
```

OUTPUT
```
PROD_DESC
------------------
ASSORTED COSTUMES
ASSORTED MASKS

2 rows selected.
```

EXISTS

The EXISTS operator is used to search for the presence of a row in a specified table that meets certain criteria.

Example	Meaning
WHERE EXISTS (SELECT EMP_ID FROM EMPLOYEE_TBL WHERE EMPLOYEE_ID = '333333333')	Searching to see whether the EMP_ID 333333333 is in the EMPLOYEE_TBL

The following example is a form of a subquery, which is further discussed during Hour 14, "Using Subqueries to Define Unknown Data."

INPUT
```
SELECT COST
FROM PRODUCTS_TBL
WHERE EXISTS ( SELECT COST
               FROM PRODUCTS_TBL
               WHERE COST > 100 );
```

OUTPUT
```
No rows selected.

----------
```

There were no rows selected because no records existed where the cost was greater than 100.

Consider the following example:

INPUT
```
SELECT COST
FROM PRODUCTS_TBL
WHERE EXISTS ( SELECT COST
               FROM PRODUCTS_TBL
               WHERE COST < 100 );
```

OUTPUT

```
COST
..........
   29.99
    7.75
     1.1
    14.5
      10
    1.35
    1.45
    1.05
    4.95
    5.95
   59.99
```

```
11 rows selected.
```

The cost was displayed for records in the table because records existed where the product cost was less than 100.

UNIQUE

The UNIQUE operator searches every row of a specified table for uniqueness (no duplicates).

Example	*Meaning*
WHERE UNIQUE (SELECT SALARY FROM EMPLOYEE_TBL WHERE EMPLOYEE_ID = '333333333')	Testing SALARY to see whether there are duplicates

ALL and ANY OPERATORS

The ALL operator is used to compare a value to all values in another value set.

Example	*Meaning*
WHERE SALARY > ALL (SELECT SALARY FROM EMPLOYEE TBL WHERE CITY =' INDIANAPOLIS')	Testing SALARY to see whether it is greater than all salaries of the employees living in Indianapolis

INPUT

```
SELECT *
FROM PRODUCTS_TBL
WHERE COST > ALL ( SELECT COST
                   FROM PRODUCTS_TBL
                   WHERE COST < 10 );
```

OUTPUT

```
PROD_ID    PROD_DESC                        COST
---------- -------------------------------  ------
11235      WITCHES COSTUME                  29.99
90         LIGHTED LANTERNS                 14.5
15         ASSORTED COSTUMES                10
2345       OAK BOOKSHELF                    59.99

4 rows selected.
```

In this output, there were five records that had a cost greater than the cost of all records having a cost less than 10.

The ANY operator is used to compare a value to any applicable value in the list according to the condition.

Example	Meaning
WHERE SALARY > ANY (SELECT SALARY FROM EMPLOYEE_TBL WHERE CITY = 'INDIANAPOLIS')	Testing SALARY to see whether it is greater than any of the salaries of employees living in Indianapolis

INPUT

```
SELECT *
FROM PRODUCTS_TBL
WHERE COST > ANY ( SELECT COST
                  FROM PRODUCTS_TBL
                  WHERE COST < 10 );
```

OUTPUT

```
PROD_ID    PROD_DESC                        COST
--------   -------------------------------  ------
11235      WITCHES COSTUME                  29.99
222        PLASTIC PUMPKIN 18 INCH           7.75
13         FALSE PARAFFIN TEETH              1.1
90         LIGHTED LANTERNS                 14.5
15         ASSORTED COSTUMES                10
9          CANDY CORN                        1.35
6          PUMPKIN CANDY                     1.45
119        ASSORTED MASKS                    4.95
1234       KEY CHAIN                         5.95
2345       OAK BOOKSHELF                    59.99

10 rows selected.
```

In this output, more records were returned than when using ALL, because the cost only had to be greater than any of the costs that were less than 10. The one record that was not displayed had a cost of 1.05, which was not greater than any of the values less than 10 (which was, in fact, 1.05).

Conjunctive Operators

NEW TERM What if you want to used multiple conditions to narrow data in an SQL statement? You must be able to combine the conditions, and you do this with what is call *conjunctive operators*. These operators are

- AND
- OR

These operators provide a means to make multiple comparisons with different operators in the same SQL statement. The following sections describe each operator's behavior.

AND

The AND operator allows the existence of multiple conditions in an SQL statement's WHERE clause. For an action to be taken by the SQL statement, whether it be a transaction or query, all conditions separated by the AND must be TRUE.

Example	*Meaning*
WHERE EMPLOYEE_ID = '333333333' AND SALARY = '20000'	The EMPLOYEE_ID must match 333333333 and the SALARY must equal 20000

INPUT
```
SELECT *
FROM PRODUCTS_TBL
WHERE COST > 10
  AND COST < 30;
```

OUTPUT
```
PROD_ID    PROD_DESC                    COST
---------- ---------------------------- ------
11235      WITCHES COSTUME              29.99
90         LIGHTED LANTERNS             14.5
```

2 rows selected.

In this output, the value for cost had to be both greater than 10 and less than 30 for data to be retrieved.

INPUT
```
SELECT *
FROM PRODUCTS_TBL
WHERE PROD_ID = '7725'
  AND PROD_ID = '2345';
```

OUTPUT
```
no rows selected
```

8

This output retrieved no data because each row of data has only one product identification.

OR

The OR operator is used to combine multiple conditions in an SQL statement's WHERE clause. For an action to be taken by the SQL statement, whether it be a transaction or query, at least one of the conditions that are separated by OR must be TRUE.

Example	Meaning
WHERE SALARY = '20000' OR SALARY = '30000'	The SALARY must match either 20000 or 30000

> Each of the comparison and logical operators can be used singularly or in combination with each other.

INPUT
```
SELECT *
FROM PRODUCTS_TBL
WHERE PROD_ID = '7725'
   OR PROD_ID = '2345'
```

OUTPUT
```
PROD_ID    PROD_DESC                              COST
---------  ------------------------------------   ------
2345       OAK BOOKSHELF                          59.99

1 rows selected.
```

In this output, either one of the conditions had to be TRUE for data to be retrieved. Two records that met either one or the other condition were found.

> When using multiple conditions and operators in an SQL statement, you may find that it improves overall readability if parentheses are used to separate statements into logical groups. However, be aware that the misuse of parentheses could adversely affect your output results.

In the next example, notice the use of the AND and two OR operators. In addition, notice the logical placement of the parentheses to make the statement more readable.

INPUT
```
SELECT *
FROM PRODUCTS_TBL
WHERE COST > 10
  AND ( PROD_ID = '222'
   OR   PROD_ID = '90'
   OR   PROD_ID = '11235' );
```

```
             PROD_ID    PROD_DESC                              COST
             ---------- ------------------------------------- ------
             11235      WITCHES COSTUME                        29.99
             90         LIGHTED LANTERNS                       14.5
```

2 rows selected.

The cost in this output had to be greater than 10, and the product identification had to be any one of the three listed. A row was not returned for PROD_ID 222, because the cost for this identification was not greater than 10.

Negating Conditions with the NOT Operator

Of all the conditions tested by the logical operators discussed here, there is a way to negate each one of these operators to change the condition's viewpoint.

The NOT operator reverses the meaning of the logical operator with which it is used. The NOT can be used with the following operators in the following methods:

- NOT EQUAL
- NOT BETWEEN
- NOT IN
- NOT LIKE
- IS NOT NULL
- NOT EXISTS
- NOT UNIQUE

Each method is discussed in the following sections. First, let's look at how to test for inequality.

Not Equal

You have learned how to test for inequality using the <> operator. Inequality is worth mentioning in this section because to test for it, you are actually negating the equality operator. The following is a second method for testing inequality available in some SQL implementations:

Example	Meaning
WHERE SALARY <> '20000'	SALARY does not equal 20000
WHERE SALARY != '20000'	SALARY does not equal 20000

In the second example, you can see that the exclamation mark is used to negate the equality comparison. The use of the exclamation mark is allowed in addition to the standard operator for inequality <> in some implementations.

8

 Check your particular implementation for the use of the exclamation mark to negate the inequality operator.

NOT BETWEEN

The BETWEEN operator is negated as follows:

Example	Meaning
WHERE Salary NOT BETWEEN '20000' AND '30000'	The value for SALARY cannot fall between 20000 and 30000, to include the values 20000 and 30000

INPUT
```
SELECT *
FROM PRODUCTS_TBL
WHERE COST NOT BETWEEN 5.95 AND 14.5;
```

OUTPUT
```
PROD_ID    PROD_DESC                          COST
---------- --------------------------------   ------
11235      WITCHES COSTUME                    29.99
13         FALSE PARAFFIN TEETH               1.1
9          CANDY CORN                         1.35
6          PUMPKIN CANDY                      1.45
87         PLASTIC SPIDERS                    1.05
119        ASSORTED MASKS                     4.95
2345       OAK BOOKSHELF                      59.99

7 rows selected.
```

 Remember that BETWEEN is inclusive; therefore, in the previous example, any rows that equal 5.95 or 14.50 are not included in the query results.

NOT IN

The IN operator is negated as NOT IN. All salaries in the following example that are not in the listed values, if any, are returned:

Example	Meaning
WHERE SALARY NOT IN ('20000', '30000', '40000')	The SALARY cannot be equal to any of the given values for action to be taken

```
INPUT      SELECT *
           FROM PRODUCTS_TBL
           WHERE PROD_ID NOT IN ('13','9','87','119');
```

```
OUTPUT     PROD_ID    PROD_DESC                          COST
           ----------  ------------------------------    ------
           11235       WITCHES COSTUME                    29.99
           222         PLASTIC PUMPKIN 18 INCH             7.75
           90          LIGHTED LANTERNS                    14.5
           15          ASSORTED COSTUMES                   10
           6           PUMPKIN CANDY                       1.45
           1234        KEY CHAIN                           5.95
           2345        OAK BOOKSHELF                       59.99

           7 rows selected.
```

In this output, records were not displayed for the listed identifications after the NOT IN operator.

NOT LIKE

The LIKE, or wildcard, operator is negated as NOT LIKE. When NOT LIKE is used, only values that are not similar are returned. Examples include:

Example	Meaning
WHERE SALARY NOT LIKE '200%'	Finds any values that do not start with 200
WHERE SALARY NOT LIKE '%200%'	Finds any values that do not have 200 in any position
WHERE SALARY NOT LIKE '_00%'	Finds any values that have 00 starting in the second position
WHERE SALARY NOT LIKE '2_%_%'	Does not find any values that start with 2 and have a length of 3 or greater

```
INPUT      SELECT PROD_DESC
           FROM PRODUCTS_TBL
           WHERE PROD_DESC NOT LIKE 'L%';
```

8

OUTPUT
```
PROD_DESC
-----------------------
WITCHES COSTUME
PLASTIC PUMPKIN 18 INCH
FALSE PARAFFIN TEETH
ASSORTED COSTUMES
CANDY CORN
PUMPKIN CANDY
PLASTIC SPIDERS
ASSORTED MASKS
KEY CHAIN
OAK BOOKSHELF

10 rows selected.
```

In this output, the product descriptions starting with the letter *L* were not displayed.

IS NOT NULL

The IS NULL operator is negated as IS NOT NULL to test for values that are not NULL.

Example	Meaning
WHERE SALARY IS NOT NULL	Only NOT NULL rows are returned

INPUT
```
SELECT EMP_ID, LAST_NAME, FIRST_NAME, PAGER
FROM EMPLOYEE_TBL
WHERE PAGER IS NOT NULL;
```

OUTPUT
```
EMP_ID     LAST_NAM FIRST_NA PAGER
---------- -------- -------- ----------
213764555 GLASS    BRANDON  3175709980
313782439 GLASS    JACOB    8887345678

2 rows selected.
```

NOT EXISTS

EXISTS is negated as NOT EXISTS.

Example	Meaning
WHERE NOT EXISTS (SELECT EMP_ID FROM EMPLOYEE_TBL WHERE EMP_ID = '333333333'	Searching to see whether the EMP_ID 3333333333 is not in the EMPLOYEE_TBL

INPUT
```
SELECT MAX(COST)
FROM PRODUCTS_TBL
WHERE NOT EXISTS ( SELECT COST
                   FROM PRODUCTS_TBL
                   WHERE COST > 100 );
```

OUTPUT
```
MAX(COST)
- - - - - - - - - - -
    59.99
```

The maximum cost for the table is displayed in this output because there were not any records that existed where the cost was greater than 100.

NOT UNIQUE

The UNIQUE operator is negated as NOT UNIQUE.

Example	Meaning
WHERE NOT UNIQUE (SELECT SALARY FROM EMPLOYEE_TBL)	Testing to see whether there are salaries in the table that are not UNIQUE

Arithmetic Operators

Arithmetic operators are used to perform mathematical functions in SQL—the same as in most other languages. There are four conventional operators for mathematical functions.

- \+ (addition)

- \- (subtraction)

- * (multiplication)

- / (division)

Addition

Addition is performed through the use of the plus (+) symbol.

Example	Meaning
SELECT SALARY + BONUS FROM EMPLOYEE_PAY_TBL;	The SALARY column is added with the BONUS column for a total for each row of data

8

```
SELECT SALARY
FROM EMPLOYEE_PAY_TBL
WHERE SALARY + BONUS
> '40000';
```

Returns all rows
that are greater than the
total of the SALARY and
BONUS columns

Subtraction

Subtraction is performed using the minus (-) symbol.

Example	Meaning
`SELECT SALARY - BONUS` `FROM EMPLOYEE_PAY_TBL;`	The BONUS column is subtracted from the SALARY column for the difference

`SELECT SALARY`
`FROM EMPLOYEE_PAY_TBL`
`WHERE SALARY -`
`BONUS > '40000';`
	Returns all rows where the SALARY minus the BONUS is greater than 40000

Multiplication

Multiplication is performed by using the asterisk (*) symbol.

Example	Meaning
`SELECT SALARY * 10` `FROM EMPLOYEE_PAY_TBL;`	The SALARY column is multiplied by 10

`SELECT SALARY`
`FROM EMPLOYEE_PAY_TBL`
`WHERE SALARY * 10`
`> '40000';`
	Returns all rows where the product of the SALARY multiplied by 10 is greater than 40000

The pay rate in the following example is multiplied by 1.1, which increases the current pay rate by 10 percent:

```
SELECT EMP_ID, PAY_RATE, PAY_RATE * 1.1
FROM EMPLOYEE_PAY_TBL
WHERE PAY_RATE IS NOT NULL;
```

```
EMP_ID       PAY_RATE PAY_RATE*1.1
-----------  -------- ------------
442346889       14.75       16.225
220984332          11         12.1
443679012          15         16.5

3 rows selected.
```

Division

Division is performed through the use of the slash (/) symbol.

Example	Meaning
SELECT SALARY / 10 FROM EMPLOYEE_PAY_TBL;	The SALARY column is divided by 10
SELECT SALARY FROM EMPLOYEE_PAY_TBL WHERE SALARY / 10 > '40000';	Returns all rows that are greater than the SALARY
SELECT SALARY FROM EMPLOYEE_PAY_TBL WHERE SALARY / 10 > '40000'	Returns all rows where the salary divided by 10 is greater than 40000

Arithmetic Operator Combinations

The arithmetic operators can be used in combinations with one another. Remember the rules of precedence in basic mathematics. Multiplication and division operations are performed first, and then addition and subtraction operations. The only way the user has control over the order of the mathematical operations is through the use of parentheses. Parentheses surrounding an expression cause that expression to be evaluated as a block.

NEW TERM *Precedence* is the order in which expressions are resolved in a mathematical expression or with embedded functions in SQL.

Expression	Result
1 + 1 * 5	6
(1 + 1) * 5	10
10 - 4 / 2 + 1	9
(10 - 4) / (2 + 1)	2

In the following examples, notice that the placement of parentheses in an expression does not affect the outcome if only multiplication and division are involved. Precedence is not a factor in these cases. Although it may not appear to make sense, it is possible that some implementations of SQL do not follow the ANSI standard in cases like this, however unlikely.

8

Expression	Result
4 * 6 / 2	12
(4 * 6) / 2	12
4 * (6 / 3)	12

The following are some more examples:

```
SELECT SALARY * 10 + 1000
FROM EMPLOYEE_PAY_TBL
WHERE SALARY > 20000;
```

```
SELECT SALARY / 52 + BONUS
FROM EMPLOYEE_PAY_TBL;
```

```
SELECT (SALARY - 1000 + BONUS) / 52 * 1.1
FROM EMPLOYEE_PAY_TBL;
```

The following is a rather wild example:

```
SELECT SALARY
FROM EMPLOYEE_PAY_TBL
WHERE SALARY < BONUS * 3 + 10 / 2 - 50;
```

Because parentheses are not used, mathematical precedence takes effect, altering the value for BONUS tremendously for the condition.

When combining arithmetic operators, remember to consider the rules of precedence. The absence of parentheses in a statement could render inaccurate results.

Summary

You have been introduced to various operators available in SQL. You have learned the hows and whys of operators. You have seen examples of operators being used by themselves and in various combinations with one another, using the conjunctive-type operators AND and OR. You have learned the basic arithmetic functions: addition, subtraction, multiplication, and division. Comparison operators are used to test equality, inequality, less-than values, and greater-than values. Logical operators include BETWEEN, IN, LIKE, EXIST, ANY, and ALL. You are already experiencing how elements are added to SQL statements to further specify conditions and better control the processing and retrieving capabilities provided with SQL.

Q&A

Q Can I have more than one AND in the WHERE clause?

A Yes. In fact, all the operators can be used multiple times. An example would be
```
SELECT SALARY
FROM EMPLOYEE_PAY_TBL
WHERE SALARY > 20000
AND BONUS BETWEEN 1000 AND 3000
AND POSITION = 'VICE PRESIDENT'
```

Q What happens if I use single quotation marks around a NUMBER datatype in a WHERE clause?

A Your query still processes. Quotation marks are not necessary for NUMBER fields.

Workshop

The following workshop is composed of a series of quiz questions and practical exercises. The quiz questions are designed to test your overall understanding of the current material. The practical exercises are intended to afford you the opportunity to apply the concepts discussed during the current hour, as well as build upon the knowledge acquired in previous hours of study. Please take time to complete the quiz questions and exercises before continuing. Refer to Appendix C, "Answers to Quizzes and Exercises," for answers.

Quiz

1. True or false: Both conditions when using the OR operator must be TRUE.

2. True or false: All specified values must match when using the IN operator.

3. True or false: The AND operator can be used in the SELECT and the WHERE clauses.

4. What, if anything, is wrong with the following SELECT statements?

a.
```
SELECT SALARY
FROM EMPLOYEE_PAY_TBL
WHERE SALARY BETWEEN 20000, 30000
```

b.
```
SELECT SALARY + DATE_HIRE
FROM EMPLOYEE_PAY_TBL
```

c.

```
SELECT SALARY, BONUS
FROM EMPLOYEE_PAY_TBL
WHERE DATE_HIRE BETWEEN 22-SEP-99
AND 23-NOV-99
AND POSITION = 'SALES'
OR POSITION = 'MARKETING'
AND EMPLOYEE_ID LIKE '%55%
```

Exercises

1. Using the following CUSTOMER_TBL:

   DESCRIBE CUSTOMER_TBL

Name	Null?	Type
CUST_ID	NOT NULL	VARCHAR2(10)
CUST_NAME	NOT NULL	VARCHAR2(30)
CUST_ADDRESS	NOT NULL	VARCHAR2(20)
CUST_CITY	NOT NULL	VARCHAR2(12)
CUST_STATE	NOT NULL	CHAR(2)
CUST_ZIP	NOT NULL	CHAR(5)
CUST_PHONE		NUMBER(10)
CUST_FAX		NUMBER(10)

   Write a SELECT statement that returns customer IDs and customer names (alpha order) for customers who live in Indiana, Ohio, Michigan, and Illinois, and whose names begin with the letters A or B.

2. Using the following PRODUCTS_TBL:

   DESCRIBE PRODUCTS_TBL

Name	Null?	Type
PROD_ID	NOT NULL	VARCHAR2(10)
PROD_DESC	NOT NULL	VARCHAR2(25)
COST	NOT NULL	NUMBER(6,2)

   Write a SELECT statement that returns the product ID, PROD_DESC, and the product cost. Limit the product cost to range from $1.00 and $12.50.

HOUR 9

Summarizing Data Results from a Query

In this hour, you learn about SQL's aggregate functions. You can perform a variety of useful functions with aggregate functions.

The highlights of this hour include

- What functions are
- How functions are used
- When to use functions
- Using aggregate functions
- Summarizing data with aggregate functions
- Results from using functions

What Are Aggregate Functions?

NEW TERM Functions are keywords in SQL used to manipulate values within columns for output purposes. A *function* is a command always used in conjunction with a column name or expression. There are several types of functions in SQL. This hour covers aggregate functions. An *aggregate function* is used to provide summarization information for an SQL statement, such as counts, totals, and averages.

The aggregate functions discussed in this hour are

- COUNT
- SUM
- MAX
- MIN
- AVG

The following queries show the data used for most of this hour's examples:

INPUT
```
SELECT *
FROM PRODUCTS_TBL;
```

OUTPUT

PROD_ID	PROD_DESC	COST
11235	WITCHES COSTUME	29.99
222	PLASTIC PUMPKIN 18 INCH	7.75
13	FALSE PARAFFIN TEETH	1.1
90	LIGHTED LANTERNS	14.5
15	ASSORTED COSTUMES	10
9	CANDY CORN	1.35
6	PUMPKIN CANDY	1.45
87	PLASTIC SPIDERS	1.05
119	ASSORTED MASKS	4.95
1234	KEY CHAIN	5.95
2345	OAK BOOKSHELF	59.99

11 rows selected.

Some employees do not have a pager number in the results of the following query:

INPUT
```
SELECT EMP_ID, LAST_NAME, FIRST_NAME, PAGER
FROM EMPLOYEE_TBL;
```

OUTPUT

EMP_ID	LAST_NAM	FIRST_NA	PAGER
311549902	STEPHENS	TINA	
442346889	PLEW	LINDA	
213764555	GLASS	BRANDON	3175709980
313782439	GLASS	JACOB	8887345678
220984332	WALLACE	MARIAH	
443679012	SPURGEON	TIFFANY	

6 rows selected.

The COUNT Function

The COUNT function is used to count rows or values of a column that do not contain a NULL value. When used with a query, the COUNT function returns a numeric value. When the COUNT function is used with the DISTINCT command, only the distinct rows are counted. ALL (opposite of DISTINCT) is the default; it is not necessary to include ALL in the syntax. Duplicate rows are counted if DISTINCT is not specified. One other option with the COUNT function is to use COUNT with an asterisk. COUNT, when used with an asterisk, counts all the rows of a table including duplicates, whether a NULL value is contained in a column or not.

The syntax for the COUNT function is as follows:

```
COUNT [ (*) | (DISTINCT | ALL) ] (COLUMN NAME)
```

> The DISTINCT command cannot be used with COUNT(*), only with the COUNT(column_name).

Example	Meaning
SELECT COUNT(EMPLOYEE_ID) FROM EMPLOYEE_PAY_ID	Counts all employee IDs
SELECT COUNT(DISTINCT SALARY) FROM EMPLOYEE_PAY_TBL	Counts only the distinct rows
SELECT COUNT(ALL SALARY) FROM EMPLOYEE_PAY_TBL	Counts all rows for SALARY
SELECT COUNT(*) FROM EMPLOYEE_TBL	Counts all rows of the EMPLOYEE table

COUNT(*) is used in the following example to get a count of all records in the EMPLOYEE_TBL table. There are six employees

```
SELECT COUNT(*)
FROM EMPLOYEE_TBL;
```

```
COUNT(*)
----------
       6
```

COUNT(EMP_ID) is used in the next example to get a count of all of the employee identifi-cations that exist in the table. The returned count is the same as the last query because all employees have an identification number.

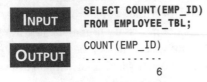

```
SELECT COUNT(EMP_ID)
FROM EMPLOYEE_TBL;
```

```
COUNT(EMP_ID)
------------
           6
```

COUNT(PAGER) is used in the following example to get a count of all of the employee records that have a pager number. Only two employees had pager numbers.

```
SELECT COUNT(PAGER)
FROM EMPLOYEE_TBL;
```

```
COUNT(PAGER)
------------
           2
```

The ORDERS_TBL table, shown next, is used in the following COUNT example:

```
SELECT *
FROM ORDERS_TBL;
```

ORD_NUM	CUST_ID	PROD_ID	QTY	ORD_DATE_
56A901	232	11235	1	22-OCT-99
56A917	12	907	100	30-SEP-99
32A132	43	222	25	10-OCT-99
16C17	090	222	2	17-OCT-99
18D778	287	90	10	17-OCT-99
23E934	432	13	20	15-OCT-99
90C461	560	1234	2	

```
7 rows selected.
```

This last example obtains a count of all distinct product identifications in the ORDERS_TBL table.

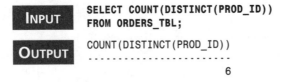

```
SELECT COUNT(DISTINCT(PROD_ID))
FROM ORDERS_TBL;
```

```
COUNT(DISTINCT(PROD_ID))
------------------------
                       6
```

The PROD_ID 222 has two entries in the table, thus reducing the distinct values from 7 to 6.

Because the COUNT function counts the rows, data types do not play a part. The rows can contain columns with any data type.

The SUM Function

The SUM function is used to return a total on the values of a column for a group of rows. The SUM function can also be used in conjunction with DISTINCT. When SUM is used with DISTINCT, only the distinct rows are totaled, which may not have much purpose. Your total is not accurate in that case, because rows of data are omitted.

The syntax for the SUM function is as follows:

SUM ([DISTINCT] COLUMN NAME)

The value of an argument must be numeric to use the SUM function. The SUM function cannot be used on columns having a data type other than numeric, such as character or date

Example	Meaning
SELECT SUM(SALARY) FROM EMPLOYEE_PAY_TBL	Totals the salaries
SELECT SUM(DISTINCT SALARY) FROM EMPLOYEE_PAY_TBL	Totals the distinct salaries

The *sum*, or total amount of all cost values, is being retrieved from the PRODUCTS_TBL table.

```
INPUT    SELECT SUM(COST)
         FROM PRODUCTS_TBL;
```

```
OUTPUT   SUM(COST)
         ----------
             163.07
```

The AVG Function

The AVG function is used to find averages for a group of rows. When used with the DISTINCT command, the AVG function returns the average of the distinct rows. The syntax for the AVG function is as follows:

```
AVG ([ DISTINCT ] COLUMN NAME)
```

> The value of the argument must be numeric for the AVG function to work.

Example	Meaning
SELECT AVG(SALARY) FROM EMPLOYEE_PAY_TBL	Returns the average salary
SELECT AVG(DISTINCT SALARY) EMPLOYEE_PAY_TBL	Returns the distinct FROM average salary

The average value for all values in the PRODUCTS_TBL table's COST column is being retrieved in the following example.

 INPUT

```
SELECT AVG(COST)
FROM PRODUCTS_TBL;
```

 OUTPUT

```
AVG(COST)
----------
13.5891667
```

> In some implementations, the results of your query may be truncated to the precision of the data type.

The next example uses two aggregate functions in the same query. Because some employees are paid hourly and others paid salary, you want to retrieve the average value for both PAY_RATE and SALARY.

INPUT
```
SELECT AVG(PAY_RATE), AVG(SALARY)
FROM EMPLOYEE_PAY_TBL;
```

OUTPUT
```
AVG(PAY_RATE) AVG(SALARY)
------------- -----------
   13.5833333       30000
```

The MAX Function

The MAX function is used to return the maximum value for the values of a column in a group of rows. NULL values are ignored when using the MAX function. The DISTINCT command is an option. However, because the maximum value for all the rows is the same as the distinct maximum value, it is useless.

SYNTAX

```
MAX([ DISTINCT ] COLUMN NAME)
```

Example	Meaning
SELECT MAX(SALARY) FROM EMPLOYEE_PAY_TBL	Returns the highest salary
SELECT MAX(DISTINCT SALARY) FROM EMPLOYEE_PAY_TBL	Returns the highest distinct salary

The following example returns the maximum value for the COST column in the PRODUCTS_TBL table:

INPUT
```
SELECT MAX(COST)
FROM PRODUCTS_TBL;
```

OUTPUT
```
MAX(COST)
---------
    59.99
```

The MIN Function

The MIN function returns the minimum value of a column for a group of rows. NULL values are ignored when using the MIN function. The DISTINCT command is an option. However, because the minimum value for all rows is the same as the minimum value for distinct rows, it is useless.

SYNTAX

```
MIN([ DISTINCT ] COLUMN NAME)
```

Example	Meaning
SELECT MIN(SALARY) FROM EMPLOYEE_PAY_TBL	Returns the lowest salary
SELECT MIN(DISTINCT SALARY) FROM EMPLOYEE_PAY_TBL	Returns the lowest distinct salary

The following example returns the minimum value for the COST column in the PRODUCTS_TBL table:

INPUT
```
SELECT MIN(COST)
FROM PRODUCTS_TBL;
```

OUTPUT
```
MIN(COST)
----------
     1.05
```

> One very important thing to keep in mind when using aggregate functions with the DISTINCT command is that your query may not return the desired results. The purpose of aggregate functions is to return summarized data based on all rows of data in a table.

The final example combines aggregate functions with the use of arithmetic operators:

INPUT
```
SELECT COUNT(ORD_NUM), SUM(QTY),
       SUM(QTY) / COUNT(ORD_NUM) AVG_QTY
FROM ORDERS_TBL;
```

OUTPUT
```
COUNT(ORD_NUM)    SUM(QTY)    AVG_QTY
--------------    --------    ----------
             7         160    22.857143
```

You have performed a count on all order numbers, figured the sum of all quantities ordered, and, by dividing the two figures, have derived the average quantity of an item per order. You also created a column alias for the computation—AVG_QTY.

Summary

Aggregate functions can be very useful and are quite simple to use. You have learned how to count values in columns, count rows of data in a table, get the maximum and minimum values for a column, figure the sum of the values in a column, and figure the average value for values in a column. Remember that NULL values are not considered when using aggregate functions, except when using the COUNT function in the format COUNT(*).

Aggregate functions are the first functions in SQL that you have learned, but more follow. Aggregate functions can also be used for group values, which is discussed the next hour. As you learn about other functions, you see that the syntaxes of most functions are similar to one another and that their concepts of use are relatively easy to understand.

Q&A

Q Why are NULL values ignored when using the MAX or MIN function?

A A NULL value means that nothing is there.

Q Why don't data types matter when using the COUNT function?

A The COUNT function only counts rows.

9

Workshop

The following workshop is composed of a series of quiz questions and practical exercises. The quiz questions are designed to test your overall understanding of the current material. The practical exercises are intended to afford you the opportunity to apply the concepts discussed during the current hour, as well as build upon the knowledge acquired in previous hours of study. Please take time to complete the quiz questions and exercises before continuing. Refer to Appendix C, "Answers to Quizzes and Exercises," for answers.

Quiz

1. True or false: The AVG function returns an average of all rows from a select column including any NULL values.

2. True or false: The SUM function is used to add column totals.

3. True or false: The COUNT(*) function counts all rows in a table.

4. Will the following SELECT statements work? If not, what will fix the statements?

    a.
    ```
    SELECT COUNT *
    FROM EMPLOYEE_PAY_TBL;
    ```

    b.
    ```
    SELECT COUNT(EMPLOYEE_ID), SALARY
    FROM EMPLOYEE_PAY_TBL;
    ```

    c.
    ```
    SELECT MIN(BONUS), MAX(SALARY)
    FROM EMPLOYEE_PAY_TBL
    WHERE SALARY > 20000;
    ```

Exercises

1. Using the following `EMPLOYEE_PAY_TBL`:

```
EMP_ID     POSITION      DATE_HIRE  PAY_RATE DATE_LAST   SALARY    BONUS
---------  ------------- ---------  -------- ----------- --------- ---------
311549902  MARKETING     23-MAY-89           01-MAY-99   30000     2000
442346889  TEAM LEADER   17-JUN-90  14.75    01-JUN-99
213764555  SALES MANAGER 14-AUG-94           01-AUG-99   40000     3000
313782439  SALESMAN      28-JUN-97                       20000     1000
220984332  SHIPPER       22-JUL-96  11       01-JUL-99
443679012  SHIPPER       14-JAN-91  15       01-JAN-99

6 rows selected.
```

Construct SQL statements to find:

   a. The average salary

   b. The maximum bonus

   c. The total salaries

   d. The minimum pay rate

   e. The total rows in the table

Hour 10

Sorting and Grouping Data

You have learned how to query the database and return data in an organized fashion. You have learned how to sort data from a query. During this hour, you learn how to break returned data from a query into groups for improved readability.

The highlights of this hour include

- Why you would want to group data
- The GROUP BY clause
- Group value functions
- The how and why of group functions
- Grouping by columns
- GROUP BY versus ORDER BY
- The HAVING clause

Why Group Data?

Grouping data is the process of combining columns with duplicate values in a logical order. For example, a database may contain information about employees; many employees live in different cities, while some employees live in the same city. You may want to execute a query that shows employee information for each particular city. You are grouping employee information by city, and a summarized report is created.

Suppose that you wanted to figure the average salary paid to employees according to each city. You would do this by using the aggregate function AVG on the SALARY column, as you learned last hour, and by using the GROUP BY clause to group the output by city.

Grouping data is accomplished through the use of the GROUP BY clause of a SELECT statement (query). Last hour, you learned how to use aggregate functions. During this lesson, you see how aggregate functions are used in conjunction with the GROUP BY clause for the database to display results more effectively.

The GROUP BY Clause

The GROUP BY clause is used in collaboration with the SELECT statement to arrange identical data into groups. The GROUP BY clause follows the WHERE clause in a SELECT statement and precedes the ORDER BY clause.

The position of the GROUP BY clause in a query is as follows:

```
SELECT
FROM
WHERE
GROUP BY
ORDER BY
```

The GROUP BY clause must follow the conditions in the WHERE clause and must precede the ORDER BY clause if one is used.

▼ SYNTAX

The following is the SELECT statement's syntax, including the GROUP BY clause:

```
SELECT COLUMN1, COLUMN2
FROM TABLE1, TABLE2
WHERE CONDITIONS
GROUP BY COLUMN1, COLUMN2
ORDER BY COLUMN1, COLUMN2
```

The following sections give examples and explanations of the GROUP BY clause's use in a variety of situations.

Grouping Selected Data

Grouping data is a simple process. The selected columns (the column list following the SELECT keyword in a query) are the columns that can be referenced in the GROUP BY clause. If a column is not found in the SELECT statement, it cannot be used in the GROUP BY clause. This is logical if you think about it—how can you group data on a report if the data is not displayed?

If the column name has been qualified, the qualified name must go into the GROUP BY clause. The column name can also be represented by a number, which is discussed later in this hour. When grouping the data, the order of columns grouped does not have to match the column order in the SELECT clause.

Group Functions

Typical group functions—those that are used with the GROUP BY clause to arrange data in groups—include AVG, MAX, MIN, SUM, and COUNT. These are the aggregate functions that you learned about during Hour 9, "Summarizing Data Results from a Query." Remember that the aggregate functions were used for single values in Hour 9; now, you use the aggregate functions for group values.

Creating Groups and Using Aggregate Functions

There are conditions that the SELECT clause has that must be met when using GROUP BY. Specifically, whatever columns are selected must appear in the GROUP BY clause, except for any aggregate values. The columns in the GROUP BY clause do not necessarily have to be in the same order as they appear in the SELECT clause. Should the columns in the SELECT clause be qualified, the qualified names of the columns must be used in the GROUP BY clause. The following are some examples of syntax for the GROUP BY clause:

Example

```
SELECT EMP_ID, CITY
FROM EMPLOYEE_TBL
GROUP BY CITY, EMP_ID;
```

 The SQL statement selects the EMP_ID and the CITY from the EMPLOYEE_TBL and groups the data returned by the CITY and then RMP_ID.

 Note the order of the columns selected, versus the order of the columns in the GROUP BY clause.

Example

```
SELECT EMP_ID, SUM(SALARY)
FROM EMPLOYEE_PAY_TBL
GROUP BY SALARY, EMP_ID;
```

ANALYSIS This SQL statement returns the EMP_ID and the total of the salary groups, as well as groups both the salaries and employee IDs.

Example

```
SELECT SUM(SALARY)
FROM EMPLOYEE_PAY_TBL;
```

ANALYSIS This SQL statement returns the total of all the salaries from the EMPLOYEE_PAY_TBL.

Example

```
SELECT SUM(SALARY)
FROM EMPLOYEE_PAY_TBL
GROUP BY SALARY;
```

ANALYSIS This SQL statement returns the totals for the different groups of salaries.

Practical examples using real data follow. In this first example, you can see that there are three distinct cities in the EMPLOYEE_TBL table.

INPUT
```
SELECT CITY
FROM EMPLOYEE_TBL;
```

OUTPUT
```
CITY
-------------
GREENWOOD
INDIANAPOLIS
WHITELAND
INDIANAPOLIS
INDIANAPOLIS
INDIANAPOLIS

6 rows selected.
```

In the following example, you select the city and a count of all records for each city. You see a count on each of the three distinct cities because you are using a GROUP BY clause.

INPUT
```
SELECT CITY, COUNT(*)
FROM EMPLOYEE_TBL
GROUP BY CITY;
```

OUTPUT

```
CITY            COUNT(*)
-------------   --------
GREENWOOD              1
INDIANAPOLIS          4
WHITELAND             1

3 rows selected.
```

The following is a query from a temporary table created based on `EMPLOYEE_TBL` and `EMPLOYEE_PAY_TBL`. You will soon learn how to join two tables for a query.

INPUT

```
SELECT *
FROM EMP_PAY_TMP;
```

OUTPUT

```
CITY          LAST_NAM FIRST_NA   PAY_RATE      SALARY
-----------   -------- ----------  -----------   ------
GREENWOOD     STEPHENS TINA                      30000
INDIANAPOLIS  PLEW     LINDA       14.75
WHITELAND     GLASS    BRANDON                   40000
INDIANAPOLIS  GLASS    JACOB                     20000
INDIANAPOLIS  WALLACE  MARIAH         11
INDIANAPOLIS  SPURGEON TIFFANY        15

6 rows selected.
```

In the following example, you retrieve the average pay rate and salary on each distinct city using the aggregate function AVG. There is no average pay rate for GREENWOOD or WHITELAND, because no employees living in those cities are paid hourly.

INPUT

```
SELECT CITY, AVG(PAY_RATE), AVG(SALARY)
FROM EMP_PAY_TMP
GROUP BY CITY;
```

OUTPUT

```
CITY          AVG(PAY_RATE) AVG(SALARY)
-----------   ------------- -----------
GREENWOOD                         30000
INDIANAPOLIS    13.5833333        20000
WHITELAND                         40000

3 rows selected.
```

In the next example, you combine the use of multiple components in a query to return grouped data. You still want to see the average pay rate and salary, but only for INDIANAPOLIS and WHITELAND. You group the data by CITY, of which you have no choice because you are using aggregate functions on the other columns. Lastly, you want to order the report by 2, and then 3, which is the average pay rate, and then average salary. Study the following details and output.

```
SELECT CITY, AVG(PAY_RATE), AVG(SALARY)
FROM EMP_PAY_TMP
WHERE CITY IN ('INDIANAPOLIS','WHITELAND')
GROUP BY CITY
ORDER BY 2,3;
```

```
CITY            AVG(PAY_RATE) AVG(SALARY)
------------    ------------- -----------
INDIANAPOLIS      13.5833333       20000
WHITELAND                          40000
```

Values are sorted before NULL values; therefore, the record for INDIANAPOLIS was displayed first. GREENWOOD was not selected, but if it were, its record would have been displayed before WHITELAND's record because GREENWOOD's average salary is $30,000 (the second sort in the ORDER BY clause was on average salary).

The last example in this section shows the use of the MAX and MIN aggregate functions with the GROUP BY clause.

```
SELECT CITY, MAX(PAY_RATE), MIN(SALARY)
FROM EMP_PAY_TMP
GROUP BY CITY;
```

```
CITY            MAX(PAY_RATE) MIN(SALARY)
------------    ------------- -----------
GREENWOOD                           30000
INDIANAPOLIS               15       20000
WHITELAND                           40000

3 rows selected.
```

Representing Column Names with Numbers

Unlike the ORDER BY clause the GROUP BY clause cannot be ordered by using an integer to represent the column name—except when using a UNION and the column names are different. The following is an example of representing column names with numbers:

```
SELECT EMP_ID, SUM(SALARY)
FROM EMPLOYEE_PAY_TBL
UNION
SELECT EMP_ID, SUM(PAY_RATE)
FROM EMPLOYEE_PAY_TBL
GROUP BY 2, 1;
```

This SQL statement returns the employee ID and the group totals for the salaries. When using the UNION operator, the results of the two SELECT statements are merged into one result set. The GROUP BY is performed on the entire result set. The order for the groupings is 2 representing salary, and 1 representing EMP_ID.

GROUP BY Versus ORDER BY

You should understand that the GROUP BY clause works the same as the ORDER BY clause in that both are used to sort data. The ORDER BY clause is specifically used to sort data from a query; the GROUP BY clause also sorts data from a query to properly group the data. Therefore, the GROUP BY clause can be used to sort data the same as ORDER BY.

There are some differences and disadvantages of using GROUP BY for sorting operations:

- All non-aggregate columns selected must be listed in the GROUP BY clause.
- Integers cannot be used in the GROUP BY to represent columns after the SELECT keyword, similar to using the ORDER BY clause.
- The GROUP BY clause is generally not necessary unless using aggregate functions.

An example of performing sort operations utilizing the GROUP BY clause in place of the ORDER BY clause is shown next:

INPUT
```
SELECT LAST_NAME, FIRST_NAME, CITY
FROM EMPLOYEE_TBL
GROUP BY LAST_NAME;
```

OUTPUT
```
SELECT LAST_NAME, FIRST_NAME, CITY
                  *
ERROR at line 1:
ORA-00979: not a GROUP BY expression
```

In this example, an error was received from the database server stating that FIRST_NAME is not a GROUP BY expression. Remember that all columns and expressions in the SELECT must be listed in the GROUP BY clause, with the exception of aggregate columns (those columns targeted by an aggregate function).

In the next example, the previous problem is solved by adding all expressions in the SELECT to the GROUP BY clause:

INPUT
```
SELECT LAST_NAME, FIRST_NAME, CITY
FROM EMPLOYEE_TBL
GROUP BY LAST_NAME, FIRST_NAME, CITY;
```

OUTPUT
```
LAST_NAM FIRST_NA CITY
-------- -------- ------------
GLASS    BRANDON  WHITELAND
GLASS    JACOB    INDIANAPOLIS
PLEW     LINDA    INDIANAPOLIS
SPURGEON TIFFANY  INDIANAPOLIS
STEPHENS TINA     GREENWOOD
WALLACE  MARIAH   INDIANAPOLIS

6 rows selected.
```

10

In this example, the same columns were selected from the same table, but all columns in the GROUP BY clause are listed as they appeared after the SELECT keyword. The results were ordered by LAST_NAME first, FIRST_NAME second, and CITY third. These results could have been accomplished easier with the ORDER BY clause; however, it may help you better understand how the GROUP BY works if you can visualize how it must first sort data to group data results.

The following example shows a SELECT from EMPLOYEE_TBL and uses the GROUP BY to order by CITY, which leads into the next example.

```
SELECT CITY, LAST_NAME
FROM EMPLOYEE_TBL
GROUP BY CITY, LAST_NAME;
```

OUTPUT

```
CITY           LAST_NAM
------------   --------
GREENWOOD      STEPHENS
INDIANAPOLIS   GLASS
INDIANAPOLIS   PLEW
INDIANAPOLIS   SPURGEON
INDIANAPOLIS   WALLACE
WHITELAND      GLASS

6 rows selected.
```

Notice the order of data in the previous results, as well as the LAST_NAME of the individual for each CITY. All employee records in the EMPLOYEE_TBL table are now counted, and the results are grouped by CITY but ordered by the count on each city first.

```
SELECT CITY, COUNT(*)
FROM EMPLOYEE_TBL
GROUP BY CITY
ORDER BY 2,1;
```

OUTPUT

```
CITY            COUNT(*)
-------------   --------
GREENWOOD              1
WHITELAND             1
INDIANAPOLIS          4
```

Notice the order of the results. The results were first sorted by the count on each city (1–4), and then by city. The count for the first two cities in the output is 1. Because the count is the same, which is the first expression in the ORDER BY clause, the city is then sorted; GREENWOOD is placed before WHITELAND.

Although GROUP BY and ORDER BY perform a similar function, there is one major difference. The GROUP BY is designed to group identical data, while the ORDER BY is designed merely to put data into a specific order. GROUP BY and ORDER BY can be used in the same SELECT statement, but must follow a specific order. The GROUP BY clause is always placed before the ORDER BY clause in the SELECT statement.

> The GROUP BY clause can be used in the CREATE VIEW statement to sort data, but the ORDER BY clause is not allowed in the CREATE VIEW statement. The CREATE VIEW statement is discussed in depth in Hour 20, "Creating and Using Views and Synonyms."

The HAVING Clause

The HAVING clause, when used in conjunction with the GROUP BY in a SELECT statement, tells GROUP BY which groups to include in the output. HAVING is to GROUP BY as WHERE is to SELECT. In other words, the WHERE clause places conditions on the selected columns, whereas the HAVING clause places conditions on groups created by the GROUP BY clause.

The following is the position of the HAVING clause in a query:

```
SELECT
FROM
WHERE
GROUP BY
HAVING
ORDER BY
```

The HAVING clause must follow the GROUP BY clause in a query and must also precede the ORDER BY clause if used.

The following is the syntax of the SELECT statement, including the HAVING clause:

```
SELECT COLUMN1, COLUMN2
FROM TABLE1, TABLE2
WHERE CONDITIONS
GROUP BY COLUMN1, COLUMN2
HAVING CONDITIONS
ORDER BY COLUMN1, COLUMN2
```

In the following example, you select the average pay rate and salary for all cities except GREENWOOD. You group the output by CITY, but only want to display those groups (cities) that have an average salary greater than $20,000. You sort the results by average salary for each city.

INPUT
```
SELECT CITY, AVG(PAY_RATE), AVG(SALARY)
FROM EMP_PAY_TMP
WHERE CITY <> 'GREENWOOD'
GROUP BY CITY
HAVING AVG(SALARY) > 20000
ORDER BY 3;
```

OUTPUT
```
CITY            AVG(PAY_RATE) AVG(SALARY)
------------    ------------- -----------
WHITELAND                           40000
```

1 row selected.

Why was only one row returned by this query?

- The city GREENWOOD was eliminated from the WHERE clause.

- INDIANAPOLIS was deducted from the output because the average salary was 20000, which is not greater than 20000.

Summary

You have learned how to group the results of a query using the GROUP BY clause. The GROUP BY clause is primarily used with aggregate SQL functions like SUM, AVG, MAX, MIN, and COUNT. The nature of GROUP BY is like that of ORDER BY in that both sort query results. The GROUP BY clause must sort data to group results logically, but can also be used exclusively to sort data, although an ORDER BY is much simpler for this purpose.

The HAVING clause, an extension to the GROUP BY clause, is used to place conditions on the established groups of a query. The WHERE clause is used to place conditions on a query's SELECT clause. During the next hour, you learn a new arsenal of functions that allow you to further manipulate query results.

Q&A

Q Is using the GROUP BY clause mandatory when using the ORDER BY clause in a SELECT statement?

A No. Using the GROUP BY clause is strictly optional, but it can be very useful when used with ORDER BY.

Q What is a group value?

A Take the CITY column from the EMPLOYEE_TBL. If you select the employee's name and city, and then group the output by city, all the cities that are identical are arranged together.

Q **Must a column appear in the SELECT statement to GROUP BY it?**

A Yes, a column must be in the SELECT statement to GROUP BY it.

Workshop

The following workshop is composed of a series of quiz questions and practical exercises. The quiz questions are designed to test your overall understanding of the current material. The practical exercises are intended to afford you the opportunity to apply the concepts discussed during the current hour, as well as build upon the knowledge acquired in previous hours of study. Please take time to complete the quiz questions and exercises before continuing. Refer to Appendix C, "Answers to Quizzes and Exercises," for answers.

Quiz

1. Will the following SQL statements work?

   a.
   ```
   SELECT SUM(SALARY), EMP_ID
   FROM EMPLOYEE_PAY_TBL
   GROUP BY 1 and 2;
   ```

   b.
   ```
   SELECT EMP_ID, MAX(SALARY)
   FROM EMPLOYEE_PAY_TBL
   GROUP BY SALARY, EMP_ID;
   ```

   c.
   ```
   SELECT EMP_ID, COUNT(SALARY)
   FROM EMPLOYEE_PAY_TBL
   ORDER BY EMP_ID
   GROUP BY SALARY;
   ```

2. True or false: You must also use the GROUP BY clause when using the HAVING clause.

3. True or false: The following SQL statement returns a total of the salaries by groups:
   ```
   SELECT SUM(SALARY)
   FROM EMPLOYEE_PAY_TBL;
   ```

4. True or false: The columns selected must appear in the GROUP BY clause in the same order.

5. True or false: The HAVING clause tells the GROUP BY which groups to include.

Exercises

1. Write an SQL statement that returns the employee ID, employee name, and city from the EMPLOYEE_TBL. Group by the CITY column first.

2. Write an SQL statement that returns the city and a count of all employees per city from EMPLOYEE_TBL. Add a HAVING clause to display only those cities that have a count of more than two employees.

Hour 11

Restructuring the Appearance of Data

During this hour, you learn how to restructure the appearance of output results using a wide array of functions, some ANSI standard functions, and other functions based on the standard and several variations used by some major SQL implementations.

This hour's highlights include

- Introduction to character functions
- How and when to use character functions
- Examples of ANSI SQL functions
- Examples of common implementation-specific functions
- Overview of conversion functions
- How and when to use conversion functions

The Concepts of ANSI Character Functions

NEW TERM   *Character functions* are functions used to represent strings in SQL in formats alternate to how they are stored in the table. The first part of this hour discusses the concepts for character functions as covered by ANSI. The second part of this hour shows real-world examples using functions that are specific to various SQL implementations. ANSI functions discussed in this hour include CONCATENATION, SUBSTRING, TRANSLATE, REPLACE, UPPER, and LOWER.

Concatenation

NEW TERM   *Concatenation* is the process of combining two separate strings into one string. For example, you may want to concatenate an individual's first and last names into a single string for the complete name.

        JOHN concatenated with SMITH = JOHN SMITH

Substring

The concept of *substring* is the capability to extract part of a string, or a "sub" of the string. For example, the following values are substrings of JOHNSON:

    J   JOHN   JO   ON   SON   ...

TRANSLATE

The TRANSLATE function is used to translate a string, character by character, into another string. There are normally three arguments with the TRANSLATE function: the string to be converted, a list of the characters to convert, and a list of the substitution characters. Implementation examples are shown in the next part of this hour.

Various Common Character Functions

Character functions are used mainly to compare, join, search, and extract a segment of a string or a value in a column. There are several character functions available to the SQL programmer.

The following sections illustrate the application of ANSI concepts in some of the leading implementations of SQL, such as in Oracle, Sybase, SQLBase, Informix, and SQL Server.

The ANSI concepts discussed in this book are just that—concepts. Standards provided by ANSI are simply guidelines for how the use of SQL in a relational database should be implemented. With that thought, keep in mind that the specific functions discussed in this hour are not necessarily the exact functions that you may use in your particular implementation. Yes, the concepts are the same, and the way the functions work are generally the same, but function names and actual syntax may differ.

Concatenation

Concatenation, along with most other functions, is represented slightly differently among various implementations. The following examples show the use of concatenation in Oracle and SQL Server.

In Oracle

```
SELECT 'JOHN' || 'SON' returns JOHNSON
```

In SQL Server

```
SELECT 'JOHN' + 'SON' returns JOHNSON
```

The syntax for Oracle is

```
COLUMN_NAME || [ '' || ] COLUMN_NAME [ COLUMN_NAME ]
```

The syntax for SQL Server is

```
COLUMN_NAME + [ '' + ] COLUMN_NAME [ COLUMN_NAME ]
```

▼ SYNTAX

11

Example	*Meaning*
SELECT CITY + STATE FROM EMPLOYEE_TBL;	This SQL Server statement concatenates the values for city and state into one value.
SELECT CITY ||', '|| STATE FROM EMPLOYEE_TBL;	This Oracle statement concatenates the values for city and state into one value, placing a comma between the values for city and state.
SELECT CITY + ' ' + STATE FROM EMPLOYEE_TBL;	This SQL Server statement concatenates the values for city and state into one value, placing a space between the two original values.

Example:

```
SELECT LAST_NAME || ', ' || FIRST_NAME NAME
FROM EMPLOYEE_TBL;
```

```
NAME
----------------
STEPHENS, TINA
PLEW, LINDA
GLASS, BRANDON
GLASS, JACOB
WALLACE, MARIAH
SPURGEON, TIFFANY

6 rows selected.
```

> Notice the use of single quotation marks and a comma in the preceding SQL statement. Most characters and symbols are allowed if enclosed by single quotations marks. Some implementations may use double quotation marks for literal string values.

TRANSLATE

The TRANSLATE function searches a string of characters and checks for a specific character, makes note of the position found, searches the replacement string at the same position, and then replaces that character with the new value. The syntax is

SYNTAX

```
TRANSLATE(CHARACTER SET, VALUE1, VALUE2)
```

Example	Meaning
SELECT TRANSLATE (CITY,'IND','ABC' FROM EMPLOYEE_TBL);	This SQL statement substitutes every occurrence of I in the string with A, replaces all occurrences of N with B, and D with C.

The following example illustrates the use of TRANSLATE with real data:

```
SELECT CITY, TRANSLATE(CITY,'IND','ABC')
FROM EMPLOYEE_TBL;
```

```
CITY          TRANSLATE(CI
------------  ------------
GREENWOOD     GREEBWOOC
INDIANAPOLIS  ABCAABAPOLAS
WHITELAND     WHATELABC
INDIANAPOLIS  ABCAABAPOLAS
INDIANAPOLIS  ABCAABAPOLAS
INDIANAPOLIS  ABCAABAPOLAS

6 rows selected.
```

Notice in this example that all occurrences of I were replaced with A, N with B, and D with C. In the city INDIANAPOLIS, IND was replaced with ABC, but in GREENWOOD, D was replaced with C. Also notice how the value WHITELAND was translated.

REPLACE

The REPLACE function is used to replace every occurrence of a character(s) with a specified character(s). The use of this function is similar to the TRANSLATE function; only one specific character or string is replaced within another string. The syntax is

```
REPLACE('VALUE', 'VALUE', [ NULL ] 'VALUE')
```

Example	Meaning
SELECT REPLACE(FIRST_ NAME, 'T', 'B') FROM EMPLOYEE_TBL	This statement returns all the first names and changes any occurrence of T to a B.

INPUT

```
SELECT CITY, REPLACE(CITY,'I','Z')
FROM EMPLOYEE_TBL;
```

OUTPUT

```
CITY            REPLACE(CITY)
------------    -------------
GREENWOOD       GREENWOOD
INDIANAPOLIS    ZNDZANAPOLZS
WHITELAND       WHZTELAND
INDIANAPOLIS    ZNDZANAPOLZS
INDIANAPOLIS    ZNDZANAPOLZS
INDIANAPOLIS    ZNDZANAPOLZS

6 rows selected.
```

UPPER

Most implementations have a way to control the case of data by using functions. The UPPER function is used to convert lowercase letters to uppercase letters for a specific string.

The syntax is as follows:

```
UPPER(character string)
```

Example	Meaning
SELECT UPPER(LAST_NAME) FROM EMPLOYEE_TBL; LAST_NAME	This SQL statement converts all characters in the column to uppercase.

INPUT
```
SELECT UPPER(CITY)
FROM EMPLOYEE_TBL;
```

OUTPUT
```
UPPER(CITY)
- - - - - - - - - - - - -
GREENWOOD
INDIANAPOLIS
WHITELAND
INDIANAPOLIS
INDIANAPOLIS
INDIANAPOLIS

6 rows selected.
```

LOWER

Converse of the UPPER function, the LOWER function is used to convert uppercase letters to lowercase letters for a specific string.

SYNTAX

The syntax is as follows:

```
LOWER(character string)
```

Example	Meaning
SELECT LOWER(LAST_NAME) FROM EMPLOYEE_TBL; LAST_NAME	This SQL statement converts all characters in the column to lowercase.

INPUT
```
SELECT LOWER(CITY)
FROM EMPLOYEE_TBL;
```

OUTPUT
```
LOWER(CITY)
- - - - - - - - - - - - -
greenwood
indianapolis
whiteland
indianapolis
indianapolis
indianapolis

6 rows selected.
```

SUBSTR

Taking an expression's substring is common in most implementations of SQL, but the function name may differ, as shown in the following Oracle and SQL Server examples.

The syntax for Oracle is

```
SUBSTR(COLUMN NAME, STARTING POSITION, LENGTH)
```

The syntax for SQL Server is

```
SUBSTRING(COLUMN NAME, STARTING POSITION, LENGTH)
```

The only difference between the two implementations is the spelling of the function name.

Example	Meaning
SELECT SUBSTRING (EMP_ID,1,3) FROM EMPLOYEE_TBL	This SQL statement returns the first three characters of EMP_ID.
SELECT SUBSTRING (EMP_ID,4,2) FROM EMPLOYEE_TBL	This SQL statement returns the fourth and fifth characters of EMP_ID.
SELECT SUBSTRING (EMP_ID,6,4) FROM EMPLOYEE_TBL	This SQL statement returns the sixth through the ninth characters of EMP_ID.

The following is an example using Microsoft SQL Server:

INPUT
```
SELECT EMP_ID, SUBSTRING(EMP_ID,1,3)
FROM EMPLOYEE_TBL;
```

OUTPUT
```
EMP_ID      SUB
.........   ...
311549902   311
442346889   442
213764555   213
313782439   313
220984332   220
443679012   443

6 rows affected.
```

The following is an example using Oracle8:

INPUT
```
SELECT EMP_ID, SUBSTR(EMP_ID,1,3)
FROM EMPLOYEE_TBL;
```

11

```
EMP_ID      SUB
----------  ---
311549902   311
442346889   442
213764555   213
313782439   313
220984332   220
443679012   443

6 rows selected.
```

Notice the difference between the feedback of the two queries. The first example returns the feedback `6 rows affected` and the second returns `6 rows selected`. You see differences such as this between implementations.

INSTR

The INSTR function is a variation of the POSITION function; it is used to search a string of characters for a specific set of characters and report the position of those characters. The syntax is as follows:

SYNTAX

```
INSTR(COLUMN NAME, 'SET',
[ START POSITION [ , OCCURRENCE ] ]);
```

Example	Meaning
SELECT INSTR(STATE ,'I',1,1) FROM EMPLOYEE_TBL;	This SQL statement returns the position of the first occurrence of the letter *I* for each state in EMPLOYEE_TBL.

INPUT

```
SELECT PROD_DESC,
       INSTR(PROD_DESC,'A',1,1)
FROM PRODUCTS_TBL;
```

OUTPUT

```
PROD_DESC                     INSTR(PROD_DESC,'A',1,1)
-----------------------       ------------------------
WITCHES COSTUME                                     0
PLASTIC PUMPKIN 18 INCH                             3
FALSE PARAFFIN TEETH                                2
LIGHTED LANTERNS                                   10
ASSORTED COSTUMES                                   1
CANDY CORN                                          2
PUMPKIN CANDY                                      10
```

```
PLASTIC SPIDERS                         3
ASSORTED MASKS                          1
KEY CHAIN                               7
OAK BOOKSHELF                           2
```

```
11 rows selected.
```

Notice that if the searched character *A* was not found in a string, the value 0 was returned for the position.

LTRIM

The LTRIM function is another way of clipping part of a string. This function and SUBSTRING are in the same family. LTRIM is used to trim characters from the left of a string. The syntax is

```
LTRIM(CHARACTER STRING [ ,'set' ])
```

Example	Meaning
SELECT LTRIM(FIRST_ NAME,'LES') FROM CUSTOMER_TBL FIRST_NAME = 'LESLIE';	This SQL statement trims the characters LES from the left of all names that are WHERE LESLIE.

INPUT

```
SELECT POSITION, LTRIM(POSITION,'SALES')
FROM EMPLOYEE_PAY_TBL;
```

OUTPUT

```
POSITION          LTRIM(POSITION,
---------------   ---------------
MARKETING         MARKETING
TEAM LEADER       TEAM LEADER
SALES MANAGER     MANAGER
SALESMAN          MAN
SHIPPER           HIPPER
SHIPPER           HIPPER
```

```
6 rows selected.
```

The S in SHIPPER was trimmed off, even though SHIPPER does not contain the string SALES. The first four characters of SALES were ignored. The searched characters must appear in the same order of the search string and must be on the far left of the string. In other words, LTRIM will trim off all characters to the left of the last occurrence in the search string.

RTRIM

Like the LTRIM, the RTRIM function is used to trim characters from the right of a string. The syntax is

SYNTAX

```
RTRIM(CHARACTER STRING [ ,'set' ])
```

Example	Meaning
SELECT RTRIM(FIRST_ NAME, 'ON') FROM EMPLOYEE_TBL WHERE FIRST_NAME = 'BRANDON';	This SQL statement returns the first name BRANDON and trims the ON, leaving BRAND as a result.

INPUT

```
SELECT POSITION, RTRIM(POSITION,'ER')
FROM EMPLOYEE_PAY_TBL;
```

OUTPUT

```
POSITION          RTRIM(POSITION,
---------------   ---------------
MARKETING         MARKETING
TEAM LEADER       TEAM LEAD
SALES MANAGER     SALES MANAG
SALESMAN          SALESMAN
SHIPPER           SHIPP
SHIPPER           SHIPP

6 rows selected.
```

The string ER was trimmed from the right of all applicable strings.

DECODE

The DECODE function is not ANSI—at least not at the time of this writing—but its use is shown here because of its great power. This function is used in SQLBase, Oracle, and possibly other implementations. DECODE is used to search a string for a value or string, and if the string is found, an alternate string is displayed as part of the query results.

The syntax is

SYNTAX

```
DECODE(COLUMN NAME, 'SEARCH1', 'RETURN1',[ 'SEARCH2', 'RETURN2' ,'DEFAULT
åVALUE'])
```

Example	Meaning
SELECT DECODE(LAST_NAME, 'SMITH', 'JONES', 'OTHER') FROM EMPLOYEE_ TBL;	This query searches the value of all last names in EMPLOYEE_TBL; if the value SMITH is found, JONES is displayed in its place. Any other names are displayed as OTHER, which is called the *default value*.

In the following example, DECODE is used on the values for CITY in EMPLOYEE_TBL:

INPUT

```
SELECT CITY,
       DECODE(CITY,'INDIANAPOLIS','INDY',
                   'GREENWOOD','GREEN', 'OTHER')
FROM EMPLOYEE_TBL;
```

OUTPUT

```
CITY         DECOD
-----------  -----
GREENWOOD    GREEN
INDIANAPOLIS INDY
WHITELAND    OTHER
INDIANAPOLIS INDY
INDIANAPOLIS INDY
INDIANAPOLIS INDY

6 rows selected.
```

The output shows the value INDIANAPOLIS displayed as INDY, GREENWOOD displayed as GREEN, and all other cities displayed as OTHER.

Miscellaneous Character Functions

The following sections show a few other character functions worth mentioning. Once again, these are functions that are fairly common among major implementations.

Finding a Value's Length

The LENGTH function is a common function used to find the length of a string, number, date, or expression in bytes. The syntax is

SYNTAX

```
LENGTH(CHARACTER STRING)
```

Example	Meaning
SELECT LENGTH	This SQL statement (LAST_NAME) returns the
FROM EMPLOYEE_TBL;	length of the last name for each employee.

INPUT

```
SELECT PROD_DESC, LENGTH(PROD_DESC)
FROM PRODUCTS_TBL;
```

OUTPUT

```
PROD_DESC                      LENGTH(PROD_DESC)
-----------------------        -----------------
WITCHES COSTUME                15
PLASTIC PUMPKIN 18 INCH        23
FALSE PARAFFIN TEETH           19
LIGHTED LANTERNS               16
ASSORTED COSTUMES              17
CANDY CORN                     10
```

11

```
PUMPKIN CANDY                    13
PLASTIC SPIDERS                  15
ASSORTED MASKS                   14
KEY CHAIN                         9
OAK BOOKSHELF                    13
```

11 rows selected.

NVL (NULL Value)

The NVL function is used to return data from one expression if another expression is NULL. NVL can be used with most data types; however, the value and the substitute must be the same data type. The syntax is

SYNTAX

```
NVL('VALUE', 'SUBSTITUTION')
```

Example	Meaning
SELECT NVL(SALARY, '00000') FROM EMPLOYEE_PAY_TBL;	This SQL statement finds NULL values and substitutes 00000 for any NULL values.

INPUT

```
SELECT PAGER, NVL(PAGER,9999999999)
FROM EMPLOYEE_TBL;
```

OUTPUT

```
PAGER        NVL(PAGER,
----------   ----------
             9999999999
             9999999999
3175709980   3175709980
8887345678   8887345678
             9999999999
             9999999999
```

6 rows selected.

Only NULL values were represented as 9999999999.

LPAD

LPAD (left pad) is used to add characters or spaces to the left of a string. The syntax is

SYNTAX

```
LPAD(CHARACTER SET)
```

The following example pads periods to the left of each product description, totaling 30 characters between the actual value and padded periods.

INPUT

```
SELECT LPAD(PROD_DESC,30,'.') PRODUCT
FROM PRODUCTS_TBL;
```

OUTPUT

```
PRODUCT
-------------------------------
...............WITCHES COSTUME
.......PLASTIC PUMPKIN 18 INCH
..........FALSE PARAFFIN TEETH
..............LIGHTED LANTERNS
.............ASSORTED COSTUMES
....................CANDY CORN
................PUMPKIN CANDY
..............PLASTIC SPIDERS
...............ASSORTED MASKS
....................KEY CHAIN
........ ........OAK BOOKSHELF

11 rows selected.
```

RPAD

SYNTAX

The RPAD (right pad) is used to add characters or spaces to the right of a string. The syntax is

```
RPAD(CHARACTER SET)
```

The following example pads periods to the right of each product description, totaling 30 characters between the actual value and padded periods.

INPUT

```
SELECT RPAD(PROD_DESC,30,'.') PRODUCT
FROM PRODUCTS_TBL;
```

OUTPUT

```
PRODUCT
-------------------------------
WITCHES COSTUME...............
PLASTIC PUMPKIN 18 INCH.......
FALSE PARAFFIN TEETH..........
LIGHTED LANTERNS..............
ASSORTED COSTUMES.............
CANDY CORN....................
PUMPKIN CANDY.................
PLASTIC SPIDERS...............
ASSORTED MASKS................
KEY CHAIN........ ........ ...
OAK BOOKSHELF........ ........

11 rows selected.
```

11

ASCII

The ASCII function is used to return the ASCII (American Standard Code for Information Interchange) representation of the leftmost character of a string. The syntax is

SYNTAX

```
ASCII(CHARACTER SET)
```

Examples:

```
ASCII('A') returns 65
ASCII('B') returns 66
ASCII('C') returns 67
```

For more information, refer to the ASCII chart in Appendix B, "ASCII Table."

Mathematical Functions

Mathematical functions are fairly standard across implementations. These are functions that allow you to manipulate numeric values in a database according to mathematical rules.

The most common functions include the following:

Absolute value	(ABS)
Rounding	(ROUND)
Square root	(SQRT)
Sign values	(SIGN)
Power	(POWER)
Ceiling and floor values	(CEIL, FLOOR)
Exponential values	(EXP)
SIN, COS, TAN	

SYNTAX

The general syntax of most mathematical functions is

```
FUNCTION(EXPRESSION)
```

Conversion Functions

NEW TERM *Conversion functions* are used to convert a data type into another data type. For example, there may be times when you want to convert character data into numeric data. You may have data that is normally stored in character format, but occasionally you want to convert the character format to numeric for the purpose of making calculations. Mathematical functions and computations are not allowed on data that is represented in character format.

The following are general types of data conversions:

- Character to numeric
- Numeric to character
- Character to date
- Date to character

The first two types of conversions are discussed in this hour. The remaining conversion types are discussed during Hour 12, "Understanding Dates and Times," after date and time storage is discussed in more detail.

Some implementations may implicitly convert data types when necessary.

Converting Character Strings to Numbers

There are two things you should notice regarding the differences between numeric data types and character string data types:

1. Arithmetic expressions and functions can be used on numeric values.
2. Numeric values are right-justified, whereas character string data types are left-justified in output results.

When a character string is converted to a numeric value, the value takes on the two attributes just mentioned.

Some implementations may not have functions to convert character strings to numbers, while some have conversion functions such as this. In either case, consult your implementation documentation for specific syntax and rules for conversions.

> Characters in a character string being converted to a number must typically
> be 0 through 9. The addition symbol, minus symbol, and period can also be
> used to represent positive numbers, negative numbers, and decimals. For
> example, the string STEVE cannot be converted to a number, whereas an
> individual's Social Security number could be stored as a character string, but
> could easily be converted to a numeric value via use of a conversion function.

The following is an example of a numeric conversion using an Oracle conversion
function:

```
SELECT EMP_ID, TO_NUMBER(EMP_ID)
FROM EMPLOYEE_TBL;
```

OUTPUT

```
EMP_ID                TO_NUMBER(EMP_ID)
----------            -----------------
311549902                     311549902
442346889                     442346889
213764555                     213764555
313782439                     313782439
220984332                     220984332
443679012                     443679012

6 rows selected.
```

The employee identification is right-justified following the conversion.

> The justification of data is the simplest way to identify a column's data type.

Converting Numbers to Strings

The conversion of numeric values to character strings is precisely the opposite of converting characters to numbers.

The following is an example of converting a numeric value to a character string using a
Transact-SQL conversion function for Microsoft SQL Server:

```
SELECT PAY = PAY_RATE, NEW_PAY = STR(PAY_RATE)
FROM EMPLOYEE_PAY_TBL
WHERE PAY_RATE IS NOT NULL;
```

```
PAY NEW_PAY
---------- -------
     17.5 17.5
    14.75 14.75
    18.25 18.25
```

```
12.8 12.8
  11 11
  15 15
```

6 rows affected.

The following is the same example using an Oracle conversion function:

INPUT
```
SELECT PAY_RATE, TO_CHAR(PAY_RATE)
FROM EMPLOYEE_PAY_TBL
WHERE PAY_RATE IS NOT NULL;
```

OUTPUT
```
  PAY_RATE TO_CHAR(PAY_RATE)
---------- -----------------
      17.5 17.5
     14.75 14.75
     18.25 18.25
      12.8 12.8
        11 11
        15 15

6 rows selected.
```

The Concept of Combining Character Functions

11

Most functions can be combined in a single SQL statement. SQL would be far too limited if function combinations were not allowed. The following examples show how some functions can be combined with one another in a query:

INPUT
```
SELECT LAST_NAME || ', ' || FIRST_NAME NAME,
       SUBSTR(EMP_ID,1,3) || '-' ||
       SUBSTR(EMP_ID,4,2) || '-' ||
       SUBSTR(EMP_ID,6,4) ID
FROM EMPLOYEE_TBL;
```

OUTPUT
```
NAME               ID
------------------ -----------
STEPHENS, TINA     311-54-9902
PLEW, LINDA        442-34-6889
GLASS, BRANDON     213-76-4555
GLASS, JACOB       313-78-2439
WALLACE, MARIAH    220-98-4332
SPURGEON, TIFFANY  443-67-9012

6 rows selected.
```

The following example combines two functions in the query (concatenation with substring). By pulling the EMP_ID column apart into three pieces, you can concatenate those pieces with dashes to render a readable Social Security number.

INPUT
```
SELECT SUM(LENGTH(LAST_NAME) + LENGTH(FIRST_NAME)) TOTAL
FROM EMPLOYEE_TBL;
```

OUTPUT
```
   TOTAL
----------
      71
```

```
1 row selected.
```

This example uses the LENGTH function and the arithmetic operator (+) to add the length of the first name to the length of the last name for each column; the SUM function then finds the total length of all first and last names.

 When embedding functions within functions in an SQL statement, remember that the innermost function is resolved first, and then each function is subsequently resolved from the inside out.

Summary

You have been introduced to various functions used in an SQL statement—usually a query—to modify or enhance the way output is represented. Those functions include character, mathematical, and conversion functions. It is very important to realize that the ANSI standard is a guideline for how SQL should be implemented by vendors, but does not dictate the exact syntax or necessarily place limits on vendors' innovations. Most vendors have standard functions and conform to the ANSI concepts, but each vendor has his or her own specific list of available functions. The function name may differ and the syntax may differ, but the concepts with all functions are the same.

Q&A

Q Are all the functions in the ANSI standard?

A No, not all functions are exactly ANSI SQL. Functions, like data types, are often implementation-dependent. Several examples of functions from selected implementations are included. However, because so many implementations use similar functions (although they may slightly differ), check your particular implementation for available functions and their usage.

Q Is the data actually changed in the database when using functions?

A No. Data is not changed in the database when using functions. Functions are typically used in queries to manipulate the output's appearance.

Workshop

The following workshop is composed of a series of quiz questions and practical exercises. The quiz questions are designed to test your overall understanding of the current material. The practical exercises are intended to afford you the opportunity to apply the concepts discussed during the current hour, as well as build upon the knowledge acquired in previous hours of study. Please take time to complete the quiz questions and exercises before continuing. Refer to Appendix C, "Answers to Quizzes and Exercises," for answers.

Quiz

Match the Descriptions with the possible Functions.

DESCRIPTIONS	FUNCTIONS
a. Used to select a portion of a character string.	|| RPAD LPAD
h Used to trim characters from either the right or left of a string.	LENGTH UPPER
c. Used to change all letters to lowercase.	LTRIM RTRIM LOWER
d. Used to find the length of a string.	SUBSTR
e. Used to combine strings.	

1. True or false: Using functions in a select statement to restructure the appearance of data in output will also affect the way the data is stored in the database.

2. True or false: The outermost function is always resolved first when functions are embedded within other functions in a query.

Exercises

1. Use the appropriate function to convert the string hello to all uppercase letters.

2. Use the appropriate function to print only the first four characters of the string JOHNSON.

3. Use the appropriate function to concatenate the strings JOHN and SON.

HOUR 12

Understanding Dates and Times

In this hour, you learn about the nature of dates and time in SQL. Not only does this hour discuss the DATETIME data type in more detail; you see how some implementations use dates, some of the common rules, and how to extract the date and time in a desired format.

The highlights of this hour include

- Understanding dates and time
- How date and time are stored
- Typical date and time formats
- How to use date functions
- How to use date conversions

As you know by now, there are many different SQL implementations. This book shows the ANSI standard and the most common non-standard functions, commands, and operators. Oracle is used for the examples. Even in Oracle, the date can be stored in different formats. You must check your particular implementation for the date storage. No matter how it is stored, your implementation should have functions that convert date formats.

How Is a Date Stored?

Each implementation has a default storage format for the date and time. This default storage often varies among different implementations, as do other data types for each implementation. The following sections begin by reviewing the standard format of the DATETIME data type and its elements. Then you see the data types for date and time in some popular implementations of SQL, including Oracle, Sybase, and Microsoft SQL Server.

Standard Data Types for Date and Time

There are three standard SQL data types for date and time (DATETIME) storage:

Data Type	Usage
DATE	Stores date literals
TIME	Stores time literals
TIMESTAMP	Stores date and time literals

Format and range of valid values for each data type:

DATE

Format: YYYY-MM-DD

Range: 0001-01-01 to 9999-12-31

TIME

Format: HH:MI:SS.*nn*...

Range: 00:00:00... to 23:59:61.999...

TIMESTAMP

Format: YYYY-MM-DD HH:MI:SS.*nn*...

Range: 0001-01-01 00:00:00... to 9999-12-31 23:59:61.999...

DATETIME Elements

DATETIME elements are those elements pertaining to date and time that are included as part of a DATETIME definition. The following is a list of the constrained DATETIME elements and a valid range of values for each element:

YEAR	0001 to 9999
MONTH	01 to 12
DAY	01 to 31
HOUR	00 to 23
MINUTE	00 to 59
SECOND	00.000... to 61.999...

Seconds can be represented as a decimal, allowing the expression of tenths of a second, hundredths of a second, milliseconds, and so on. Each of these elements, except for the last, is self explanatory; they are elements of time that we deal with on a daily basis. You may question the fact that a minute can contain more than 60 seconds. According to the ANSI standard, this 61,999 seconds is due to the possible insertion or omission of a leap second in a minute, which in itself is a rare occurrence. Refer to your implementation on the allowed values because date and time storage may vary widely.

Implementation Specific Data Types

As with other data types, each implementation provides its own representation and syntax. This section shows how three products (Oracle, Sybase, and SQLBase) have been implemented with date and time.

Product	Data Type	Use
Oracle	DATE	Stores both date and time information
Sybase	DATETIME	Stores both date and time information
	SMALLDATETIME	Stores both date and time information, but includes a smaller date range than DATETIME
SQLBase	DATETIME	Stores both date and time information
	TIMESTAMP	Stores both date and time information
	DATE	Stores a date value
	TIME	Stores a time value

12

Each implementation has its own specific data type(s) for date and time information. However, most implementations comply with the ANSI standard in the fact that all elements of the date and time are included in their associated data types. The way the date is internally stored is implementation-dependent.

Date Functions

Date functions are available in SQL depending on the options with each specific implementation. *Date functions*, similar to character string functions, are used to manipulate the representation of date and time data. Available date functions are often used to format the output of dates and time in an appealing format, compare date values with one another, compute intervals between dates, and so on.

The Current Date

You may have already raised the question: How do I get the current date from the database? The need to retrieve the current date from the database may originate from several situations, but the current date is normally returned either to compare to a stored date or to return the value of the current date as some sort of timestamp.

NEW TERM The current date is ultimately stored on the host computer for the database, and is called the *system date*. The database, which interfaces with the appropriate operating system, has the capability to retrieve the system date for its own purpose or to resolve database requests, such as queries.

Take a look at a couple of methods of attaining the system date based on commands from two different implementations.

Sybase uses a function called GETDATE() to return the system date. This function is used in a query as follows. The output is what would return if today's current date was New Year's Eve for 1999.

INPUT
```
SELECT GETDATE()
```

OUTPUT
```
Dec 31, 1999
```

Most options discussed in this book for Sybase's and Microsoft's implementations are applicable to both implementations, because both use SQL Server for their database server. Both implementations also use an extension to standard SQL known as Transact-SQL.

Oracle uses what is calls a *pseudocolumn*, SYSDATE, to retrieve the current date. SYSDATE acts as any other column in a table and can be selected from any table in the database, although it is not actually part of the table's definition.

To return the system date in Oracle, the following statement returns the output if today was New Year's Eve before 2000:

INPUT

```
SELECT SYSDATE FROM TABLE_NAME
```

OUTPUT

```
31-DEC-99
```

Time Zones

The use of time zones may be a factor when dealing with date and time information. For instance, a time of 6:00 p.m. in central United States does not equate to the same time in Australia, although the actual point in time is the same. Some of us who live within the daylight savings time zone are used to adjusting our clocks twice a year. If time zones are considerations when maintaining data in your case, you may find it necessary to consider time zones and perform time conversions, if available with your SQL implementation.

The following are some common time zones and their abbreviations:

Abbreviation	Definition
AST, ADT	Atlantic standard, daylight time
BST, BDT	Bering standard, daylight time
CST, CDT	Central standard, daylight time
EST, EDT	Eastern standard, daylight time
GMT	Greenwich mean time
HST, HDT	Alaska/Hawaii standard, daylight time
MST, MDT	Mountain standard, daylight time
NST	Newfoundland standard, daylight time
PST, PDT	Pacific standard, daylight time
YST, YDT	Yukon standard, daylight time

12

Some implementations have functions that allow you to deal with different time zones. However, not all implementations may support the use of time zones. Be sure to verify the use of time zones in your particular implementation, as well as the need in the case of your database.

Adding Time to Dates

Days, months, and other parts of time can be added to dates for the purpose of comparing dates to one another, or to provide more specific conditions in the WHERE clause of a query.

Intervals can be used to add periods of time to a DATETIME value. As defined by the standard, intervals are used to manipulate the value of a DATETIME value, as in the following examples:

INPUT

```
DATE '1999-12-31' + INTERVAL '1' DAY
```

OUTPUT

```
'2000-01-01'
```

INPUT

```
DATE '1999-12-31' + INTERVAL '1' MONTH
```

OUTPUT

```
'2000-01-31'
```

The following is an example using the SQL Server function DATEADD:

INPUT

```
SELECT DATEADD(MONTH, 1, DATE_HIRE)
FROM EMPLOYEE_PAY_TBL
```

OUTPUT

```
DATE_HIRE  ADD_MONTH
---------- ----------
23-MAY-89  23-JUN-89
17-JUN-90  17-JUL-90
14-AUG-94  14-SEP-94
28-JUN-97  28-JUL-97
22-JUL-96  22-AUG-96
14-JAN-91  14-FEB-91

6 rows affected.
```

The following example uses the Oracle function ADD_MONTHS:

INPUT

```
SELECT DATE_HIRE, ADD_MONTHS(DATE_HIRE,1)
FROM EMPLOYEE_PAY_TBL;
```

OUTPUT

```
DATE_HIRE ADD_MONTH
----- -------
23-MAY-89 23-JUN-89
17-JUN-90 17-JUL-90
14-AUG-94 14-SEP-94
28-JUN-97 28-JUL-97
22-JUL-96 22-AUG-96
14-JAN-91 14-FEB-91

6 rows selected.
```

To add one day to a date in Oracle, use the following:

INPUT

```
SELECT DATE_HIRE, DATE_HIRE + 1
FROM EMPLOYEE_PAY_TBL
WHERE EMP_ID = '311549902';
```

OUTPUT

```
DATE_HIRE DATE_HIRE
--------- ---------
23-MAY-89 24-MAY-89

1 row selected.
```

Notice that these examples in SQL Server and Oracle, though they differ syntactically from the ANSI examples, derive their results based on the same concept as described by the SQL standard.

Comparing Dates and Time Periods

OVERLAPS is a powerful standard SQL conditional operator for DATETIME values. The OVERLAPS operator is used to compare two timeframes and return the Boolean value TRUE or FALSE, depending on whether the two timeframes overlap. The following comparison returns the value TRUE:

```
(TIME '01:00:00' , TIME '05:59:00')
OVERLAPS
(TIME '05:00:00' , TIME '07:00:00')
```

The following comparison returns the value FALSE:

```
(TIME '01:00:00' , TIME '05:59:00')
OVERLAPS
(TIME '06:00:00 , TIME '07:00:00')
```

Miscellaneous Date Functions

The following list shows some powerful date functions that exist in the implementations for SQL Server and Oracle.

12

SQL SERVER

DATEPART	Returns the integer value of a DATEPART for a date
DATENAME	Returns the text value of a DATEPART for a date
GETDATE()	Returns the system date
DATEDIFF	Returns the difference between two dates for specified date parts, such as days, minutes, and seconds

ORACLE

NEXT_DAY	Returns the next day of the week as specified (for example, FRIDAY) since a given date
MONTHS_BETWEEN	Returns the number of months between two given dates

Date Conversions

The conversion of dates takes place for any number of reasons. Conversions are mainly used to alter the data type of values defined as a DATETIME value or any other valid data type of a particular implementation.

Typical reasons for date conversions are as follows:

- To compare date values of different data types
- To format a date value as a character string
- To convert a character string into a date format

The ANSI CAST operator is used to convert data types into other data types.

SYNTAX

The basic syntax is as follows:

```
CAST ( EXPRESSION AS NEW_DATA_TYPE )
```

Specific examples according to the syntax of some implementations are illustrated in the following subsections, covering

- The representation of parts of a DATETIME value
- Conversions of dates to character strings
- Conversions of character strings to dates

Date Pictures

NEW TERM A *date picture* is composed of formatting elements used to extract date and time information from the database in a desired format. Date pictures may not be available in all SQL implementations.

Without the use of a date picture and some type of conversion function, the date and time information is retrieved from the database in a default format, such as:

```
1999-12-31
31-DEC-99
1999-12-31 23:59:01.11
...
```

What if you wanted the date displayed as the following? You have to convert the date from a DATETIME format into a character string format:

```
December 31, 1997
```

This is accomplished by implementation-specific functions for this very purpose, further illustrated in the following sections.

Sybase date pictures:

yy	year
qq	quarter
mm	month
dy	day of year
wk	week
dw	weekday
hh	hour
mi	minute
ss	second
ms	millisecond

Oracle date pictures:

AD	anno Domini
AM	ante meridian
BC	Before Christ
CC	Century
D	Number of the day in the week

12

DD	Number of the day in the month
DDD	Number of the day in the year
DAY	The day spelled out (*MONDAY*)
Day	The day spelled out (*Monday*)
day	The day spelled out (*monday*)
DY	The three-letter abbreviation of day (*MON*)
Dy	The three-letter abbreviation of day (*Mon*)
dy	The three-letter abbreviation of day (*mon*)
HH	Hour of the day
HH12	Hour of the day
HH24	Hour of the day for a 24-hour clock
J	Julian days since 12-31-4713 b.c.
MI	Minute of the hour
MM	The number of the month
MON	The three-letter abbreviation of the month (*JAN*)
Mon	The three-letter abbreviation of the month (*Jan*)
mon	The three-letter abbreviation of the month (*jan*)
MONTH	The month spelled out (*JANUARY*)
Month	The month spelled out (*January*)
month	The month spelled out (*january*)
PM	post meridian
Q	The number of the quarter
RM	The Roman numeral for the month
RR	The two digits of the year
SS	The second of a minute
SSSSS	The seconds since midnight
SYYYY	The signed year; if b.c. 500, b.c. = -500
W	The number of the week in a month
WW	The number of the week in a year
Y	The last digit of the year
YY	The last two digits of the year
YYY	The last three digits of the year

YYYY	The year
YEAR	The year spelled out (*NINETEEN-NINETY-NINE*)
Year	The year spelled out (*Nineteen-Ninety-Nine*)
year	The year spelled out (*nineteen-ninety-nine*)

Converting Dates to Character Strings

DATETIME values are converted to character strings to alter the appearance of output from a query. A conversion function is used to achieve this. Two examples, the first using SQL Server, of converting date and time data into a character string as designated by a query follow:

INPUT
```
SELECT DATE_HIRE = DATENAME(MONTH, DATE_HIRE)
FROM EMPLOYEE_PAY_TBL
```

OUTPUT
```
DATE_HIRE
-----
May
June
August
June
July
Jan

6 rows affected.
```

The following is an Oracle date conversion using the TO_CHAR function:

INPUT
```
SELECT DATE_HIRE, TO_CHAR(DATE_HIRE,'Month dd, yyyy') HIRE
FROM EMPLOYEE_PAY_TBL;
```

OUTPUT
```
DATE_HIRE HIRE
------ ---------
23-MAY-89 May       23, 1989
17-JUN-90 June      17, 1990
14-AUG-94 August    14, 1994
28-JUN-97 June      28, 1997
22-JUL-96 July      22, 1996
14-JAN-91 January   14, 1991

6 rows selected.
```

12

Converting Character Strings to Dates

The following example illustrates a method from one implementation of converting a character string into a date format. When the conversion is complete, the data can be stored in a column defined as having some form of a DATETIME data type.

INPUT
```
SELECT TO_DATE('JANUARY 01 1998','MONTH DD YYYY')
FROM EMPLOYEE_PAY_TBL;
```

OUTPUT
```
TO_DATE('
- - - - -
01-JAN-99
01-JAN-99
01-JAN-99
01-JAN-99
01-JAN-99
01-JAN-99

6 rows selected.
```

You may be wondering why six rows were selected from this query when only one date value was provided. The reason is because the conversion of the literal string was selected from the EMPLOYEE_PAY_TBL, which has six rows of data. Hence, the conversion of the literal string was selected against each record in the table.

Summary

You have an understanding of DATETIME values based on the fact that ANSI has provided a standard. However, as with many SQL elements, most implementations have deviated from the exact functions and syntax of standard SQL commands, although the concepts always remain the same as far as the basic representation and manipulation of date and time information. Last hour, you saw how functions varied depending on each implementation. This hour, you have seen some of the differences between date and time data types, functions, and operators. Keep in mind that not all examples discussed in this hour work with your particular implementation, but the concepts of dates and times are the same and should be applicable to any implementation.

Q&A

Q **Why do implementations choose to deviate from a single standard set of data types and functions?**

A Implementations differ as far as the representation of data types and functions mainly because of the way each vendor has chosen to internally store data and provide the most efficient means of data retrieval. However, all implementations should provide the same means for the storage of date and time values based on the required elements prescribed by ANSI, such as the year, month, day, hour, minute, second, and so on.

Q What if I want to store date and time information differently than what is available in my implementation?

A Dates can be stored in nearly any type of format if you choose to define the column for a date as a variable length character. The main thing to remember is that when comparing date values to one another, it is usually required to first convert the character string representation of the date to a valid DATETIME format for your implementation; that is, if appropriate conversion functions are available.

Workshop

The following workshop is composed of a series of quiz questions and practical exercises. The quiz questions are designed to test your overall understanding of the current material. The practical exercises are intended to afford you the opportunity to apply the concepts discussed during the current hour, as well as build upon the knowledge acquired in previous hours of study. Please take time to complete the quiz questions and exercises before continuing. Refer to Appendix C, "Answers to Quizzes and Exercises," for answers.

Quiz

1. From where is the system date and time normally derived?
2. List the standard internal elements of a DATETIME value.
3. What could be a major factor concerning the representation and comparison of date and time values if your company is an international organization?
4. Can a character string date value be compared to a date value defined as a valid DATETIME data type?

Exercises

Provide SQL code for the exercises given the following information:

Use SYSDATE to represent the current date and time.

Use the table called DATES.

Use the TO_CHAR function to convert dates to character strings with the following syntax:

```
TO_CHAR('EXPRESSION','DATE_PICTURE')
```

Use the TO_DATE function to convert character strings to dates, with the following syntax:

```
TO_DATE('EXPRESSION','DATE_PICTURE')
```

12

Date picture information:

DATE PICTURE	MEANING
MONTH	Month spelled out
DAY	Day spelled out
DD	Day of month, number
MM	Month of year, number
YY	Two-digit year
YYYY	Four-digit year
MI	Minutes of the hour
SS	Seconds of the minute

1. Assuming today is 1999-12-31, convert the current date to the format December 31 1999.

2. Convert the following string to DATE format:
   'DECEMBER 31 1999'

3. Write the code to return the day of the week on which New Year's Eve of 1999 falls. Assume that the date is stored in the format 31-DEC-99, which is a valid DATETIME data type.

PART IV
Building Sophisticated Database Queries

Hour

HOUR 13

Joining Tables in Queries

To this point, all database queries you have executed have extracted data from a single table. During this hour, you learn how to join tables in a query so that data can be retrieved from multiple tables.

The highlights of this hour include

- An introduction to the table join
- The different types of joins
- How and when joins are used
- Numerous practical examples of table joins
- The effects of improperly joined tables
- Renaming tables in a query using an alias

Selecting Data from Multiple Tables

Having the capability to select data from multiple tables is one of SQL's most powerful features. Without this capability, the entire relational database concept would not be feasible. Single-table queries are sometimes quite informative, but in the real world, the most practical queries are those whose data is acquired from multiple tables within the database.

As you witnessed in the hour on normalization, a relational database is broken up into smaller, more manageable tables for simplicity and the sake of overall management ease. As tables are divided into smaller tables, the related tables are created with common columns—*primary keys*. These keys are used to join related tables to one another.

NEW TERM A *join* combines two or more tables to retrieve data from multiple tables.

You might ask why you should normalize tables if, in the end, you are only going to rejoin the tables to retrieve the data you want. You rarely select all data from all tables, so it is better to pick and choose according to the needs of each individual query. Although performance may suffer slightly due to a normalized database, overall coding and maintenance are much simpler.

Types of Joins

While different implementations have many ways of joining tables, you concentrate on the most common joins in this lesson. The types of joins that you learn are

```
EQUIJOINS
NATURAL JOINS
NON-EQUIJOINS
OUTER JOINS
SELF JOINS
```

Component Locations of a Join Condition

As you have learned from previous hours, the SELECT and FROM clauses are both required SQL statement elements; the WHERE clause is a required element of an SQL statement when joining tables. The tables being joined are listed in the FROM clause. The join is performed in the WHERE clause. Several operators can be used to join tables, such as =, <, >, <>, <=, >=, !=, BETWEEN, LIKE, and NOT; they can all be used to join tables. However, the most common operator is the equal symbol.

Joins of Equality

Perhaps the most used and important of the joins is the EQUIJOIN, also referred to as an INNER JOIN. The EQUIJOIN joins two tables with a common column in which each is usually the primary key.

SYNTAX

The syntax for an EQUIJOIN is

```
SELECT TABLE1.COLUMN1, TABLE2.COLUMN2...
FROM TABLE1, TABLE2 [, TABLE3 ]
WHERE TABLE1.COLUMN_NAME = TABLE2.COLUMN_NAME
[ AND TABLE1.COLUMN_NAME = TABLE3.COLUMN_NAME ]
```

> Take note of the example SQL statements. Indentation is used in the SQL statements to improve overall readability. Indentation is not required, but is recommended.

Look at the following example:

```
SELECT EMPLOYEE_TBL.EMP_ID,
       EMPLOYEE_PAY_TBL.DATE_HIRE
FROM EMPLOYEE_TBL,
     EMPLOYEE_PAY_TBL
WHERE EMPLOYEE_TBL.EMP_ID = EMPLOYEE_PAY_TBL.EMP_ID;
```

This SQL statement returns the employee identification and the employee's date of hire. The employee identification is selected from the EMPLOYEE_TBL (although it exists in both tables, you must specify one table), while the hire date is selected from the EMPLOYEE_PAY_TBL. Because the employee identification exists in both tables, both columns must be justified with the table name. By justifying the columns with the table names, you tell the database server where to get the data.

Data in the following example is selected from tables EMPLOYEE_TBL and EMPLOYEE_PAY_TBL tables because desired data resides in each of the two tables. An equality join is used.

INPUT

```
SELECT EMPLOYEE_TBL.EMP_ID, EMPLOYEE_TBL.LAST_NAME,
       EMPLOYEE_PAY_TBL.POSITION
FROM EMPLOYEE_TBL, EMPLOYEE_PAY_TBL
WHERE EMPLOYEE_TBL.EMP_ID = EMPLOYEE_PAY_TBL.EMP_ID;
```

OUTPUT

```
EMP_ID     LAST_NAM POSITION
---------- -------- -------------
311549902 STEPHENS MARKETING
442346889 PLEW     TEAM LEADER
213764555 GLASS    SALES MANAGER
```

13

```
313782439 GLASS     SALESMAN
220984332 WALLACE   SHIPPER
443679012 SPURGEON  SHIPPER

6 rows selected.
```

NEW TERM Notice that each column in the SELECT clause is preceded by the associated table name in order to identify each column. This is called *qualifying columns in a query*. Qualifying columns is only necessary for columns that exist in more than one table referenced by a query. You usually qualify all columns for consistency and to avoid any questions when debugging or modifying SQL code.

Natural Joins

A NATURAL JOIN is nearly the same as the EQUIJOIN; however, the NATURAL JOIN differs from the EQUIJOIN by eliminating duplicate columns in the joining columns. The JOIN condition is the same, but the columns selected differ.

The syntax is as follows:

SYNTAX
```
SELECT TABLE1.*, TABLE2.COLUMN_NAME
       [ TABLE3.COLUMN_NAME ]
FROM TABLE1, TABLE2 [ TABLE3 ]
WHERE TABLE1.COLUMN_NAME = TABLE2.COLUMN_NAME
[ AND TABLE1.COLUMN_NAME = TABLE3.COLUMN ]
```

Look at the following example:

```
SELECT EMPLOYEE_TBL.*, EMPLOYEE_PAY_TBL.SALARY
FROM EMPLOYEE_TBL,
     EMPLOYEE_PAY_TBL
WHERE EMPLOYEE_TBL.EMP_ID = EMPLOYEE_PAY_TBL.EMP_ID;
```

This SQL statement returns all columns from EMPLOYEE_TBL and SALARY from the EMPLOYEE_PAY_TBL. The EMP_ID is in both tables, but is retrieved only from the EMPLOYEE_TBL because both contain the same information and do not need to be selected.

The following example selects all columns from the EMPLOYEE_TBL table and only one column from the EMPLOYEE_PAY_TBL table. Remember that the asterisk (*) represents all columns of a table.

INPUT
```
SELECT EMPLOYEE_TBL.*, EMPLOYEE_PAY_TBL.POSITION
FROM EMPLOYEE_TBL, EMPLOYEE_PAY_TBL
WHERE EMPLOYEE_TBL.EMP_ID = EMPLOYEE_PAY_TBL.EMP_ID;
```

OUTPUT

```
EMP_ID     LAST_NAM FIRST_NA M ADDRESS        CITY         ST ZIP   PHONE
--------   -------- -------- - ------------   ------------ -- ----- ----------
PAGER       POSITION
----------  --------------
311549902 STEPHENS TINA     D RR 3 BOX 17A   GREENWOOD    IN 47890 3178784465
            MARKETING

442346889 PLEW     LINDA    C 3301 BEACON    INDIANAPOLIS IN 46224 3172978990
            TEAM LEADER

213764555 GLASS    BRANDON  S 1710 MAIN ST   WHITELAND    IN 47885 3178984321
3175709980 SALES MANAGER

313782439 GLASS    JACOB      3789 RIVER BLVD INDIANAPOLIS IN 45734 3175457676
8887345678 SALESMAN

220984332 WALLACE  MARIAH     7889 KEYSTONE   INDIANAPOLIS IN 46741 3173325986
            SHIPPER

443679012 SPURGEON TIFFANY    5 GEORGE COURT  INDIANAPOLIS IN 46234 3175679007
            SHIPPER
```

        6 rows selected.

> Notice how the output has wrapped in the previous example. The wrap
> occurred because the length of the line has exceeded the limit for the line.

Using Table Aliases

NEW TERM The use of *table aliases* means to rename a table in a particular SQL statement. The renaming is a temporary change. The actual table name does not change in the database. As we will learn later in this hour, giving the tables aliases is a necessity for the SELF JOIN. Giving tables aliases is most often used to save keystrokes, which results in the SQL statement being shorter and easier to read. In addition, fewer keystrokes means fewer keystroke errors. Giving tables aliases also means that the columns being selected must be qualified with the table alias. The following are some examples of table aliases and the corresponding columns:

13

```
SELECT E.EMP_ID, EP.SALARY, EP.DATE_HIRE, E.LAST_NAME
FROM EMPLOYEE_TBL E,
     EMPLOYEE_PAY_TBL EP
WHERE E.EMP_ID = EP.EMP_ID
AND EP.SALARY > 20000;
```

ANALYSIS The tables have been given aliases in the preceding SQL statement. The EMPLOYEE_TBL has been renamed E. The EMPLOYEE_PAY_TBL has been renamed EP. The choice of what to rename the tables is arbitrary. The letter E is chosen because the EMPLOYEE_TBL starts with E. Because the EMPLOYEE_PAY_TBL also begins with the letter E, you could not use E again. Instead, the first letter (E) and the first letter of the second word in the name (PAY) are used as the alias. The selected columns were justified with the corresponding table alias. Note that SALARY was used in the WHERE clause and must also be justified with the table alias.

Joins of Non-Equality

NON-EQUIJOIN joins two or more tables based on a specified column value not equaling a specified column value in another table. The syntax for the NON-EQUIJOIN is

SYNTAX
```
FROM TABLE1, TABLE2 [, TABLE3 ]
WHERE TABLE1.COLUMN_NAME != TABLE2.COLUMN_NAME
[ AND TABLE1.COLUMN_NAME != TABLE2.COLUMN_NAME ]
```

An example is as follows:

```
SELECT EMPLOYEE_TBL.EMP_ID, EMPLOYEE_PAY_TBL.DATE_HIRE
FROM EMPLOYEE_TBL,
     EMPLOYEE_PAY_TBL
WHERE EMPLOYEE_TBL.EMP_ID != EMPLOYEE_PAY_TBL.EMP_ID;
```

ANALYSIS The preceding SQL statement returns the employee identification and the date of hire for all employees who do not have a corresponding record in both tables. The following example is a join of non-equality:

INPUT
```
SELECT E.EMP_ID, E.LAST_NAME, P.POSITION
FROM EMPLOYEE_TBL E,
     EMPLOYEE_PAY_TBL P
WHERE E.EMP_ID <> P.EMP_ID;
```

OUTPUT
```
EMP_ID     LAST_NAM POSITION
.......... ........ ............
442346889  PLEW     MARKETING
213764555  GLASS    MARKETING
313782439  GLASS    MARKETING
220984332  WALLACE  MARKETING
443679012  SPURGEON MARKETING
311549902  STEPHENS TEAM LEADER
213764555  GLASS    TEAM LEADER
```

```
313782439 GLASS     TEAM LEADER
220984332 WALLACE   TEAM LEADER
443679012 SPURGEON  TEAM LEADER
311549902 STEPHENS  SALES MANAGER
442346889 PLEW      SALES MANAGER
313782439 GLASS     SALES MANAGER
220984332 WALLACE   SALES MANAGER
443679012 SPURGEON  SALES MANAGER
311549902 STEPHENS  SALESMAN
442346889 PLEW      SALESMAN
213764555 GLASS     SALESMAN
220984332 WALLACE   SALESMAN
443679012 SPURGEON  SALESMAN
311549902 STEPHENS  SHIPPER
442346889 PLEW      SHIPPER
213764555 GLASS     SHIPPER
313782439 GLASS     SHIPPER
443679012 SPURGEON  SHIPPER
311549902 STEPHENS  SHIPPER
442346889 PLEW      SHIPPER
213764555 GLASS     SHIPPER
313782439 GLASS     SHIPPER
220984332 WALLACE   SHIPPER

30 rows selected.
```

You may be curious why 30 rows were retrieved when only 6 rows exist in each table. For every record in EMPLOYEE_TBL, there is a corresponding record in EMPLOYEE_PAY_TBL. Because non-equality was tested in the join of the two tables, each row in the first table is paired with all rows from the second table, except for its own corresponding row. This means that each of the 6 rows are paired with 5 unrelated rows in the second table; 6 rows multiplied by 5 rows equals 30 rows total.

In the previous section's test for equality example, each of the six rows in the first table were paired with only one row in the second table (each row's corresponding row); six rows multiplied by one row yields a total of six rows.

> When using NON-EQUIJOINs, you may receive several rows of data that are of no use to you. Check your results carefully.

Outer Joins

An OUTER JOIN is used to return all rows that exist in one table, even though corresponding rows do not exist in the joined table. The (+) symbol is used to denote an OUTER JOIN in a query. The (+) is placed at the end of the table name in the WHERE clause. The table with the (+) should be the table that does not have matching rows. In many implementations, the OUTER JOIN is broken down into joins called LEFT OUTER JOIN, RIGHT OUTER JOIN, and FULL OUTER JOIN. The OUTER JOIN in these implementations is normally optional.

> You must check your particular implementation for exact usage and syntax of the OUTER JOIN. The (+) symbol is used by some major implementations, but is non-standard.

 SYNTAX

The general syntax is

```
FROM TABLE1
{RIGHT | LEFT | FULL} [OUTER] JOIN
ON TABLE2
```

The Oracle syntax is

```
FROM TABLE1, TABLE2 [, TABLE3 ]
WHERE TABLE1.COLUMN_NAME[(+)] = TABLE2.COLUMN_NAME[(+)]
[ AND TABLE1.COLUMN_NAME[(+)] = TABLE3.COLUMN_NAME[(+)]]
```

> The OUTER JOIN can only be used on one side of a join condition; however, you can use an OUTER JOIN on more than one column of the same table in the join condition.

The concept of the OUTER JOIN is explained in the next two examples. In the first example, the product description and the quantity ordered are selected; both values are extracted from two separate tables. One important factor to keep in mind is that there may not be a corresponding record in the ORDERS_TBL table for every product. A regular join of equality is performed:

INPUT

```
SELECT P.PROD_DESC, O.QTY
FROM PRODUCTS_TBL P,
     ORDERS_TBL O
WHERE P.PROD_ID = O.PROD_ID;
```

OUTPUT

```
PROD_DESC                          QTY
---------------------------------- ---
WITCHES COSTUME                      1
PLASTIC PUMPKIN 18 INCH             25
PLASTIC PUMPKIN 18 INCH              2
LIGHTED LANTERNS                    10
FALSE PARAFFIN TEETH                20
KEY CHAIN                            1

6 rows selected.
```

Only 6 rows were selected, but there are 10 distinct products. You want to display all products, whether the products have been placed on order or not.

The next example accomplishes the desired output through the use of an OUTER JOIN. Oracle's syntax is used for the OUTER JOIN.

INPUT

```
SELECT P.PROD_DESC, O.QTY
FROM PRODUCTS_TBL P,
     ORDERS_TBL O
WHERE P.PROD_ID = O.PROD_ID(+);
```

OUTPUT

```
PROD_DESC                           QTY
----------------------------------- ---
WITCHES COSTUME                       1
ASSORTED MASKS
FALSE PARAFFIN TEETH                 20
ASSORTED COSTUMES
PLASTIC PUMPKIN 18 INCH              25
PLASTIC PUMPKIN 18 INCH               2
PUMPKIN CANDY
PLASTIC SPIDERS
CANDY CORN
LIGHTED LANTERNS                     10
KEY CHAIN                             1
OAK BOOKSHELF

12 rows selected.
```

All products were returned by the query, even though they may not have had a quantity ordered. The outer join is inclusive of all rows of data in the PRODUCTS_TBL table, whether a corresponding row exists in the ORDERS_TBL table or not.

Self Joins

The SELF JOIN is used to join a table to itself, as if the table were two tables, temporarily renaming at least one table in the SQL statement. The syntax is as follows:

```
SELECT A.COLUMN_NAME, B.COLUMN_NAME, [ C.COLUMN_NAME ]
FROM TABLE1 A, TABLE2 B [, TABLE3 C ]
WHERE A.COLUMN_NAME = B.COLUMN_NAME
[ AND A.COLUMN_NAME = C.COLUMN_NAME ]
```

The following is an example:

```
SELECT A.LAST_NAME, B.LAST_NAME, A.FIRST_NAME
FROM EMPLOYEE_TBL A,
     EMPLOYEE_TBL B
WHERE A.LAST_NAME = B.LAST_NAME;
```

13

ANALYSIS   The preceding SQL statement returns the employees' first name for all the
employees with the same last name from the EMPLOYEE_TBL. Self joins are useful
when all of the data you want to retrieve resides in one table, but you must somehow
compare records in the table to other records in the table.

Another common example used to explain a self join is as follows. Suppose you have a
table that stores an employee identification number, the employee's name, and the
employee identification number of the employee's manager. You may want to produce a
list of all employees and their managers' names. The problem is that the manager name
does not exist in the table, only the employee name:

```
SELECT * FROM EMP;

ID   NAME       MGR_ID
---- ---------- ------
1    JOHN       0
2    MARY       1
3    STEVE      1
4    JACK       2
5    SUE        2
```

In the following example, we have included the table EMP twice in the FROM clause of the
query, giving the table two aliases for the purpose of the query. By providing two aliases,
it is as if you are selecting from two distinct tables. All managers are also employees, so
the join condition between the two tables compares the value of the employee identification number from the first table with the manager identification number in the second
table. The first table acts as a table that stores employee information, whereas the second
table acts as a table that stores manager information:

```
SELECT E1.NAME, E2.NAME
FROM EMP E1, EMP E2
WHERE E1.MGR_ID = E2.ID;

NAME       NAME
---------- ----------
MARY       JOHN
STEVE      JOHN
JACK       MARY
SUE        MARY
```

Joining on Multiple Keys

Most join operations that occur involve the merging of data based on a key in one table
and a key in another table. Depending on how your database has been designed, you may
have to join on more than one key field to accurately depict that data in your database.
You may have a table that has a primary key that is comprised of more than one column.

You may also have a foreign key in a table that consists of more than one column, which references the multiple column primary key.

Consider the following tables that are used here for examples only:

```
SQL> desc prod
 Name                                     Null?    Type
 ---------------------------------------- -------- ----------------------------
 SERIAL_NUMBER                            NOT NULL NUMBER(10)
 VENDOR_NUMBER                            NOT NULL NUMBER(10)
 PRODUCT_NAME                             NOT NULL VARCHAR2(30)
 COST                                     NOT NULL NUMBER(8,2)

SQL> desc ord
 Name                                     Null?    Type
 ---------------------------------------- -------- ----------------------------
 ORD_NO                                   NOT NULL NUMBER(10)
 PROD_NUMBER                              NOT NULL NUMBER(10)
 VENDOR_NUMBER                            NOT NULL NUMBER(10)
 QUANTITY                                 NOT NULL NUMBER(5)
 ORD_DATE                                 NOT NULL DATE
```

The primary key in PROD is the combination of the columns SERIAL_NUMBER and VENDOR_NUMBER. Perhaps two products can have the same serial number within the distribution company, but each serial number is unique per vendor.

The foreign key in ORD is also the combination of the columns SERIAL_NUMBER and VENDOR_NUMBER.

When selecting data from both tables (PROD and ORD), the join operation may appear as follows:

```
SELECT P.PRODUCT_NAME, O.ORD_DATE, O.QUANTITY
FROM PROD P, ORD O
WHERE P.SERIAL_NUMBER = O.SERIAL_NUMBER
  AND P.VENDOR_NUMBER = O.VENDOR_NUMBER;
```

Join Considerations

Several things should be considered before using joins. Some considerations include what columns(s) to join on, if there is no common column to join on, and performance issues. Performance issues are discussed in Hour 18, "Managing Database Users."

Using a BASE TABLE

What to join on? Should you have the need to retrieve data from two tables that do not have a common column to join, you must use another table that has a common column or columns to both tables to join on. That table becomes the BASE TABLE. A BASE TABLE

13

is used to join one or more tables that have common columns, or to join tables that do not have common columns. Use the following three tables for an example of a base table:

CUSTOMER_TBL

CUST_ID	VARCHAR2(10)	NOT NULL	**PRIMARY KEY**
CUST_NAME	VARCHAR2(30)	NOT NULL	
CUST_ADDRESS	VARCHAR2(20)	NOT NULL	
CUST_CITY	VARCHAR2(15)	NOT NULL	
CUST_STATE	CHAR(2)	NOT NULL	
CUST_ZIP	NUMBER(5)	NOT NULL	
CUST_PHONE	NUMBER(10)		
CUST_FAX	NUMBER(10)		

ORDERS_TBL

ORD_NUM	VARCHAR2(10)	NOT NULL	**PRIMARY KEY**
CUST_ID	VARCHAR2(10)	NOT NULL	
PROD_ID	VARCHAR2(10)	NOT NULL	
QTY	NUMBER(6)	NOT NULL	
ORD_DATE	DATE		

PRODUCTS_TBL

PROD_ID	VARCHAR2(10)	NOT NULL	**PRIMARY KEY**
PROD_DESC	VARCHAR2(40)	NOT NULL	
COST	NUMVER(6,2)	NOT NULL	

You have a need to use the CUSTOMERS_TBL and the PRODUCTS_TBL. There is no common column in which to join the tables. Now look at the ORDERS_TBL. The ORDERS_TBL has CUST_ID to join with the CUSTOMERS_TBL, which also has CUST_ID. The PRODUCTS_TBL has PROD_ID, which is also in the ORDERS_TBL. The JOIN conditions and results look like the following:

INPUT

```
SELECT C.CUST_NAME, P.PROD_DESC
FROM CUSTOMER_TBL C,
     PRODUCTS_TBL P,
     ORDERS_TBL O
WHERE C.CUST_ID = O.CUST_ID
  AND P.PROD_ID = O.PROD_ID;
```

OUTPUT

```
CUST_NAME                        PROD_DESC
-----------------------------    ------------------------
LESLIE GLEASON                   WITCHES COSTUME
SCHYLERS NOVELTIES               PLASTIC PUMPKIN 18 INCH
WENDY WOLF                       PLASTIC PUMPKIN 18 INCH
GAVINS PLACE                     LIGHTED LANTERNS
SCOTTYS MARKET                   FALSE PARAFFIN TEETH
ANDYS CANDIES                    KEY CHAIN

6 rows selected.
```

> Note the use of table aliases and their use on the columns in the WHERE clause.

The Cartesian Product

NEW TERM   The *Cartesian Product* is a result of a CARTESIAN JOIN or "no join." If you select from two or more tables and do not JOIN the tables, your output is all possible rows from all the tables selected from. If your tables were large, the result could be hundreds of thousands, or even millions, of rows of data. A WHERE clause is highly recommended for SQL statements retrieving data from two or more tables. The Cartesian Product is also known as a *cross join*.

SYNTAX

The syntax is

```
FROM TABLE1, TABLE2 [, TABLE3 ]
WHERE TABLE1, TABLE2 [, TABLE3 ]
```

The following is an example of a cross join, or the dreaded Cartesian Product:

13

INPUT

```
SELECT E.EMP_ID, E.LAST_NAME, P.POSITION
FROM EMPLOYEE_TBL E,
     EMPLOYEE_PAY_TBL P;
```

OUTPUT

```
EMP_ID     LAST_NAM POSITION
---------  -------- --------------
311549902 STEPHENS MARKETING
442346889 PLEW     MARKETING
213764555 GLASS    MARKETING
```

```
313782439  GLASS     MARKETING
220984332  WALLACE   MARKETING
443679012  SPURGEON  MARKETING
311549902  STEPHENS  TEAM LEADER
442346889  PLEW      TEAM LEADER
213764555  GLASS     TEAM LEADER
313782439  GLASS     TEAM LEADER
220984332  WALLACE   TEAM LEADER
443679012  SPURGEON  TEAM LEADER
311549902  STEPHENS  SALES MANAGER
442346889  PLEW      SALES MANAGER
213764555  GLASS     SALES MANAGER
313782439  GLASS     SALES MANAGER
220984332  WALLACE   SALES MANAGER
443679012  SPURGEON  SALES MANAGER
311549902  STEPHENS  SALESMAN
442346889  PLEW      SALESMAN
213764555  GLASS     SALESMAN
313782439  GLASS     SALESMAN
220984332  WALLACE   SALESMAN
443679012  SPURGEON  SALESMAN
311549902  STEPHENS  SHIPPER
442346889  PLEW      SHIPPER
213764555  GLASS     SHIPPER
313782439  GLASS     SHIPPER
220984332  WALLACE   SHIPPER
443679012  SPURGEON  SHIPPER
311549902  STEPHENS  SHIPPER
442346889  PLEW      SHIPPER
213764555  GLASS     SHIPPER
313782439  GLASS     SHIPPER
220984332  WALLACE   SHIPPER
443679012  SPURGEON  SHIPPER

36 rows selected.
```

Data is being selected from two separate tables, yet no JOIN operation is performed. Because you have not specified how to join rows in the first table with rows in the second table, the database server pairs every row in the first table with every row in the second table. Because each table has 6 rows of data each, the product of 36 rows selected is achieved from 6 rows multiplied by 6 rows.

To fully understand exactly how the Cartesian Product is derived, study the following example.

INPUT   **SQL> SELECT X FROM TABLE1;**

OUTPUT
```
X
-
A
B
C
D

4 rows selected.
```

INPUT
SQL> SELECT V FROM TABLE2;

OUTPUT
```
X
-
A
B
C
D

4 rows selected.
```

INPUT
SQL> SELECT TABLE1.X, TABLE2.X
  2* FROM TABLE1, TABLE2;

OUTPUT
```
X X
- -
A A
B A
C A
D A
A B
B B
C B
D B
A C
B C
C C
D C
A D
B D
C D
D D

16 rows selected.
```

Be careful to always join all tables in a query. If two tables in a query have not been joined and each table contains 1,000 rows of data, the Cartesian Product consists of 1,000 rows multiplied by 1,000 rows, which results in a total of 1,000,000 rows of data returned.

13

Summary

You have been introduced to one of the most robust features of SQL—the table join. Imagine the limits if you were not able to extract data from more than one table in a single query. You were shown several types of joins, each serving its own purpose depending on conditions placed on the query. Joins are used to link data from tables based on equality and non-equality. OUTER JOINs are very powerful, allowing data retrieved from one table, even though associated data is not found in a joined table. SELF JOINs are used to join a table to itself. Beware of the cross join, more commonly known as the Cartesian Product. The Cartesian Product is the result set of a multiple table query without a join, often yielding a large amount of unwanted output. When selecting data from more than one table, be sure to properly join the tables according to the related columns (normally primary keys). Failure to properly join tables could result in incomplete or inaccurate output.

Q&A

Q **When joining tables, must they be joined in the same order that they appear in the FROM clause?**

A No, they do not have to appear in the same order; however, performance benefits may be experienced depending on the order of tables in the FROM clause and the order that tables are joined.

Q **When using a BASE TABLE to join unrelated tables, must I select any columns from the base table?**

A No, the use of a BASE TABLE to join unrelated tables does not mandate columns for selection from the base table.

Q **Can I join on more than one column between tables?**

A Yes, some queries may require you to join on more than one column per table to provide a complete relationship between rows of data in the joined tables.

Workshop

The following workshop is composed of a series of quiz questions and practical exercises. The quiz questions are designed to test your overall understanding of the current material. The practical exercises are intended to afford you the opportunity to apply the concepts discussed during the current hour, as well as build upon the knowledge acquired in previous hours of study. Please take time to complete the quiz questions and exercises before continuing. Refer to Appendix C, "Answers to Quizzes and Exercises," for answers.

Quiz

1. What type of join would you use to return records from one table, regardless of the existence of associated records in the related table?

2. The join conditions are located in what part of the SQL statement?

3. What type of join do you use to evaluate equality among rows of related tables?

4. What happens if you select from two different tables but fail to join the tables?

5. Use the following tables:

ORDERS_TBL

ORD_NUM	VARCHAR2(10)	NOT NULL	PRIMARY KEY
CUST_ID	VARCHAR2(10)	NOT NULL	
PROD_ID	VARCHAR2(10)	NOT NULL	
QTY	NUMBER(6)	NOT NULL	
ORD_DATE	DATE		

PRODUCTS_TBL

PROD_ID	VARCHAR2(10)	NOT NULL	PRIMARY KEY
PROD_DESC	VARCHAR2(40)	NOT NULL	
COST	NUMBER(6,2)	NOT NULL	

Is the following syntax correct for using an OUTER JOIN?

```
SELECT C.CUST_ID, C.CUST_NAME, O.ORD_NUM
FROM CUSTOMER_TBL C, ORDERS_TBL O
WHERE C.CUST_ID(+) = O.CUST_ID(+)
```

Exercises

Perform the exercises using the following tables:

EMPLOYEE_TBL

EMP_ID	VARCHAR2(9)	NOT NULL	PRIMARY KEY
LAST_NAME	VARCHAR2(15)	NOT NULL	
FIRST_NAME	VARCHAR2(15)	NOT NULL	
MIDDLE_NAME	VARCHAR2(15)		
ADDRESS	VARCHAR2(30)	NOT NULL	
CITY	VARCHAR2(15)	NOT NULL	
STATE	CHAR(2)	NOT NULL	

13

ZIP	NUMBER(5)	NOT NULL
PHONE	CHAR(10)	
PAGER	CHAR(10)	

EMPLOYEE_PAY_TBL

EMP_ID	VARCHAR2(9)	NOT NULL	PRIMARY KEY
POSITION	VARCHAR2(15)	NOT NULL	
DATE_HIRE	DATE		
PAY_RATE	NUMBER(4,2)	NOT NULL	
DATE_LAST-RAISE	DATE		
SALARY	NUMBER(6,2)		
BONUS	NUMBER(4,2)		

    CONSTRAINT EMP_FK FOREIGN KEY (EMP_ID) REFERENCED
        EMPLOYEE_TBL (EMP_ID)

CUSTOMER_TBL

CUST_ID	VARCHAR2(10)	NOT NULL	PRIMARY KEY
CUST_NAME	VARCHAR2(30)	NOT NULL	
CUST_ADDRESS	VARCHAR2(20)	NOT NULL	
CUST_CITY	VARCHAR2(15)	NOT NULL	
CUST_STATE	CHAR(2)	NOT NULL	
CUST_ZIP	NUMBER(5)	NOT NULL	
CUST_PHONE	NUMBER(10)		
CUST_FAX	NUMBER(10)		

ORDERS_TBL

ORD_NUM	VARCHAR2(10)	NOT NULL	PRIMARY KEY
CUST_ID	VARCHAR2(10)	NOT NULL	
PROD_ID	VARCHAR2(10)	NOT NULL	
QTY	NUMBER(6)	NOT NULL	
ORD_DATE	DATE		

PRODUCTS_TBL

PROD_ID	VARCHAR2(10)	NOT NULL	PRIMARY KEY
PROD_DESC	VARCHAR2(40)	NOT NULL	
COST	NUMBER(6,2)	NOT NULL	

1. Write a SQL statement to return the EMP_ID, LAST_NAME, and FIRST_NAME from the EMPLOYEE_TBL and SALARY and BONUS from the EMPLOYEE_PAY_TBL.

2. Select from the CUSTOMERS_TBL the columns: CUST_ID, CUST_NAME. Select from the PRODUCTS_TBL the columns: PROD_ID, COST. Select from the ORDERS_TBL the ORD_NUM and QTY columns. Join all three of the tables into one SQL statement.

13

Hour **14**

Using Subqueries to Define Unknown Data

During this hour, you are presented with the concept of using subqueries to return results from a database query more effectively.

The highlights of this hour include

- What a subquery is
- The justifications of using subqueries
- Examples of subqueries in regular database queries
- Using subqueries with data manipulation commands
- Embedded subqueries

What Is a Subquery?

NEW TERM   A *subquery* is a query embedded within the WHERE clause of another query to fur-
            ther restrict data returned by the query. A subquery is a query within another
query, also known as a *nested query*. A subquery is used to return data that will be used
in the main query as a condition to further restrict the data to be retrieved. Subqueries are
used with the SELECT, INSERT, UPDATE, and DELETE statements.

A subquery can be used in some cases in place of a join operation by indirectly linking
data between the tables based on one or more conditions. When a subquery is used in a
query, the subquery is resolved first, and then the main query is resolved according to the
condition(s) as resolved by the subquery. The results of the subquery are used to process
expressions in the WHERE clause of the main query. The subquery can either be used in
the WHERE clause or the HAVING clause of the main query. Logical and relational operators, such as =, >, <, <>, IN, NOT IN, AND, OR, and so on, can be used within the subquery
as well to evaluate a subquery in the WHERE or HAVING clause.

> The same rules that apply to standard queries also apply to subqueries. Join
> operations, functions, conversions, and other options can be used within a
> subquery.

There are a few rules that subqueries must follow:

- Subqueries must be enclosed within parentheses.
- A subquery can have only one column in the SELECT clause, unless multiple
  columns are in the main query for the subquery to compare its selected columns.
- An ORDER BY cannot be used in a subquery, although the main query can use an
  ORDER BY. The GROUP BY can be used to perform the same function as the ORDER
  BY in a subquery.
- Subqueries that return more than one row can only be used with multiple value
  operators, such as the IN operator.
- The SELECT list cannot include any references to values that evaluate to a BLOB,
  ARRAY, CLOB, or NCLOB.
- A subquery cannot be immediately enclosed in a set function.
- The BETWEEN operator cannot be used with a subquery; however, the BETWEEN can
  be used within the subquery.

SYNTAX

The basic syntax for a subquery is as follows:

```
SELECT COLUMN_NAME
FROM TABLE
WHERE COLUMN_NAME = (SELECT COLUMN_NAME
                        FROM TABLE
                        WHERE CONDITIONS);
```

> Notice the use of indentation in our examples. The use of indentation is merely for readability. We have found that when looking for errors in SQL statements, the neater your statements are, the easier it is to read and find any errors in syntax.

The following examples show how the BETWEEN operator can and cannot be used with a subquery:

The following is an example of a correct use of BETWEEN in the subquery:

```
SELECT COLUMN_NAME
FROM TABLE
WHERE COLUMN_NAME OPERATOR (SELECT COLUMN_NAME
                              FROM TABLE)
                              WHERE VALUE BETWEEN VALUE)
```

The following is an example of an illegal use of BETWEEN with a subquery:

```
SELECT COLUMN_NAME
FROM TABLE
WHERE COLUMN_NAME BETWEEN VALUE AND (SELECT COLUMN_NAME
                                       FROM TABLE)
```

Subqueries with the SELECT Statement

Subqueries are most frequently used with the SELECT statement, although they can be used within a data manipulation statement as well. The subquery, when used with the SELECT statement, retrieves data for the main query to use to solve the main query.

▼ SYNTAX

The basic syntax is as follows:

```
SELECT COLUMN_NAME [, COLUMN_NAME ]
FROM TABLE1 [, TABLE2 ]
WHERE COLUMN_NAME OPERATOR
                (SELECT COLUMN_NAME [, COLUMN_NAME ]
                 FROM TABLE1 [, TABLE2 ]
                 [ WHERE ])
```

14

The following is an example:

```
SELECT E.EMP_ID, E.LAST_NAME, E.FIRST_NAME, EP.PAY_RATE
FROM EMPLOYEE_TBL E, EMPLOYEE_PAY_TBL EP
WHERE E.EMP_ID = EP.EMP_ID
AND EP.PAY_RATE > (SELECT PAY_RATE
                   FROM EMPLOYEE_PAY_TBL
                   WHERE EMP_ID = '313782439')
```

ANALYSIS The preceding SQL statement returns the employee identification, last name, first name, and pay rate for all employees who have a pay rate greater than that of the employee with the identification 313782439. In this case, you do not necessarily know (or care) what the exact pay rate is for this particular employee; you only care about the pay rate for the purpose of getting a list of employees who bring home more than the employee specified in the subquery.

The next query selects the pay rate for a particular employee. This query is used as the subquery in the following example.

INPUT
```
SELECT PAY_RATE
FROM EMPLOYEE_PAY_TBL
WHERE EMP_ID = '220984332';
```

OUTPUT
```
  PAY_RATE
----------
        11
```

```
1 row selected.
```

The previous query is used as a subquery in the WHERE clause of the following query.

INPUT
```
SELECT E.EMP_ID, E.LAST_NAME, E.FIRST_NAME, EP.PAY_RATE
FROM EMPLOYEE_TBL E, EMPLOYEE_PAY_TBL EP
WHERE E.EMP_ID = EP.EMP_ID
  AND EP.PAY_RATE > (SELECT PAY_RATE
                     FROM EMPLOYEE_PAY_TBL
                     WHERE EMP_ID = '220984332');
```

OUTPUT
```
EMP_ID     LAST_NAM FIRST_NA  PAY_RATE
---------- -------- --------- --------
442346889  PLEW     LINDA        14.75
443679012  SPURGEON TIFFANY         15
```

```
2 rows selected.
```

The result of the subquery is 11 (shown in the last example), so the last condition of the WHERE clause is evaluated as

```
AND EP.PAY_RATE > 11
```

You did not know the value of the pay rate for the given individual when you executed the query. However, the main query was able to compare each individual's pay rate to the subquery results.

Subqueries are frequently used to place conditions on a query when the exact conditions are unknown. The salary for 220984332 was unknown, but the subquery was designed to do the footwork for you.

Subqueries with the INSERT Statement

Subqueries also can be used in conjunction with data manipulation language (DML) statements. The INSERT statement is the first instance you examine. The INSERT statement uses the data returned from the subquery to insert into another table. The selected data in the subquery can be modified with any of the character, date, or number functions.

SYNTAX

The basic syntax is as follows:

```
INSERT INTO TABLE_NAME [ (COLUMN1 [, COLUMN2 ]) ]
SELECT [ *|COLUMN1 [, COLUMN2 ]
FROM TABLE1 [, TABLE2 ]
[ WHERE VALUE OPERATOR ]
```

The following is an example of the INSERT statement with a subquery:

INPUT

```
INSERT INTO RICH_EMPLOYEES
SELECT E.EMP_ID, E.LAST_NAME, E.FIRST_NAME, EP.PAY_RATE
FROM EMPLOYEE_TBL E, EMPLOYEE_PAY_TBL EP
WHERE E.EMP_ID = EP.EMP_ID
  AND EP.PAY_RATE > (SELECT PAY_RATE
                     FROM EMPLOYEE_PAY_TBL
                     WHERE EMP_ID = '220984332');
```

OUTPUT

```
2 rows created.
```

This INSERT statement inserts the EMP_ID, LAST_NAME, FIRST_NAME, and PAY_RATE into a table called RICH_EMPLOYEES for all records of employees who have a pay rate greater than the pay rate of the employee with identification 220984332.

Remember to use the COMMIT and ROLLBACK commands when using DML commands such as the INSERT statement.

14

Subqueries with the UPDATE Statement

The subquery can be used in conjunction with the UPDATE statement. Either single or multiple columns in a table can be updated when using a subquery with the UPDATE statement.

The basic syntax is as follows:

```
UPDATE TABLE
SET COLUMN_NAME [, COLUMN_NAME) ] =
    (SELECT )COLUMN_NAME [, COLUMN_NAME) ]
    FROM TABLE
    [ WHERE ]
```

Examples showing the use of the UPDATE statement with a subquery follow. The first query returns the employee identification of all employees that reside in Indianapolis. You can see that there are four individuals who meet this criteria.

INPUT

```
SELECT EMP_ID
FROM EMPLOYEE_TBL
WHERE CITY = 'INDIANAPOLIS';
```

OUTPUT

```
EMP_ID
..........
442346889
313782439
220984332
443679012

4 rows selected.
```

The first query is used as the subquery in the following UPDATE statement. The first query proves how many employee identifications are returned by the subquery. The following is the UPDATE with the subquery:

INPUT

```
UPDATE EMPLOYEE_PAY_TBL
SET PAY_RATE = PAY_RATE * 1.1
WHERE EMP_ID IN (SELECT EMP_ID
                 FROM EMPLOYEE_TBL
                 WHERE CITY = 'INDIANAPOLIS');
```

OUTPUT

```
4 rows updated.
```

As expected, four rows are updated. One very important thing to notice is that, unlike the example in the first section, this subquery returns multiple rows of data. Because you expect multiple rows to be returned, you have used the IN operator instead of the equal sign. Remember that IN is used to compare an expression to values in a list. If the equal sign was used, an error would have been returned.

Be sure to use the correct operator when evaluating a subquery. For example, an operator used to compare an expression to one value, such as the equal sign, cannot be used to evaluate a subquery that returns more than one row of data.

Subqueries with the DELETE Statement

The subquery also can be used in conjunction with the DELETE statement.

The basic syntax is as follows:

```
DELETE FROM TABLE_NAME
[ WHERE OPERATOR [ VALUE ]
              (SELECT COLUMN_NAME
               FROM TABLE_NAME)
               [ WHERE) ]
```

In this example, you delete BRANDON GLASS's record from the EMPLOYEE_PAY_TBL table. You do not know Brandon's employee identification number, but you can use a subquery to get his identification from the EMPLOYEE_TBL table, which contains the FIRST_NAME and LAST_NAME columns.

```
DELETE FROM EMPLOYEE_PAY_TBL
WHERE EMP_ID = (SELECT EMP_ID
               FROM EMPLOYEE_TBL
               WHERE LAST_NAME = 'GLASS'
                 AND FIRST_NAME = 'BRANDON');
```

OUTPUT

1 row deleted.

Do not forget the use of the WHERE clause with the UPDATE and DELETE statements. All rows are updated or deleted from the target table if the WHERE clause is not used. See Hour 5, "Manipulating Data."

Embedding a Subquery Within a Subquery

A subquery can be embedded within another subquery, just as you can embed the subquery within a regular query. When a subquery is used, that subquery is resolved before the main query. Likewise, the lowest level subquery is resolved first in embedded or nested subqueries, working out to the main query.

14

You must check your particular implementation for limits on the number of subqueries, if any, that can be used in a single statement. It may differ between vendors.

▼ SYNTAX

The basic syntax for embedded subqueries is as follows:

```
SELECT COLUMN_NAME [, COLUMN_NAME ]
FROM TABLE1 [, TABLE2 ]
WHERE COLUMN_NAME OPERATOR (SELECT COLUMN_NAME
                           FROM TABLE
                           WHERE COLUMN_NAME OPERATOR
                                  (SELECT COLUMN_NAME
                                  FROM TABLE
                                  [ WHERE COLUMN_NAME OPERATOR VALUE ]))
```

▲

The following example uses two subqueries, one embedded within the other. You want to find out what customers have placed orders where the quantity multiplied by the cost of a single order is greater than the sum of the cost of all products.

INPUT
```
SELECT CUST_ID, CUST_NAME
FROM CUSTOMER_TBL
WHERE CUST_ID IN (SELECT O.CUST_ID)
            FROM, ORDERS_TBL O, PRODUCTS_TBL P
            WHERE O PROD_ID = P.PROD_ID
               AND O.QTY + P.COST < (SELECT SUM(COST)
                                     FROM PRODUCTS_TBL));
```

OUTPUT
```
CUST_ID     CUST_NAME
.........   .................
090         WENDY WOLF
232         LESLIE GLEASON
287         GAVINS PLACE
43          SCHYLERS NOVELTIES
432         SCOTTYS MARKET
560         ANDYS CANDIES

6 rows selected.
```

Six rows that met the criteria of both subqueries were selected.

The following two examples show the results of each of the subqueries to aid your understanding of how the main query was resolved.

INPUT
```
SELECT SUM(COST) FROM PRODUCTS_TBL;
```

OUTPUT

```
SUM(COST)
----------
    138.08
```

1 row selected.

INPUT

```
SELECT O.CUST_ID
FROM ORDERS_TBL O, PRODUCTS_TBL P
WHERE O.PROD_ID = P.PROD_ID
  AND O.QTY * P.COST > 72.14;
```

OUTPUT

```
CUST_ID
-------
43
287
```

2 rows selected.

In essence, the main query (after the resolution of the subqueries) is evaluated, as shown in the following example, the substitution of the second subquery:

INPUT

```
SELECT CUST_ID, CUST_NAME
FROM CUSTOMER_TBL
WHERE CUST_ID IN (SELECT O.CUST_ID
                  FROM ORDERS_TBL O, PRODUCTS_TBL P
                  WHERE O.PROD_ID = P.PROD_ID
                    AND O.QTY * P.COST > 72.14);
```

The following shows the substitution of the first subquery:

INPUT

```
SELECT CUST_ID, CUST_NAME
FROM CUSTOMER_TBL
WHERE CUST_ID IN ('287','43');
```

The following is the final result:

OUTPUT

```
CUST_ID     CUST_NAME
----------  ------------------

43          SCHYLERS NOVELTIES
287         GAVINS PLACE
```

2 rows selected.

The use of multiple subqueries results in slower response time and may result in reduced accuracy of the results due to possible mistakes in the statement coding.

14

Correlated Subqueries

NEW TERM Correlated subqueries are common in many SQL implementations. The concept of correlated subqueries is discussed as an ANSI standard SQL topic and is covered briefly in this hour. A *correlated subquery* is a subquery that is dependent upon information in the main query.

In the following example, the table join between CUSTOMER_TBL and ORDERS_TBL in the subquery is dependent on the alias for CUSTOMER_TBL (C) in the main query. This query returns the name of all customers that have ordered more than 10 units of one or more items.

INPUT
```
SELECT C.CUST_NAME
FROM CUSTOMER_TBL C
WHERE 10 < (SELECT SUM(O.QTY)
                FROM ORDERS_TBL O
                WHERE O.CUST_ID = C.CUST_ID);
```

OUTPUT
```
CUST_NAME
-----------------

SCOTTYS MARKET
SCHYLERS NOVELTIES
MARYS GIFT SHOP
```

> In the case of a correlated subquery, the reference to the table in the main query must be accomplished before the subquery can be resolved.

The subquery is slightly modified in the next statement to show you the total quantity of units ordered for each customer, allowing the previous results to be verified.

INPUT
```
SELECT C.CUST_NAME, SUM(O.QTY)
FROM CUSTOMER_TBL C,
     ORDERS_TBL O
WHERE C.CUST_ID = O.CUST_ID
GROUP BY C.CUST_NAME;
```

OUTPUT

CUST_NAME	SUM(O.QTY)
ANDYS CANDIES	1
GAVINS PLACE	10
LESLIE GLEASON	1
MARYS GIFT SHOP	100
SCHYLERS NOVELTIES	25
SCOTTYS MARKET	20
WENDY WOLF	2

```
7 rows selected.
```

The GROUP BY clause in this example is required because another column is being selected with the aggregate function SUM. This gives you a sum for each customer. In the original subquery, a GROUP BY clause is not required because SUM is used to achieve a total for the entire query, which is run against the record for each individual customer.

Summary

By simple definition and general concept, a subquery is a query that is performed within another query to place further conditions on a query. A subquery can be used in an SQL statement's WHERE clause or HAVING clause. Queries are typically used within other queries (Data Query Language), but can also be used in the resolution of Data Manipulation Language statements such as INSERT, UPDATE, and DELETE. All basic rules for DML apply when using subqueries with DML commands.

The subquery's syntax is virtually the same as that of a standalone query, with a few minor restrictions. One of these restrictions is that the ORDER BY clause cannot be used within a subquery; a GROUP BY clause can be used, however, which renders virtually the same effect. Subqueries are used to place conditions that are not necessarily known for a query, providing more power and flexibility with SQL.

Q&A

Q In the examples of subqueries, I noticed quite a bit of indentation. Is this necessary in the syntax of a subquery?

A Absolutely not. The indentation is used merely to break the statement into separate parts, making the statement more readable and easier to follow.

Q Is there a limit on the number of embedded subqueries that can be used in a single query?

A Limitations such as the number of embedded subqueries allowed and the number of tables joined in a query are specific to each implementation. Some implementations may not have limits, although the use of too many embedded subqueries could drastically hinder SQL statement performance. Most limitations are affected by the actual hardware, CPU speed, and system memory available, although there are many other considerations.

Q It seems that debugging a query with subqueries can prove to be very confusing, especially with embedded subqueries. What is the best way to debug a query with subqueries?

A The best way to debug a query with subqueries is to evaluate the query in sections. First, evaluate the lowest-level subquery, and then work your way to the main query (the same way the database evaluates the query). When you evaluate each

14

subquery individually, you can substitute the returned values for each subquery to check your main query's logic. An error with a subquery is often the use of the operator used to evaluate the subquery, such as (=), IN, >, <, and so on.

Workshop

The following workshop is composed of a series of quiz questions and practical exercises. The quiz questions are designed to test your overall understanding of the current material. The practical exercises are intended to afford you the opportunity to apply the concepts discussed during the current hour, as well as build upon the knowledge acquired in previous hours of study. Please take time to complete the quiz questions and exercises before continuing. Refer to Appendix C, "Answers to Quizzes and Exercises," for answers.

Quiz

1. What is the function of a subquery when used with a SELECT statement?

2. Can you update more than one column when using the UPDATE statement in conjunction with a subquery?

3. Are the following syntaxes correct? If not, what is the correct syntax?

   a.
   ```
   SELECT CUST_ID, CUST_NAME
         FROM CUSTOMER_TBL
         WHERE CUST_ID =
                     (SELECT CUST_ID
                             FROM ORDERS_TBL
                             WHERE ORD_NUM = '16C17');
   ```

   b.
   ```
   SELECT EMP_ID, SALARY
         FROM EMPLOYEE_PAY_TBL
         WHERE SALARY BETWEEN '20000'
                     AND (SELECT SALARY
                             FROM EMPLOYEE_ID
                             WHERE SALARY = '40000');
   ```

   c.
   ```
   UPDATE PRODUCTS_TBL
       SET COST = 1.15
       WHERE CUST_ID =
                   (SELECT CUST_ID
                   FROM ORDERS_TBL
                   WHERE ORD_NUM = '32A132');
   ```

4. What would happen if the following statement were run?

```
DELETE FROM EMPLOYEE_TBL
WHERE EMP_ID IN
            (SELECT EMP_ID
            FROM EMPLOYEE_PAY_TBL);
```

Exercises

Use the following tables to complete the exercises:

EMPLOYEE_TBL

EMP_ID	VARCHAR2(9)	NOT NULL	PRIMARY KEY
LAST_NAME	VARCHAR2(15)	NOT NULL	
FIRST_NAME	VARCHAR2(15)	NOT NULL	
MIDDLE_NAME	VARCHAR2(15)		
ADDRESS	VARCHAR2(30)	NOT NULL	
CITY	VARCHAR2(15)	NOT NULL	
STATE	CHAR(2)	NOT NULL	
ZIP	NUMBER(5)	NOT NULL	
PHONE	CHAR(10)		
PAGER	CHAR(10)		

EMPLOYEE_PAY_TBL

EMP_ID	VARCHAR2(9)	NOT NULL	PRIMARY KEY
POSITION	VARCHAR2(15)	NOT NULL	
DATE_HIRE	DATE		
PAY_RATE	NYMBER(4,2)	NOT NULL	
DATE_LAST_RAISE	DATE		

CONSTRAINT EMP_FK FOREIGN KEY (EMP_ID_ REFERENCES
  EMPLOYEE_TBL (EMP_ID)

CUSTOMER_TBL

CUST_ID	VARCHAR2(10)	NOT NULL	PRIMARY KEY
CUST_NAME	VARCHAR2(30)	NOT NULL	
CUST_ADDRESS	VARCHAR2(20)	NOT NULL	
CUST_CITY	VARCHAR2(15)	NOT NULL	

14

CUST_STATE	CHAR(2)	NOT NULL	
CUST_ZIP	NUMBER(5)	NOT NULL	
CUST_PHONE	NUMBER(10)		
CUST_FAX	NUMBER(10)		

ORDERS_TBL

ORD_NUM	VARCHAR2(10)	NOT NULL	**PRIMARY KEY**
CUST_ID	VARCHAR2(10)	NOT NULL	
PROD_ID	VARCHAR2(10)	NOT NULL	
QTY	NUMBER(6)	NOT NULL	
ORD_DATE	DATE		

PRODUCTS_TBL

PROD_ID	VARCHAR2(10)	NOT NULL	**PRIMARY KEY**
PROD_DESC	VARCHAR2(40)	NOT NULL	
COST	NUMBER(6,2)	NOT NULL	

1. Using a subquery, write an SQL statement to update the CUSTOMER_TBL table, changing the customer name to DAVIDS MARKET, who has an order with order number 23E934.

2. Using a subquery, write a query that returns all the names of all employees who have a pay rate greater than JOHN DOE, whose employee identification number is 343559876.

3. Using a subquery, write a query that lists all products that cost more than the average cost of all products.

HOUR 15

Combining Multiple Queries into One

During this hour, you learn how to combine SQL queries into one by using the UNION, UNION ALL, INTERSECT, and EXCEPT operators. Once again, you must check your particular implementation for any variations in the use of the UNION, UNION ALL, INTERSECT, and EXCEPT operators.

The highlights of this hour include

- An overview of the operators used to combine queries
- When to use the commands to combine queries
- Using the GROUP BY with the compound operators
- Using the ORDER BY with the compound operators
- How to retrieve accurate data

Single Queries Versus Compound Queries

The single query is one SELECT statement, while the compound query includes two or more SELECT statements.

Compound queries are formed by using some type of operator that is used to join the two queries. The UNION operator in the following examples is used to join two queries.

A single SQL statement could be written as follows:

```
SELECT EMP_ID, SALARY, PAY_RATE
FROM EMPLOYEE_PAY_TBL
WHERE SALARY IS NOT NULL OR
PAY_RATE IS NOT NULL;
```

This is the same statement using the UNION operator:

```
SELECT EMP_ID, SALARY
FROM EMPLOYEE_PAY_TBL
WHERE SALARY IS NOT NULL
UNION
SELECT EMP_ID, PAY_RATE
FROM EMPLOYEE_PAY_TBL
WHERE PAY_RATE IS NOT NULL;
```

The previous statements return pay information for all employees who are paid either hourly or salaried.

> If you executed the second query, the output has two column headings: EMP_ID and SALARY. Each individual's pay rate is listed under the SALARY column. When using the UNION operator, column headings are determined by column names or column aliases used in the first SELECT of the UNION.

Why Would I Ever Want to Use a Compound Query?

Compound operators are used to combine and restrict the results of two SELECT statements. These operators can be used to return or suppress the output of duplicate records. Compound operators can bring together similar data that is stored in different fields.

Compound queries allow you to combine the results of more than one query to return a single set of data. Compound queries are often simpler to write than a single query with complex conditions. Compound queries also allow for more flexibility regarding the never-ending task of data retrieval.

Compound Query Operators

15

The compound query operators vary among database vendors. The ANSI standard includes the UNION, UNION ALL, EXCEPT, and INTERSECT operators, all of which are discussed in the following sections.

The UNION Operator

The UNION operator is used to combine the results of two or more SELECT statements without returning any duplicate rows. In other words, if a row of output exists in the results of one query, the same row is not returned, even though it exists in the second query that combined with a UNION operator. To use UNION, each SELECT must have the same number of columns selected, the same number of column expressions, the same data type, and have them in the same order—but they do not have to be the same length.

The syntax is as follows:

```
SELECT COLUMN1 [, COLUMN2 ]
FROM TABLE1 [, TABLE2 ]
[ WHERE ]
UNION
SELECT COLUMN1 [, COLUMN2 ]
FROM TABLE1 [, TABLE2 ]
[ WHERE ]
```

Look at the following example:

```
SELECT EMP_ID FROM EMPLOYEE_TBL
UNION
SELECT EMP_ID FROM EMPLOYEE_PAY_TBL;
```

ANALYSIS Those employee IDs that are in both tables appear only once in the results.

This hour's examples begin with a simple SELECT from two tables:

INPUT

```
SELECT PROD_DESC FROM PRODUCTS_TBL;
```

OUTPUT

```
PROD_DESC
- - - - - - - - - - - - - - - - - - - - - -
WITCHES COSTUME
PLASTIC PUMPKIN 18 INCH
FALSE PARAFFIN TEETH
LIGHTED LANTERNS
ASSORTED COSTUMES
CANDY CORN
PUMPKIN CANDY
```

```
PLASTIC SPIDERS
ASSORTED MASKS
KEY CHAIN
OAK BOOKSHELF
```

11 rows selected.

INPUT

SELECT PROD_DESC FROM PRODUCTS_TMP;

> The PRODUCTS_TMP table was created in Hour 3, "Managing Database Objects." Refer back to Hour 3 if you need to re-create this table.

OUTPUT

```
PROD_DESC
--------------------
WITCHES COSTUME
PLASTIC PUMPKIN 18 INCH
FALSE PARAFFIN TEETH
LIGHTED LANTERNS
ASSORTED COSTUMES
CANDY CORN
PUMPKIN CANDY
PLASTIC SPIDERS
ASSORTED MASKS
KEY CHAIN
OAK BOOKSHELF
```

11 rows selected.

Now, combine the same two queries with the UNION operator, making a compound query.

INPUT

**SELECT PROD_DESC FROM PRODUCTS_TBL
UNION
SELECT PROD_DESC FROM PRODUCTS_TMP;**

OUTPUT

```
PROD_DESC
-------------------------
ASSORTED COSTUMES
ASSORTED MASKS
CANDY CORN
FALSE PARAFFIN TEETH
LIGHTED LANTERNS
PLASTIC PUMPKIN 18 INCH
PLASTIC SPIDERS
PUMPKIN CANDY
WITCHES COSTUME
KEY CHAIN
OAK BOOKSHELF
```

11 rows selected.

In the first query, nine rows of data were returned, and six rows of data were returned from the second query. Nine rows of data are returned when the UNION operator combines the two queries. Only nine rows are returned because duplicate rows of data are not returned when using the UNION operator.

The next example shows an example of combining two unrelated queries with the UNION operator:

INPUT

```
SELECT PROD_DESC FROM PRODUCTS_TBL
UNION
SELECT LAST_NAME FROM EMPLOYEE_TBL;
```

OUTPUT

```
PROD_DESC
----------------------
ASSORTED COSTUMES
ASSORTED MASKS
CANDY CORN
FALSE PARAFFIN TEETH
GLASS
KEY CHAIN
LIGHTED LANTERNS
OAK BOOKSHELF
PLASTIC PUMPKIN 18 INCH
PLASTIC SPIDERS
PLEW
PUMPKIN CANDY
SPURGEON
STEPHENS
WALLACE
WITCHES COSTUME

16 rows selected.
```

The PROD_DESC and LAST_NAME values are listed together, and the column heading taken is from the column name in the first query.

The UNION ALL Operator

The UNION ALL operator is used to combine the results of two SELECT statements including duplicate rows. The same rules that apply to UNION apply to the UNION ALL operator. The UNION and UNION ALL operators are the same, although one returns duplicate rows of data where the other does not.

The syntax is as follows:

▼ SYNTAX

```
SELECT COLUMN1 [, COLUMN2 ]
FROM TABLE1 [, TABLE2 ]
[ WHERE ]
UNION ALL
```

```
SELECT COLUMN1 [, COLUMN2 ]
FROM TABLE1 [, TABLE2 ]
[ WHERE ]
```
▲

Look at the following example:

```
SELECT EMP_ID FROM EMPLOYEE_TBL
UNION ALL
SELECT EMP_ID FROM EMPLOYEE_PAY_TBL
```

ANALYSIS The preceding SQL statement returns all employee IDs from both tables and shows duplicates.

The following is the same compound query in the previous section with the UNION ALL operator:

INPUT
```
SELECT PROD_DESC FROM PRODUCTS_TBL
UNION ALL
SELECT PROD_DESC FROM PRODUCTS_TMP;
```

OUTPUT
```
PROD_DESC
-----------------------
WITCHES COSTUME
PLASTIC PUMPKIN 18 INCH
FALSE PARAFFIN TEETH
LIGHTED LANTERNS
ASSORTED COSTUMES
CANDY CORN
PUMPKIN CANDY
PLASTIC SPIDERS
ASSORTED MASKS
KEY CHAIN
OAK BOOKSHELF
WITCHES COSTUME
PLASTIC PUMPKIN 18 INCH
FALSE PARAFFIN TEETH
LIGHTED LANTERNS
ASSORTED COSTUMES
CANDY CORN
PUMPKIN CANDY
PLASTIC SPIDERS
ASSORTED MASKS
KEY CHAIN
OAK BOOKSHELF

22 rows selected.
```

Notice that there were 22 rows returned in this query (9+6) because duplicate records are retrieved with the UNION ALL operator.

The INTERSECT Operator

The INTERSECT operator is used to combine two SELECT statements, but returns rows only from the first SELECT statement that are identical to a row in the second SELECT statement. Just as with the UNION operator, the same rules apply when using the INTERSECT operator.

SYNTAX ▼

The syntax is as follows:

```
SELECT COLUMN1 [, COLUMN2 ]
FROM TABLE1 [, TABLE2 ]
[ WHERE ]
INTERSECT
SELECT COLUMN1 [, COLUMN2 ]
FROM TABLE1 [, TABLE2 ]
[ WHERE ]
```

Look at the following example:

```
SELECT CUST_ID FROM CUSTOMER_TBL
INTERSECT
SELECT CUST_ID FROM ORDERS_TBL;
```

The preceding SQL statement returns the customer identification for those customers who have placed an order.

The following example illustrates the INTERSECT using the two original queries in this hour:

INPUT

```
SELECT PROD_DESC FROM PRODUCTS_TBL
INTERSECT
SELECT PROD_DESC FROM PRODUCTS_TMP;
```

OUTPUT

```
PROD_DESC
--------------------
ASSORTED COSTUMES
ASSORTED MASKS
CANDY CORN
FALSE PARAFFIN TEETH
KEY CHAIN
LIGHTED LANTERNS
OAK BOOKSHELF
PLASTIC PUMPKIN 18 INCH
PLASTIC SPIDERS
PUMPKIN CANDY
WITCHES COSTUME

11 rows selected.
```

15

Only eleven rows are returned, because only eleven rows were identical between the output of the two single queries.

The EXCEPT Operator

The EXCEPT operator combines two SELECT statements and returns rows from the first SELECT statement that are not returned by the second SELECT statement. Once again, the same rules that apply to the UNION operator also apply to the EXCEPT operator.

The syntax is as follows:

```
SELECT COLUMN1 [, COLUMN2 ]
FROM TABLE1 [, TABLE2 ]
[ WHERE ]
EXCEPT
SELECT COLUMN1 [, COLUMN2 ]
FROM TABLE1 [, TABLE2 ]
[ WHERE ]
```

Study the following example:

```
SELECT PROD_DESC FROM PRODUCTS_TBL
EXCEPT
SELECT PROD_DESC FROM PRODUCTS_TMP;
```

OUTPUT

```
PROD_DESC
----------------------
PLASTIC PUMPKIN 18 INCH
PLASTIC SPIDERS
PUMPKIN CANDY

3 rows selected.
```

According to the results, there were three rows of data returned by the first query that were not returned by the second query.

> The EXCEPT operator is known as the MINUS operator in some implementations. Check your implementation for the operator name that performs the EXCEPT operator's function.

INPUT

```
SELECT PROD_DESC FROM PRODUCTS_TBL
MINUS
SELECT PROD_DESC FROM PRODUCTS_TMP;
```

OUTPUT

```
PROD_DESC
----------------------
PLASTIC PUMPKIN 18 INCH
PLASTIC SPIDERS
PUMPKIN CANDY

3 rows selected.
```

15

Using an ORDER BY with a Compound Query

The ORDER BY clause can be used with a compound query. However, the ORDER BY can only be used to order the results of both queries. Therefore, there can be only one ORDER BY clause in a compound query, even though the compound query may consist of multiple individual queries or SELECT statements. The ORDER BY must reference the columns being ordered by an alias or by the number of column order.

▼ SYNTAX

The syntax is as follows:

```
SELECT COLUMN1 [, COLUMN2 ]
FROM TABLE1 [, TABLE2 ]
[ WHERE ]
OPERATOR{UNION | EXCEPT | INTERSECT | UNION ALL}
SELECT COLUMN1 [, COLUMN2 ]
FROM TABLE1 [, TABLE2 ]
[ WHERE ]
[ ORDER BY ]
```

Examine the following example:

```
SELECT EMP_ID FROM EMPLOYEE_TBL
UNION
SELECT EMP_ID FROM EMPLOYEE_PAY_TBL
ORDER BY 1;
```

ANALYSIS The results of the compound query are sorted by the first column of each individual query. Duplicate records can easily be recognized by sorting compound queries.

> The column in the ORDER BY clause is referenced by the number 1 instead of the actual column name.

The preceding SQL statement returns the employee ID from the EMPLOYEE_TBL and the EMPLOYEE_PAY_TBL, but does not show duplicates and orders by the employee ID.

The following example shows the use of the ORDER BY clause with a compound query. The column name can be used in the ORDER BY clause if the column sorted by has the same name in all individual queries of the statement.

INPUT

```
SELECT PROD_DESC FROM PRODUCTS_TBL
UNION
SELECT PROD_DESC FROM PRODUCTS_TBL
ORDER BY PROD_DESC;
```

OUTPUT

```
PROD_DESC
----------------------
ASSORTED COSTUMES
ASSORTED MASKS
CANDY CORN
FALSE PARAFFIN TEETH
KEY CHAIN
LIGHTED LANTERNS
OAK BOOKSHELF
PLASTIC PUMPKIN 18 INCH
PLASTIC SPIDERS
PUMPKIN CANDY
WITCHES COSTUME

11 rows selected.
```

The following query uses a numeric value in place of the actual column name in the ORDER BY clause:

INPUT

```
SELECT PROD_DESC FROM PRODUCTS_TBL
UNION
SELECT PROD_DESC FROM PRODUCTS_TBL
ORDER BY 1;
```

OUTPUT

```
PROD_DESC
----------------------
ASSORTED COSTUMES
ASSORTED MASKS
CANDY CORN
FALSE PARAFFIN TEETH
KEY CHAIN
LIGHTED LANTERNS
OAK BOOKSHELF
PLASTIC PUMPKIN 18 INCH
PLASTIC SPIDERS
PUMPKIN CANDY
WITCHES COSTUME

11 rows selected.
```

Using a GROUP BY with a Compound Query

Unlike the ORDER BY, the GROUP BY can be used in each SELECT statement of a compound query, but also can be used following all individual queries. In addition, the HAVING clause (sometimes used with the GROUP BY clause) can be used in each SELECT statement of a compound statement.

▼ SYNTAX

The syntax is as follows:

```
SELECT COLUMN1 [, COLUMN2 ]
FROM TABLE1 [, TABLE2 ]
[ WHERE ]
[ GROUP BY ]
[ HAVING ]
OPERATOR {UNION | EXCEPT | INTERSECT | UNION ALL}
SELECT COLUMN1 [, COLUMN2 ]
FROM TABLE1 [, TABLE2 ]
[ WHERE ]
[ GROUP BY ]
[ HAVING ]
[ ORDER BY ]
```

In the following example, you select a literal string to represent customer records, employee records, and product records. Each individual query is simply a count of all records in each appropriate table. The GROUP BY clause is used to group the results of the entire report by the numeric value 1, which represents the first column in each individual query.

INPUT

```
SELECT 'CUSTOMERS' TYPE, COUNT(*)
FROM CUSTOMER_TBL
UNION
SELECT 'EMPLOYEES' TYPE, COUNT(*)
FROM EMPLOYEE_TBL
UNION
SELECT 'PRODUCTS' TYPE, COUNT(*)
FROM PRODUCTS_TBL
GROUP BY 1;
```

OUTPUT

```
TYPE          COUNT(*)
-----------  --------
CUSTOMERS         15
EMPLOYEES          6
PRODUCTS           9

3 rows selected.
```

The following query is identical to the previous query, except that the ORDER BY clause is used as well:

```
SELECT 'CUSTOMERS' TYPE, COUNT(*)
FROM CUSTOMER_TBL
UNION
SELECT 'EMPLOYEES' TYPE, COUNT(*)
FROM EMPLOYEE_TBL
UNION
SELECT 'PRODUCTS' TYPE, COUNT(*)
FROM PRODUCTS_TBL
GROUP BY 1
ORDER BY 2;
```

OUTPUT

```
TYPE          COUNT(*)
----------    --------
EMPLOYEES            6
PRODUCTS             9
CUSTOMERS           15

3 rows selected.
```

This is sorted by column 2, which was the count on each table. Hence, the final output is sorted by the count from least to greatest.

Retrieving Accurate Data

Be cautious when using the compound operators. Incorrect or incomplete data may be returned if you were using the INTERSECT operator and you used the wrong SELECT statement as the first individual query. In addition, consider whether duplicate records are wanted when using the UNION and UNION ALL operators. What about EXCEPT? Do you need any of the rows that were not returned by the second query? As you can see, the wrong compound query operator or the wrong order of individual queries in a compound query can easily cause misleading data to be returned.

Incomplete data returned by a query qualifies as incorrect data.

Summary

You have been introduced to compound queries. All SQL statements previous to this hour have consisted of a single query. Compound queries allow multiple individual queries to be used together as a single query to achieve the data result set desired as output. The compound query operators discussed included UNION, UNION ALL, INTERSECT, and EXCEPT (MINUS). UNION returns the output of two single queries without displaying duplicate rows of data. UNION ALL simply displays all output of single queries, regardless of existing duplicate rows. INTERSECT is used to return identical rows between two queries. EXCEPT (the same as MINUS) is used to return the results of one query that do not exist in another query. Compound queries provide greater flexibility when trying to satisfy the requirements of various queries, which, without the use of compound operators, could result in very complex queries.

Q&A

Q **How are the columns referenced in the GROUP BY clause when using the GROUP BY clause with a compound query?**

A The columns can be referenced by the actual column name or by the number of the column placement in the query if the column names are not identical in the two queries.

Q **I understand what the EXCEPT operator does, but would the outcome change if I were to reverse the SELECT statements?**

A Yes. The order of the individual queries is very important when using the EXCEPT or MINUS operator. Remember that all rows are returned from the first query that are not returned by the second query. Changing the order of the two individual queries in the compound query could definitely affect the results.

Q **Must the data type and the length of columns in a compound query be the same in both queries?**

A No. Only the data type must be the same. The length can differ.

Workshop

The following workshop is composed of a series of quiz questions and practical exercises. The quiz questions are designed to test your overall understanding of the current material. The practical exercises are intended to afford you the opportunity to apply the concepts discussed during the current hour, as well as build upon the knowledge acquired in previous hours of study. Please take time to complete the quiz questions and exercises before continuing. Refer to Appendix C, "Answers to Quizzes and Exercises," for answers.

Quiz

1. Is the syntax correct for the following compound queries? If not, what would correct the syntax? Use the EMPLOYEE_TBL and the EMPLOYEE_PAY_TBL shown as follows:

```
EMPLOYEE_TBL
─────────────
    EMP_ID              VARCHAR2(9)      NOT NULL,
    LAST_NAME           VARCHAR2(15)     NOT NULL,
    FIRST_NAME          VARCHAR2(15)     NOT NULL,
    MIDDLE_NAME         VARCHAR2(15),
    ADDRESS             VARCHAR2(30)     NOT NULL,
    CITY                VARCHAR2(15)     NOT NULL,
    STATE               CHAR(2)          NOT NULL,
    ZIP                 NUMBER(5)        NOT NULL,
    PHONE               CHAR(10),
    PAGER               CHAR(10),

CONSTRAINT EMP_PK PRIMARY KEY (EMP_ID)

EMPLOYEE_PAY_TBL
─────────────────
    EMP_ID              VARCHAR2(9)      NOT NULL,    PRIMARY KEY
    POSITION            VARCHAR2(15)     NOT NULL,
    DATE_HIRE           DATE,
    PAY_RATE            NUMBER(4,2)      NOT NULL,
    DATE_LAST_RAISE     DATE,
    SALARY              NUMBER(8,2),
    BONUS               NUMBER(6,2),

CONSTRAINT EMP_FK FOREIGN KEY (EMP_ID)
REFERENCES EMPLOYEE_TBL (EMP_ID)
```

a.

```
SELECT EMP_ID, LAST_NAME, FIRST_NAME
FROM EMPLOYEE_TBL
UNION
SELECT EMP_ID, POSITION, DATE_HIRE
FROM EMPLOYEE_PAY_TBL;
```

b.

```
SELECT EMP_ID FROM EMPLOYEE_TBL
UNION ALL
SELECT EMP_ID FROM EMPLOYEE_PAY_TBL
ORDER BY EMP_ID;
```

c.

```
SELECT EMP_ID FROM EMPLOYEE_PAY_TBL
INTERSECT
SELECT EMP_ID FROM EMPLOYEE_TBL
ORDER BY 1;
```

2. Match the correct operator to the following statements.

	STATEMENT	OPERATOR
a.	Show duplicates	UNION
b.	Return only rows from the first query that match those in the second query	INTERSECT UNION ALL EXCEPT
c.	Return no duplicates	
d.	Return only rows from the first query not returned by the second	

Exercises

Use the CUSTOMER_TBL and the ORDERS_TBL as listed:

CUSTOMER_TBL

CUST_IN	VARCHAR2(10)	NOT NULL	PRIMARY KEY,
CUST_NAME	VARCHAR2(30)	NOT NULL,	
CUST_ADDRESS	VARCHAR2(20)	NOT NULL,	
CUST_CITY	VARCHAR2(15)	NOT NULL,	
CUST_STATE	CHAR(2)	NOT NULL,	
CUST_ZIP	NUMBER(5)	NOT NULL,	
CUST_PHONE	NUMBER(10),		
CUST_FAX	NUMBER(10)		

ORDERS_TBL

ORD_NUM	VARCHAR2(10)	NOT NULL	PRIMARY KEY,
CUST_ID	VARCHAR2(10)	NOT NULL,	
PROD_ID	VARCHAR2(10)	NOT NULL,	
QTY	NUMBER(6)	NOT NULL,	
ORD_DATE	DATE		

1. Write a compound query to find the customers that have placed an order.
2. Write a compound query to find the customers that have not placed an order.

PART V
SQL Performance Tuning

Hour

HOUR 16

Using Indexes to Improve Performance

During this hour, you learn how to improve SQL statement performance by creating and using indexes.

You begin with the CREATE INDEX command and learn how to use indexes that have been created on tables.

The highlights of this hour include

- How to create an index
- How indexes work
- The different types of indexes
- When to use indexes
- When not to use indexes

What Is an Index?

Simply put, an *index* is a pointer to data in a table. An index in a database is very similar to an index in the back of a book. For example, if you want to reference all pages in a book that discuss a certain topic, you first refer to the index, which lists all topics alphabetically, and are then referred to one or more specific page numbers. An index in a database works the same way in that a query is pointed to the exact physical location of data in a table. You are actually being directed to the data's location in an underlying file of the database, but as far as you are concerned, you are referring to a table.

New Term Which would be faster, looking through a book page by page for some information or searching the book's index and getting a page number? Of course, using the book's index is the most efficient method. A lot of time can be saved if that book is large. Say you have a small book of just a few pages. In this case, it may be faster to check the pages for the information than to flip back and forth between the index and pages of the book. When a database does not use an index, it is performing what is typically called a *full table scan*, the same as flipping through a book page by page. Full table scans are discussed in Hour 17, "Improving Database Performance."

An index is stored separately from the table for which the index was created. An index's main purpose is to improve the performance of data retrieval. Indexes can be created or dropped with no effect on the data. However, once dropped, performance of data retrieval may be slowed. An index does take up physical space and often grows larger than the table itself.

How Do Indexes Work?

When an index is created, it records the location of values in a table that are associated with the column that is indexed. Entries are added to the index when new data is added to the table. When a query is executed against the database and a condition is specified on a column in the WHERE clause that is indexed, the index is first searched for the values specified in the WHERE clause. If the value is found in the index, the index returns the exact location of the searched data in the table. Figure 16.1 illustrates how an index functions.

Suppose the following query was issued:

```
SELECT *
FROM TABLE_NAME
WHERE NAME = 'SMITH';
```

As shown in Figure 16.1, the NAME index is referenced to resolve the location of all names equal to 'SMITH'. After the location is determined, the data can be quickly retrieved from the table. The data, in this case names, is alphabetized in the index.

A full table scan would occur if there were no index on the table and the same query was executed, which means that every row of data in the table would be read to retrieve information pertaining to all individuals with the name SMITH.

FIGURE 16.1

Table access using an index.

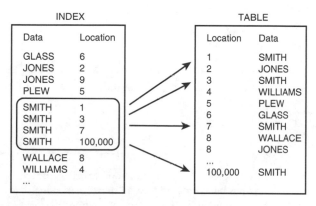

16

The CREATE INDEX Command

The CREATE INDEX statement, as with many other statements in SQL, varies greatly among different relational database vendors. Most relational database implementations use the CREATE INDEX statement:

SYNTAX

```
CREATE INDEX INDEX_NAME ON TABLE_NAME
```

The syntax is where the vendors start varying greatly on the CREATE INDEX statement options. Some implementations allow the specification of a storage clause (as with the CREATE TABLE statement), ordering (DESC||ASC), and the use of clusters. You must check your particular implementation for its correct syntax.

Types of Indexes

There are different types of indexes that can be created on tables in a database, all of which serve the same goal—to improve database performance by expediting data retrieval. This hour discusses single-column indexes, composite indexes, and unique indexes.

> Indexes can be created during table creation in some implementations. Most implementations accommodate a command, aside from the CREATE TABLE command, used to create indexes. You must check your particular implementation for the exact syntax for the command, if any, that is available to create an index.

Single-Column Indexes

Indexing on a single column of a table is the simplest and most common manifestation of an index. Obviously, a single-column index is one that is created based on only one table column. The basic syntax is as follows:

```
CREATE INDEX INDEX_NAME
ON TABLE_NAME (COLUMN_NAME)
```

For example, if you want to create an index on the EMPLOYEE_TBL table for employees' last names, the command used to create the index would look like the following:

```
CREATE INDEX NAME_IDX
ON EMPLOYEE_TBL (LAST_NAME);
```

> You should plan your tables and indexes. Do not assume that because an index has been created that all performance issues are resolved. The index may not help at all (it may actually hinder performance) and may just take up disk space.

> Single-column indexes are most effective when used on columns that are frequently used alone in the WHERE clause as query conditions. Good candidates for a single-column index are an individual identification number, a serial number, or a system-assigned key.

Unique Indexes

NEW TERM *Unique indexes* are used not only for performance, but also for data integrity. A unique index does not allow any duplicate values to be inserted into the table. Otherwise, the unique index performs the same way a regular index performs. The syntax is as follows:

```
CREATE UNIQUE INDEX INDEX_NAME
ON TABLE_NAME (COLUMN_NAME)
```

If you want to create a unique index on the EMPLOYEE_TBL table for an employee's last name, the command used to create the unique index would look like the following:

```
CREATE UNIQUE INDEX NAME_IDX
ON EMPLOYEE_TBL (LAST_NAME);
```

The only problem with this index is that every individual's last name in the EMPLOYEE_TBL table must be unique—pretty impractical. However, a unique index should be created for a column, such as an individual's Social Security number, because each of these numbers for each individual is unique.

You may be wondering, "What if an employee's SSN were the primary key for a table?" An index is usually implicitly created when you define a primary key for a table. However, a company can use a fictitious number for an employee ID, but maintain each employees' SSN for tax purposes. You probably want to index this column and ensure that all entries into this column are unique values.

16

The unique index can only be created on a column in a table whose values are unique. In other words, you cannot create a unique index on an existing table with data that already contains records on the indexed key.

Composite Indexes

NEW TERM A *composite index* is an index on two or more columns of a table. You should consider performance when creating a composite index because the order of columns in the index has a measurable effect on data retrieval speed. Generally, the most restrictive value should be placed first for optimum performance. However, the columns that will always be specified should be placed first. The syntax is as follows:

```
CREATE INDEX INDEX_NAME
ON TABLE_NAME (COLUMN1, COLUMN2)
```

An example of a composite index follows:

```
CREATE INDEX ORD_IDX
ON ORDERS_TBL (CUST_ID, PROD_ID);
```

In this example, you create a composite index based on two columns in the ORDERS_TBL table: CUST_ID and PROD_ID. You assume that these two columns are frequently used together as conditions in the WHERE clause of a query.

Composite indexes are most effective on table columns that are used together frequently as conditions in a query's WHERE clause.

Single-Column Versus Composite Indexes

In deciding whether to create a single-column index or a composite index, take into consideration the column(s) that you may use very frequently in a query's WHERE clause as filter conditions. Should there be only one column used, a single-column index should be the choice. Should there be two or more columns that are frequently used in the WHERE clause as filters, the composite index would be the best choice.

Implicit Indexes

NEW TERM *Implicit indexes* are indexes that are automatically created by the database server when an object is created. Indexes are automatically created for primary key constraints and unique constraints. Why are indexes automatically created for these constraints? Imagine that you are the database server. A user adds a new product to the database. The product identification is the primary key on the table, which means that it must be a unique value. To efficiently check to make sure the new value is unique among hundreds or thousands of records, the product identifications in the table must be indexed. Therefore, when you create a primary key or unique constraint, an index is automatically created for you.

When Should Indexes Be Considered?

Unique indexes are implicitly used in conjunction with a primary key for the primary key to work. Foreign keys are also excellent candidates for an index because they are often used to join the parent table. Most, if not all, columns used for table joins should be indexed.

Columns that are frequently referenced in the ORDER BY and GROUP BY clauses should be considered for indexes. For example, if you are sorting on an individual's name, it would be quite beneficial to have any index on the name column. It renders an automatic alphabetical order on every name, thus simplifying the actual sort operation and expediting the output results.

Furthermore, indexes should be created on columns with a high number of unique values, or columns when used as filter conditions in the WHERE clause return a low percentage of rows of data from a table. This is where trial and error may come into play. Just as production code and database structures should always be tested before their implementation into production, so should indexes. This testing is time that should be spent trying different combinations of indexes, no indexes, single-column indexes, and composite indexes. There is no cut-and-dried rule for using indexes. The effective use of indexes requires a thorough knowledge of table relationships, query and transaction requirements, and the data itself.

When Should Indexes Be Avoided?

Although indexes are intended to enhance a database's performance, there are times when they should be avoided. The following guidelines indicate when the use of an index should be reconsidered:

- Indexes should not be used on small tables.

- Indexes should not be used on columns that return a high percentage of data rows when used as a filter condition in a query's WHERE clause. For instance, you would not have an entry for the word "the" or "and" in the index of a book.

- Tables that have frequent, large batch update jobs run can be indexed. However, the batch job's performance is slowed considerably by the index. The conflict of having an index on a table that is frequently loaded or manipulated by a large batch process can be corrected by dropping the index before the batch job, and then re-creating the index after the job has completed.

- Indexes should not be used on columns that contain a high number of NULL values.

- Columns that are frequently manipulated should not be indexed. Maintenance on the index can become excessive.

> Caution should be taken when creating indexes on a table's extremely long keys because performance is inevitably slowed by high I/O costs.

You can see in Figure 16.2 that an index on a column, such as sex, may not prove beneficial. For example, suppose the following query was submitted to the database:

```
SELECT *
FROM TABLE_NAME
WHERE GENDER = 'FEMALE';
```

By referring to Figure 16.2, which is based on the previous query, you can see that there is constant activity between the table and its index. Because a high number of data rows is returned WHERE GENDER = 'FEMALE' (or MALE), the database server constantly has to read the index, and then the table, and then the index, and then the table, and so on. In this case, it may be more efficient for a full table scan to occur because a high percentage of the table must be read anyway.

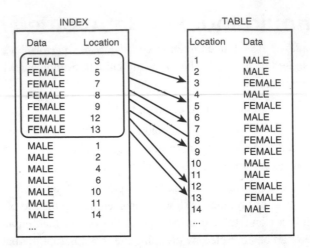

FIGURE 16.2

When to avoid using an index.

As a general rule, you do not want to use an index on a column used in a query's condition that will return a high percentage of data rows from the table. In other words, do not create an index on a column, such as sex, or any column that contains very few distinct values.

> Indexes can be very good for performance, but in some cases may actually hurt performance. Refrain from creating indexes on columns that will contain few unique values, such as sex, state of residence, and so on.

Dropping an Index

An index can be dropped rather simply. Check your particular implementation for the exact syntax, but most major implementations use the DROP command. Care should be taken when dropping an index because performance may be slowed drastically (or improved!). The syntax is as follows:

```
DROP INDEX INDEX_NAME
```

The most common reason for dropping an index is in an attempt to improve performance. Remember that if you drop an index, you can also re-create it. Indexes may need to be rebuilt sometimes to reduce fragmentation. It is often necessary to experiment with the use of indexes in a database to determine the route to best performance, which may involve creating an index, dropping it, and eventually re-creating it, with or without modifications.

Summary

You have learned that indexes can be used to improve the overall performance of queries and transactions performed within the database. Database indexes, like an index of a book, allow specific data to be quickly referenced from a table. The most common method for creating indexes is through use of the CREATE INDEX command. There are different types of indexes available among various SQL implementations. Unique indexes, single-column indexes, and composite indexes are among those different types of indexes. There are many factors to consider when deciding on the index type used to best meet the needs of your database. The effective use of indexes often requires some experimentation, a thorough knowledge of table relationships and data, and a little patience—but patience now can save minutes, hours, or even days of work later.

16

Q&A

Q Does an index actually take up space the way a table does?

A Yes. An index takes up physical space in a database. In fact, an index can become much larger than the table for which the index was created.

Q If you drop an index for a batch job to complete faster, how long does it take to re-create the index?

A Many factors are involved, such as the size of the index being dropped, CPU usage, and the machine's power.

Q Should all indexes be unique indexes?

A No. Unique indexes allow no duplicate values. There may be a need for the allowance of duplicate values in a table.

Workshop

The following workshop is composed of a series of quiz questions and practical exercises. The quiz questions are designed to test your overall understanding of the current material. The practical exercises are intended to afford you the opportunity to apply the concepts discussed during the current hour, as well as build upon the knowledge acquired in previous hours of study. Please take time to complete the quiz questions and exercises before continuing. Refer to Appendix C, "Answers to Quizzes and Exercises," for answers.

Quiz

1. What are some major disadvantages of using indexes?
2. Why is the order of columns in a composite important?
3. Should a column with a large percentage of NULLs be indexed?
4. Is the main purpose of an index to stop duplicate values in a table?
5. True or false: The main reason for a composite index is for aggregate function usage in an index.

Exercises

1. For the following situations, decide whether an index should be used and, if so, what type of index should be used.

   a. Several columns, but a rather small table.

   b. Medium-sized table, no duplicates should be allowed.

   c. Several columns, very large table, several columns used as filters in the WHERE clause.

   d. Large table, many columns, a lot of data manipulation.

HOUR 17

Improving Database Performance

During this hour, you learn how to tune your SQL statement for maximum performance using some very simple methods.

The highlights of this hour include

- What SQL statement tuning is
- Database tuning versus SQL statement tuning
- Formatting your SQL statement
- Properly joining tables
- The most restrictive condition
- Full table scans
- Invoking the use of indexes
- Avoiding the use of OR and HAVING
- Avoiding large sort operations

What Is SQL Statement Tuning?

SQL statement tuning is the process of optimally building SQL statements to achieve results in the most effective and efficient manner. SQL tuning begins with the basic arrangement of the elements in a query. Simple formatting plays a rather large role in the optimization of a statement.

SQL statement tuning mainly involves tweaking a statement's FROM and WHERE clauses. It is in these two clauses that the database server decides how to evaluate a query. To this point, you have learned the FROM and WHERE clauses' basics. Now it is time to learn how to fine-tune them for better results and happier users.

Database Tuning Versus SQL Tuning

Before continuing with your SQL statement tuning lesson, it is important to understand the difference between tuning a database and tuning the SQL statements that access the database.

NEW TERM   *Database tuning* is the process of tuning the actual database, which encompasses the allocated memory, disk usage, CPU, I/O, and underlying database processes. Tuning a database also involves the management and manipulation of the database structure itself, such as the design and layout of tables and indexes. There are many other considerations when tuning a database, but these tasks are normally accomplished by the database administrator. The objective of database tuning is to ensure that the database has been designed in a way that best accommodates expected activity within the database.

NEW TERM   *SQL tuning* is the process of tuning the SQL statements that access the database. These SQL statements include database queries and transactional operations such as inserts, updates, and deletes. The objective of SQL statement tuning is to formulate statements that most effectively access the database in its current state, taking advantage of database and system resources and indexes.

> Both database tuning and SQL statement tuning must be performed to achieve optimal results when accessing the database. A poorly tuned database may very well render wasted effort in SQL tuning, and vice versa.

Formatting Your SQL Statement

Formatting your SQL statement sounds like an obvious statement; as obvious as it may sound, it is worth mentioning. There are several things that a newcomer to SQL will probably not take into consideration when building an SQL statement. The following sections discuss the listed considerations; some are common sense, others are not so obvious:

- Formatting SQL statements for readability
- The order of tables in the FROM clause
- The placement of the most restrictive conditions in the WHERE clause
- The placement of join conditions in the WHERE clause

> Most relational database implementations have what is called an *SQL optimizer*, which evaluates an SQL statement and determines the best method for executing the statement based on the way an SQL statement is written and the availability of indexes in the database. Not all optimizers are the same. Please check your implementation or consult the database administrator to learn how the optimizer reads SQL code. You should understand how the optimizer works to effectively tune an SQL statement.

17

Formatting a Statement for Readability

Formatting an SQL statement for readability is pretty obvious, but many SQL statements have not been written neatly. Although the neatness of a statement does not affect the actual performance (the database does not care how neat the statement appears), careful formatting is the first step in tuning a statement. When you look at an SQL statement with tuning intentions, making the statement readable is always the first thing to do. How can you determine if the statement is written well if it is difficult to read?

Some basic rules for making a statement readable include:

- *Always begin a new line with each clause in the statement*—For example, place the FROM clause on a separate line from the SELECT clause. Place the WHERE clause on a separate line from the FROM clause, and so on.
- *Use tabs or spaces for indentation when arguments of a clause in the statement exceed one line.*
- *Use tabs and spaces consistently.*
- *Use table aliases when multiple tables are used in the statement*—The use of the full table name to qualify each column in the statement quickly clutters the statement and makes reading it difficult.
- *Use remarks sparingly in SQL statements if they are available in your specific implementation*—Remarks are great for documentation, but too many of them clutter a statement.

- *Begin a new line with each column name in the SELECT clause if many columns are being selected.*
- *Begin a new line with each table name in the FROM clause if many tables are being used.*
- *Begin a new line with each condition of the WHERE clause*—You can easily see all conditions of the statement and the order in which they are used.

The following is an example of an unreadable statement:

INPUT

```
SELECT CUSTOMER_TBL.CUST_ID, CUSTOMER_TBL.CUST_NAME,
CUSTOMER_TBL.CUST_PHONE, ORDERS_TBL.ORD_NUM, ORDERS_TBL.QTY
FROM CUSTOMER_TBL, ORDERS_TBL
WHERE CUSTOMER_TBL.CUST_ID = ORDERS_TBL.CUST_ID
AND ORDERS_TBL.QTY > 1 AND CUSTOMER_TBL.CUST_NAME LIKE 'G%'
ORDER BY CUSTOMER_TBL.CUST_NAME;
```

OUTPUT

```
CUST_ID    CUST_NAME                       CUST_PHONE ORD_NUM
QTY
---------- ------------------------------- ---------- ----------------
287        GAVINS PLACE                    3172719991 18D778
10

1 row selected.
```

The following is an example of a reformatted statement for improved readability:

INPUT

```
SELECT C.CUST_ID,
       C.CUST_NAME,
       C.CUST_PHONE,
       O.ORD_NUM,
       O.QTY
FROM ORDERS_TBL O,
     CUSTOMER_TBL C
WHERE O.CUST_ID = C.CUST_ID
  AND O.QTY > 1
  AND C.CUST_NAME LIKE 'G%'
ORDER BY 2;
```

OUTPUT

```
CUST_ID    CUST_NAME                       CUST_PHONE ORD_NUM
QTY
---------- ------------------------------- ---------- ---------------- -
--
287        GAVINS PLACE                    3172719991 18D778
10

1 row selected.
```

Both statements are exactly the same, but the second statement is much more readable. The second statement has been greatly simplified by using table aliases, which have been defined in the query's FROM clause. Spacing has been used to align the elements of each clause, making each clause stand out.

Again, making a statement more readable does not directly improve its performance, but it assists you in making modifications and debugging a lengthy and otherwise possibly complex statement. Now you can easily identify the columns being selected, the tables being used, the table joins that are being performed, and the conditions that are placed on the query.

Proper Arrangement of Tables in the FROM Clause

The arrangement or order of tables in the FROM clause may make a difference, depending on how the optimizer reads the SQL statement. For example, it may be more beneficial to list the smaller tables first and the larger tables last. Some users with lots of experience have found that listing the larger tables last in the FROM clause proves to be more efficient.

The following is an example FROM clause:

```
FROM SMALLEST TABLE,
     LARGEST TABLE
```

Check your particular implementation for performance tips, if any, when listing multiple tables in the FROM clause.

Proper Order of Join Conditions

As you learned in Hour 13, "Joining Tables in Queries," most joins use a BASE TABLE to link tables that have one or more common columns on which to join. The BASE TABLE is the main table that most or all tables are joined to in a query. The column from the BASE TABLE is normally placed on the right side of a join operation in the WHERE clause. The tables being joined to the BASE TABLE are normally in order from smallest to largest, similar to the tables listed in the FROM clause.

Should there not be a BASE TABLE, the tables should be listed from smallest to largest, with the largest tables on the right side of the join operation in the WHERE clause. The join conditions should be in the first position(s) of the WHERE clause followed by the filter clause(s), as shown in the following:

```
FROM TABLE1,                        Smallest Table
     TABLE2,                                to
     TABLE3                  Largest Table, also BASE TABLE
WHERE TABLE1.COLUMN = TABLE3.COLUMN       Join condition
  AND TABLE2.COLUMN = TABLE3.COLUMN       Join condition
[ AND CONDITION1 ]                     Filter condition
[ AND CONDITION2 ]                     Filter condition
```

In this example, TABLE3 is used as the BASE TABLE. TABLE1 and TABLE2 are joined to TABLE3 for both simplicity and proven efficiency.

> Because joins typically return a high percentage of rows of data from the table(s), join conditions should be evaluated after more restrictive conditions.

The Most Restrictive Condition

The most restrictive condition is typically the driving factor in achieving optimal performance for an SQL query. What is the most restrictive condition? The condition in the WHERE clause of a statement that returns the fewest rows of data. Conversely, the least restrictive condition is the condition in a statement that returns the most rows of data. This hour is concerned with the most restrictive condition simply because it is this condition that filters the data that is to be returned by the query the most.

It should be your goal for the SQL optimizer to evaluate the most restrictive condition first because a smaller subset of data is returned by the condition, thus reducing the query's overhead. The effective placement of the most restrictive condition in the query requires knowledge of how the optimizer operates. The optimizers worked with, in some cases, seem to read from the bottom of the WHERE clause up. Therefore, you want to place the most restrictive condition last in the WHERE clause, which is the condition that is first read by the optimizer.

```
FROM TABLE1,                        Smallest Table
     TABLE2,                                to
     TABLE3                  Largest Table, also BASE TABLE
WHERE TABLE1.COLUMN = TABLE3.COLUMN       Join condition
  AND TABLE2.COLUMN = TABLE3.COLUMN       Join condition
[ AND CONDITION1 ]                     Least restrictive
[ AND CONDITION2 ]                     Most restrictive
```

> If you do not know how your particular implementation's SQL optimizer works, the DBA does not know, or you do not have sufficient documentation, you can execute a large query that takes a while to run, and then rearrange conditions in the WHERE clause. Be sure to record the time it takes the query to complete each time you make changes. You should only have to run a couple of tests to figure out whether the optimizer reads the WHERE clause from the top to bottom or bottom to top.

The following is an example using a phony table:

Table:	TEST
Row count:	95,867
Conditions:	WHERE LAST_NAME = 'SMITH'
	returns 2,000 rows
	WHERE CITY = 'INDIANAPOLIS'
	returns 30,000 rows
Most restrictive condition is:	WHERE LAST_NAME = 'SMITH'

QUERY1:

INPUT
```
SELECT COUNT(*)
FROM TEST
WHERE LAST_NAME = 'SMITH'
  AND CITY = 'INDIANAPOLIS';
```

OUTPUT
```
  COUNT(*)
----------
     1,024
```

QUERY2:

INPUT
```
SELECT COUNT(*)
FROM TEST
WHERE CITY = 'INDIANAPOLIS'
  AND LAST_NAME = 'SMITH';
```

OUTPUT
```
  COUNT(*)
----------
     1,024
```

Suppose that QUERY1 completed in 20 seconds, whereas QUERY2 completed in 10 seconds. Because QUERY2 returned faster results and the most restrictive condition was listed last in the WHERE clause, it would be safe to assume that the optimizer reads the WHERE clause from the bottom up.

It is a good practice to try to use an indexed column as the most restrictive condition in a query. Indexes generally improve a query's performance.

Full Table Scans

A full table scan occurs when an index is either not used or there is no index on the table(s) being used by the SQL statement. Full table scans usually return data much slower than when an index is used. The larger the table, the slower that data is returned when a full table scan is performed. The query optimizer decides whether to use an index when executing the SQL statement. The index is used—if it exists—in most cases.

Some implementations have sophisticated query optimizers that can decide whether an index should be used. Decisions such as this are based on statistics that are gathered on database objects, such as the size of an object and the estimated number of rows that are returned by a condition with an indexed column. Please refer to your implementation documentation for specifics on the decision-making capabilities of your relational database's optimizer.

When and How to Avoid Full Table Scans

Full table scans should be avoided when reading large tables. For example, a full table scan is performed when a table that does not have an index is read, which usually takes a considerably longer time to return the data. An index should be considered for most larger tables. On small tables, as previously mentioned, the optimizer may choose the full table scan over using the index, if the table is indexed. In the case of a small table with an index, consideration should be given to dropping the index and reserving the space that was used for the index for other needy objects in the database.

The easiest and most obvious way to avoid a full table scan—outside of ensuring that indexes exist on the table—is to use conditions in a query's WHERE clause to filter data to be returned.

The following is a reminder of data that should be indexed:

- Columns used as primary keys
- Columns used as foreign keys
- Columns frequently used to join tables
- Columns frequently used as conditions in a query
- Columns that have a high percentage of unique values

> Sometimes full table scans are good. Full table scans should be performed on queries against small tables or queries whose conditions return a high percentage of rows. The easiest way to force a full table scan is to avoid creating an index on the table.

Other Performance Considerations

There are other performance considerations that should be noted when tuning SQL statements. The following concepts are discussed in the next sections:

- Using the LIKE operator and wildcards
- Avoiding the OR operator
- Avoiding the HAVING clause
- Avoiding large sort operations
- Using stored procedures

Using the LIKE Operator and Wildcards

The LIKE operator is a useful tool that is used to place conditions on a query in a flexible manner. The placement and use of wildcards in a query can eliminate many possibilities of data that should be retrieved. Wildcards are very flexible for queries that search for similar data (data that is not equivalent to an exact value specified).

Suppose you want to write a query using the EMPLOYEE_TBL selecting the EMP_ID, LAST_NAME, FIRST_NAME, and STATE columns. You need to know the employee identification, name, and state for all the employees with the last name Stevens. Three SQL statement examples with different wildcard placements serve as examples.

QUERY1:

```
SELECT EMP_ID, LAST_NAME, FIRST_NAME, STATE
FROM EMPLOYEE_TBL
WHERE LAST_NAME LIKE '%E%';
```

QUERY2:

```
SELECT EMP_ID, LAST_NAME, FIRST_NAME, STATE
FROM EMPLOYEE_TBL
WHERE LAST_NAME LIKE '%EVENS%';
```

QUERY3:

```
SELECT EMP_ID, LAST_NAME, FIRST NAME, STATE
FROM EMPLOYEE_TBL
WHERE LAST_NAME LIKE 'ST%';
```

The SQL statements do not necessarily return the same results. More than likely, QUERY1 will return more rows than the other two queries. QUERY2 and QUERY3 are more specific as to the data desired for return, thus eliminating more possibilities than QUERY1 and speeding data retrieval time. Additionally, QUERY3 is probably faster than QUERY2 because the first letters of the string for which you are searching are specified (and the column LAST_NAME is likely to be indexed). QUERY3 can take advantage of an index.

> With QUERY1, you might retrieve all individuals with the last name Stevens; but can't Stevens also be spelled different ways? QUERY2 picks up all individuals with the last name Stevens and its various spellings. QUERY3 also picks up any last name starting with St; this is the only way to assure that you receive all the Stevens (Stephens).

Avoiding the OR Operator

Rewriting the SQL statement using the IN predicate instead of the OR operator consistently and substantially improves data retrieval speed. Your implementation will tell you about tools you can use to time or check the performance between the OR operator and the IN predicate. An example of how to rewrite an SQL statement taking the OR operator out and replacing the OR operator with the IN predicate follows:

> Hour 8, "Using Operators to Categorize Data," can be referenced for the use of the OR operator and the IN predicate.

The following is a query using the OR operator:

```
SELECT EMP_ID, LAST_NAME, FIRST_NAME
FROM EMPLOYEE_TBL
WHERE CITY = 'INDIANAPOLIS'
   OR CITY = 'BROWNSBURG'
   OR CITY = 'GREENFIELD';
```

The following is the same query using the IN operator:

```
SELECT EMP_ID, LAST_NAME, FIRST_NAME
FROM EMPLOYEE_TBL
WHERE CITY IN ('INDIANAPOLIS', 'BROWNSBURG',
               'GREENFIELD');
```

The SQL statements retrieve the very same data; however, through testing and experience, you find that the data retrieval is measurably faster by replacing OR conditions with the IN, as in the second query.

Avoiding the HAVING Clause

The HAVING clause is a useful clause; however, you can't use it without cost. Using the HAVING clause causes the SQL optimizer extra work, which results in extra time. If possible, SQL statements should be written without the use of the HAVING clause.

Avoid Large Sort Operations

Large sort operations mean the use of the ORDER BY, GROUP BY, and HAVING clauses. Subsets of data must be stored in memory or to disk (if there is not enough space in allotted memory) whenever sort operations are performed. You must often sort data. The main point is that these sort operations affect an SQL statement's response time.

Use Stored Procedures

Stored procedures should be created for SQL statements executed on a regular basis—particularly large transactions or queries. Stored procedures are simply SQL statements that are compiled and permanently stored in the database in an executable format.

NEW TERM Normally, when an SQL statement is issued in the database, the database must check the syntax and convert the statement into an executable format within the database (called *parsing*). The statement, once parsed, is stored in memory; however, it is not permanent. This means that when memory is needed for other operations, the statement may be ejected from memory. In the case of stored procedures, the SQL statement is always available in an executable format and remains in the database until it is dropped like any other database object. Stored procedures are discussed in more detail in Hour 22, "Advanced SQL Topics."

Disabling Indexes During Batch Loads

When a user submits a transaction to the database (INSERT, UPDATE, or DELETE), an entry is made to both the database table and any indexes associated with the table being modified. This means that if there is an index on the EMPLOYEE table, and a user updates the EMPLOYEE table, an update also occurs to the index associated with the EMPLOYEE table. In a transactional environment, the fact that a write to an index occurs every time a write to the table occurs is usually not an issue.

During batch loads, however, an index can actually cause serious performance degradation. A batch load may consist of hundreds, thousands, or millions of manipulation statements or transactions. Because of their volume, batch loads take a long time to complete and are normally scheduled during off-peak hours—usually during weekends or evenings. To optimize performance during a batch load—which may equate to decreasing the time it takes the batch load to complete from 12 hours to 6 hours—it is recommended that the indexes associated with the table affected during the load are dropped.

When the indexes are dropped, changes are written to the tables much faster, so the job completes faster. When the batch load is complete, the indexes should be rebuilt. During the rebuild of the indexes, the indexes will be populated with all of the appropriate data from the tables. Although it may take a while for an index to be created on a large table, the overall time expended if you drop the index and rebuild it is less.

Another advantage to rebuilding an index after a batch load completes is the reduction of fragmentation that is found in the index. When a database grows, records are added, removed, and updated, and fragmentation can occur. For any database that experiences a lot of growth, it is a good idea to periodically drop and rebuild large indexes. When an index is rebuilt, the number of physical extents that comprise the index are decreased, there is less disk I/O involved to read the index, the user gets results faster, and everyone is happy.

Performance Tools

Many relational databases have built-in tools that assist in SQL statement and database performance tuning. For example, Oracle has a tool called EXPLAIN PLAN that shows the user the execution plan of an SQL statement. There is another tool in Oracle that measures the actual elapsed time of a SQL statement—TKPROF. In SQL Server, there are numerous SET commands that can be used to measure the performance of the database and SQL statements. Check with your DBA and implementation documentation for more information on tools that may be available to you.

Summary

You have learned the meaning of tuning SQL statements in a relational database. You have learned that there are two basic types of tuning: database tuning and SQL statement tuning—both of which are vital to the efficient operation of the database and SQL statements within it. Each is equally important and cannot be optimally tuned without the other. Tuning the database falls to the DBA, whereas tuning SQL statements falls to the individuals writing the statements. This book is more concerned with the latter.

You have read about methods for tuning an SQL statement, starting with a statement's actual readability, which does not directly improve performance but aids the programmer in the development and management of statements. One of the main issues in SQL statement performance is the use of indexes. There are times to use indexes and times to avoid using them. A full table scan is performed when a table is read and an index is not used. In a full table scan, each row of data in a table is completely read. Other considerations for statement tuning, such as the arrangement of elements in a query, were discussed. Of foremost importance is the placement of the most restrictive condition in a statement's WHERE clause. For all measures taken to improve SQL statement performance, it is important to understand the data itself, database design and relationships, and the users' needs as far as accessing the database.

Like building indexes on tables, SQL statement tuning often involves extensive testing, which can be qualified as trial and error. There is no one way to tune a database or SQL statements within a database. All databases are different, as the business needs for each company are different. These differences affect the data within the database and the methods in which the data is retrieved. It is your job to crack the riddle of the most efficient SQL statement design for optimal database performance.

Q&A

Q **By following what I have learned about performance, what realistic performance gains, as far as data retrieval time, can I really expect to see?**

A Realistically, you could see performance gains from fractions of a second to minutes, hours, or even days.

Q **How can I test my SQL statements for performance?**

A Each implementation should have a tool or system to check performance. Oracle7 was used to test the SQL statements in this book. Oracle has several tools for use in checking performance. Some of these tools are called FXPLAIN PLAN, TKPROF, and SET commands. Check your particular implementation for tools that are similar to Oracle's.

17

Workshop

The following workshop is composed of a series of quiz questions and practical exercises. The quiz questions are designed to test your overall understanding of the current material. The practical exercises are intended to afford you the opportunity to apply the concepts discussed during the current hour, as well as build upon the knowledge acquired in previous hours of study. Please take time to complete the quiz questions and exercises before continuing. Refer to Appendix C, "Answers to Quizzes and Exercises," for answers.

Quiz

1. Would the use of a unique index on a small table be of any benefit?
2. What happens when the optimizer chooses not to use an index on a table when a query has been executed?
3. Should the most restrictive clause(s) be placed before the join condition(s) or after the join conditions in the WHERE clause?

Exercises

Rewrite the following SQL statements to improve their performance. Use the
EMPLOYEE_TBL and the EMPLOYEE_PAY_TBL as described here:

EMPLOYEE_TBL

Column	Type	Constraint
EMP_ID	VARCHAR2(9)	NOT NULL PRIMARY KEY,
LAST_NAME	VARCHAR2(15)	NOT NULL,
FIRST_NAME	VARCHAR2(15)	NOT NULL,
MIDDLE_NAME	VARCHAR2(15),	
ADDRESS	VARCHAR2(30)	NOT NULL,
CITY	VARCHAR2(15)	NOT NULL,
STATE	CHAR(2)	NOT NULL,
ZIP	NUMBER(5)	NOT NULL,
PHONE	CHAR(10),	
PAGER	CHAR(10),	

    CONSTRAINT EMP_PK PRIMARY KEY (EMP_ID)

EMPLOYEE_PAY_TBL

Column	Type	Constraint
EMP_ID	VARCHAR2(9)	NOT NULL PRIMARY KEY,
POSITION	VARCHAR2(15)	NOT NULL,
DATE_HIRE	DATE,	
PAY_RATE	NUMBER(4,2)	NOT NULL,
DATE_LAST_RAISE	DATE,	
SALARY	NUMBER(8,2),	
BONUS	NUMBER(8,2),	

    CONSTRAINT EMP_FK FOREIGN KEY (EMP_ID)
      REFERENCES EMPLOYEE_TBL (EMP_ID)

a.

```
SELECT EMP_ID, LAST_NAME, FIRST_NAME,
        PHONE
  FROM EMPLOYEE_TBL
  WHERE SUBSTR(PHONE, 1, 3) = '317' OR
        SUBSTR(PHONE, 1, 3) = '812' OR
        SUBSTR(PHONE, 1, 3) = '765';
```

b.

```
SELECT LAST_NAME, FIRST_NAME
   FROM EMPLOYEE_TBL
   WHERE LAST_NAME LIKE '%ALL%';
```

c.

```
SELECT E.EMP_ID, E.LAST_NAME, E.FIRST_NAME,
          EP.SALARY
   FROM EMPLOYEE_TBL E,
   EMPLOYEE_PAY_TBL EP
   WHERE LAST_NAME LIKE 'S%'
   AND E.EMP_ID = EP.EMP_ID;
```

17

PART VI

Using SQL to Manage Users and Security

Hour

Hour 18

Managing Database Users

During this hour, you learn about one of the most fundamental purposes for any relational database: managing database users. You will learn the concepts behind creating users in SQL, user security, the user versus the schema, user profiles, user attributes, and tools users utilize.

The highlights of this hour include

- Types of users
- User management
- The user's place in the database
- The user versus the schema
- User sessions
- Altering a user's attributes
- User profiles
- Dropping users from the database
- Tools utilized by users

The SQL standard refers to a database user identification as an *Authorization Identifier* (authID). In most major implementations, authIDs are referred to simply as *users*. This book refers to Authorization Identifiers as users, database users, usernames, or database user accounts. The SQL standard states that the Authorization Identifier is a name by which the system knows the database user.

Users Are the Reason

Users are the reason for the season—the season of designing, creating, implementing, and maintaining any database. The user's needs are taken into consideration when the database is designed, and the final goal in implementing a database is making the database available to users, who in turn utilize the database that you and possibly many others have had a hand in developing.

A common perception of users is that if there were no users, nothing bad would ever happen to the database. Although this statement reeks with truth, the database was nevertheless created to hold data so that users can function in their day-to-day jobs.

Although user management is often the database administrator's implicit task, other individuals sometimes take a part in the user management process. User management is vital in the life of a relational database and is ultimately managed through the use of SQL concepts and commands, although varied from vendor to vendor.

Types of Users

There are several types of database users:

- Data entry clerks
- Programmers
- System engineers
- Database administrators
- System analysts
- Developers
- Testers
- Management
- End user

Each type of user has its own set of job functions (and problems), all of which are critical to their daily survival and job security. Furthermore, each type of user has different levels of authority and its own place in the database.

Who Manages Users?

A company's management staff is responsible for the day-to-day management of users; however, the database administrator or other assigned individuals are ultimately responsible for the management of users within the database.

The *database administrator* usually handles the creation of the database user accounts, roles, privileges, profiles, as well as dropping those user accounts from the database. Because it can become an overwhelming task in a large and active environment, some companies have a security officer who assists the database administrator with the user management process.

The *security officer*, if one is assigned, is usually responsible for the paperwork, relaying to the database administrator a user's job requirements, and letting the database administrator know when a user no longer requires access to the database.

The *system analyst*, or system administrator, is usually responsible for the operating system security, which entails creating users and assigning appropriate privileges. The security officer also may assist the system analyst in the same way he or she does the database administrator.

18

The User's Place in the Database

A user should be given the roles and privileges necessary to accomplish his or her job. No user should have database access that extends beyond the scope of his or her job duties. Protecting the data is the whole reason for setting up user accounts and security. Data can be damaged or lost, even if unintentionally, if the wrong user has access to the wrong data. When the user no longer requires database access, that user's account should be either removed from the database or disabled.

All users have their place in the database; some have more responsibilities than others. Database users are like parts of a human body—all work together in unison (at least that is the way it is supposed to be) to accomplish some goal.

How Does a User Differ from a Schema?

NEW TERM   A database's objects are associated with database user accounts, called schemas. A *schema* is a set of database objects that a database user owns. This database user is called the *schema owner*. The difference between a regular database user and a schema owner is that a schema owner owns objects within the database, whereas most users do not own objects. Most users are given database accounts to access data that is contained in other schemas.

The Management Process

A stable user management system is mandatory for data security in any database system. The user management system starts with the new user's immediate supervisor, who should initiate the access request, and then go through the company's approval authorities, at which time the request, if accepted by management, is routed to the security officer or database administrator, who takes action. A good notification process is necessary; the supervisor and the user must be notified that the user account has been created and that access to the database has been granted. The user account password should only be given to the user, who should immediately change the password upon initial login to the database.

You must check your particular implementation for the creation of users. Also refer to company policies and procedures when creating and managing users. The following section compares the user creation processes in Oracle, Sybase, and Microsoft SQL Server.

Creating Users

The creation of database users involves the use of SQL-type commands within the database. There is no one standard command for creating database users in SQL; each implementation has a method for doing so. Some implementations have similar commands, while others vary in syntax. The basic concept is the same, regardless of the implementation.

When the database administrator or assigned security officer receives a user account request, the request should be analyzed for the necessary information. The information should include your particular company's requirements for establishing a user ID.

Some items that should be included are Social Security number, full name, address, phone number, office or department name, assigned database, and sometimes, a suggested user ID.

There are syntactical examples of creating users compared between two different implementations shown in the following sections.

Creating Users in Oracle

Steps for creating a user account in an Oracle database:

1. Create the database user account with default settings.

2. Grant appropriate privileges to the user account.

The following is the syntax for creating a user:

SYNTAX

```
CREATE USER USER_ID
IDENTIFIED BY [PASSWORD | EXTERNALLY ]
[ DEFAULT TABLESPACE TABLESPACE_NAME ]
[ TEMPORARY TABLESPACE TABLESPACE_NAME ]
[ QUOTA (INTEGER (K | M) | UNLIMITED) ON TABLESPACE_NAME ]
[ PROFILE PROFILE_TYPE ]
[PASSWORD EXPIRE |ACCOUNT [LOCK | UNLOCK]
```

> The previous syntax for creating users can be used to add a user to an Oracle database, as well as a few other, major relational database implementations.

NEW TERM If you are not using Oracle, do not overly concern yourself with some of the options in this syntax. A *tablespace* is a logical area that houses database objects, such as tables and indexes. The DEFAULT TABLESPACE is the tablespace in which objects created by the particular user reside. The TEMPORARY TABLESPACE is the tablespace used for sort operations (table joins, ORDER BY, GROUP BY) from queries executed by the user. The QUOTA is space limits placed on a particular tablespace to which the user has access. PROFILE is a particular database profile that has been assigned to the user.

The following is the syntax for granting privileges to the user account:

SYNTAX

```
GRANT PRIV1 [ , PRIV2, ... ] TO USERNAME | ROLE [, USERNAME ]
```

The GRANT statement can grant one or more privileges to one or more users in the same statement. The privilege(s) can also be granted to a role, which in turn can be granted to a user(s).

Creating Users in Sybase and Microsoft SQL Server

The steps for creating a user account in a Sybase and Microsoft SQL Server database follow:

1. Create the database user account for SQL Server and assign a password and a default database for the user.

2. Add the user to the appropriate database(s).

3. Grant appropriate privileges to the user account.

The following is the syntax for creating the user account:

```
SP_ADDLOGIN USER_ID ,PASSWORD [, DEFAULT_DATABASE ]
```

The following is the syntax for adding the user to a database:

```
SP_ADDUSER USER_ID [, NAME_IN_DB [, GRPNAME ] ]
```

The following is the syntax for granting privileges to the user account:

```
GRANT PRIV1 [ , PRIV2, ... ] TO USER_ID
```

> The discussion of privileges within a relational database are further elaborated on during Hour 19, "Managing Database Security."

CREATE SCHEMA

Schemas are created via the CREATE SCHEMA statement.

The following is the syntax:

```
CREATE SCHEMA [ SCHEMA_NAME ] [ USER_ID ]
            [ DEFAULT CHARACTER SET CHARACTER_SET ]
            [PATH SCHEMA NAME [ ,SCHEMA NAME] ]
            [ SCHEMA_ELEMENT_LIST ]
```

The following is an example:

```
CREATE SCHEMA USER1
CREATE TABLE TBL1
  (COLUMN1    DATATYPE    [NOT NULL],
   COLUMN2    DATATYPE    [NOT NULL]...)
CREATE TABLE TBL2
  (COLUMN1    DATATYPE    [NOT NULL],
   COLUMN2    DATATYPE    [NOT NULL]...)
GRANT SELECT ON TBL1 TO USER2
GRANT SELECT ON TBL2 TO USER2
[ OTHER DDL COMMANDS ... ]
```

The following is the application of the CREATE SCHEMA command in one implementation:

```
CREATE SCHEMA AUTHORIZATION USER1
CREATE TABLE EMP
   (ID        NUMBER         NOT NULL,
    NAME      VARCHAR2(10)   NOT NULL)
CREATE TABLE CUST
   (ID        NUMBER         NOT NULL,
    NAME      VARCHAR2(10)   NOT NULL)
GRANT SELECT ON TBL1 TO USER2
GRANT SELECT ON TBL2 TO USER2
/
```

```
Schema created.
```

The AUTHORIZATION keyword is added to the CREATE SCHEMA command. This example was performed in an Oracle database. This goes to show you, as you have also seen in this book's previous examples, that vendors' syntax for commands often varies in their implementations.

Some implementations may not support the CREATE SCHEMA command. However, schemas can be implicitly created when a user creates objects. The CREATE SCHEMA command is simply a single-step method of accomplishing this task. After objects have been created by a user, the user can grant privileges that allow access to the user's objects to other users.

18

Dropping a Schema

A schema can be removed from the database using the DROP SCHEMA statement. There are two options that must be considered when dropping a schema. First, the RESTRICT option. If RESTRICT is specified, an error occurs if objects currently exist in the schema. The second option is CASCADE. The CASCADE option must be used if any objects currently exist in the schema. Remember that when you drop a schema, you also drop all database objects associated with that schema.

The syntax is as follows:

```
DROP SCHEMA SCHEMA_NAME { RESTRICT | CASCADE }
```

> The absence of objects in a schema is possible because objects, such as tables, can be dropped using the DROP TABLE command. Some implementations may have a procedure or command that drops a user, which can also be used to drop a schema. If the DROP SCHEMA command is not available in your implementation, you can remove a schema by removing the user that owns the schema objects.

Altering Users

A very important part of managing users is the ability to alter a user's attributes after user creation. Life for the database administrator would be a lot simpler if personnel with user accounts were never promoted, never left the company, or if the addition of new employees was minimized. In the real world, high personnel turnover, as well as users' duties, is a reality and a significant factor in user management. Nearly everyone changes jobs or job duties, therefore, user privileges in a database must be adjusted to fit a user's needs.

The following is one implementation's example of altering the current state of a user.

For Oracle:

```
ALTER USER USER_ID [ IDENTIFIED BY PASSWORD | EXTERNALLY |GLOBALLY AS 'CN=USER']
[ DEFAULT TABLESPACE TABLESPACE_NAME ]
[ TEMPORARY TABLESPACE TABLESPACE_NAME ]
[ QUOTA  INTEGER K|M |UNLIMITED ON TABLESPACE_NAME ]
[ PROFILE PROFILE_NAME ]
[PASSWORD EXPIRE]
[ACCOUNT [LOCK |UNLOCK]]
[ DEFAULT ROLE ROLE1 [, ROLE2 ] | ALL
[ EXCEPT ROLE1 [, ROLE2 | NONE ] ]
```

Many of the user's attributes can be altered in this syntax. Unfortunately, not all implementations provide a simple command that allows the manipulation of database users. Some implementations also provide GUI tools that allow users to be created, modified, and removed.

> You must check your particular implementation for the correct syntax for altering users. Oracle's ALTER USER syntax is shown here. In most major implementations, there is a tool used to alter or change a user's roles, privileges, attributes, and password.

A user can change an established password. You must check your particular implementation for the exact syntax or tool used to reset a password. The ALTER USER command is typically used in Oracle.

User Sessions

A user database *session* is the time that begins at database login time and ends when a user logs out. During the time a user is logged in to the database (a user session), the user can perform various actions, such as queries and transactions.

An SQL session is initiated when a user connects from the client to the server using the CONNECT statement. Upon the establishment of the connection and the initiation of the session, any number of transactions can be started and performed until the connection is disconnected; at that time, the database user session terminates.

Users can explicitly connect and disconnect from the database, starting and terminating SQL sessions, using commands such as the following:

```
CONNECT TO DEFAULT | STRING1 [ AS STRING2 ] [ USER STRING3 ]

DISCONNECT DEFAULT | CURRENT | ALL | STRING

SET CONNECTION DEFAULT | STRING
```

18

Remember that the syntax varies between implementations. In addition, most database users do not manually issue the commands to connect or disconnect from the database. Most users access the database through a vendor-provided or third-party tool that prompts the user for a username and password, which in turn connects to the database and initiates a database user session.

User sessions can be—and often are—monitored by the database administrator or other personnel having interest in user activities. A user session is associated with a particular user account when a user is monitored. A database user session is ultimately represented as a process on the host operating system.

Removing User Access

Removing a user from the database or disallowing a user's access can easily be accomplished through a couple of simple commands. Once again, however, variations among different implementations are numerous, so you must check your particular implementation for the syntax or tools used to accomplish user removal or access revocation.

Methods for removing user database access:

- Change the user's password.
- Drop the user account from the database.
- Revoke appropriate previously granted privileges from the user.

The DROP command can be used in some implementations to drop a user from the database:

```
DROP USER USER_ID [ CASCADE ]
```

The REVOKE command is the counterpart of the GRANT command in many implementations, allowing privileges that have been granted to a user to be revoked. An example syntax for this command in some implementations follows:

```
REVOKE PRIV1 [ ,PRIV2, ... ] FROM USERNAME
```

Tools Utilized by Database Users

Some people say that you do not need to know SQL to perform database queries. In a sense, they may be correct; however, knowing SQL definitely helps querying a database, even when using Graphical User Interface (GUI) tools. Even though GUI tools are good and should be used when available, it is most beneficial to understand what is happening behind the scenes, so that you can maximize the efficiency of utilizing these user-friendly tools.

Many GUI tools that aid the database user automatically generate SQL code by navigating through windows, responding to prompts, and selecting options. There are reporting tools that generate reports. Forms can be created for users to query, update, insert, or delete data from a database. There are tools that convert data into graphs and charts. There are database administration tools used to monitor database performance, and some that allow remote connectivity to a database. Database vendors provide some of these tools, while others are provided as third-party tools from other vendors.

Summary

All databases have users, whether it be one or thousands. The user is the reason for the database. There are three basic steps in the management of users. First, the database user account must be created. Second, privileges must be granted to the user to accommodate the tasks the user must perform within the database. Finally, a user account must either be removed from the database or certain privileges within the database must be revoked from a user.

Some of the most common tasks of managing users have been touched on; too much detail is avoided here, because most databases differ in the user management process. However, it is important to discuss user management due to its relationship with SQL. Many of the commands used to manage users have not been defined or discussed in great detail by the ANSI standard, but the concept remains the same.

Q&A

Q Is there an SQL standard for adding users to a database?

A Some commands and concepts are provided by ANSI, although each implementation and each company has its own commands, tools, and rules for creating or adding users to a database.

Q Can user access be temporarily suspended without removing the user ID completely from the database?

A Yes. User access can temporarily be suspended by simply changing the user's password or by revoking privileges that allow the user to connect to the database. The functionality of the user account can be reinstated by changing and issuing the password to the user, or by granting privileges to the user that may have been revoked.

Q Can a user change his or her own password?

A Yes, in most major implementations. Upon user creation or addition to the database, a generic password is usually given to the user and must be changed as quickly as possible by the user to a password of his or her choice. After this has been accomplished, even the database administrator does not know the user's password.

Workshop

The following workshop is composed of a series of quiz questions and practical exercises. The quiz questions are designed to test your overall understanding of the current material. The practical exercises are intended to afford you the opportunity to apply the concepts discussed during the current hour, as well as build upon the knowledge acquired in previous hours of study. Please take time to complete the quiz questions and exercises before continuing. Refer to Appendix C, "Answers to Quizzes and Exercises," for answers.

Quiz

1. What command is used to establish a session?

2. Which option must be used to drop a schema that still contains database objects?

3. What statement is used to remove a database privilege?

4. What command creates a grouping or collection of tables, views, and privileges?

Exercise

1. Describe or list the steps that allow a new employee database access.

Hour **19**

Managing Database Security

During this hour, you learn the basics of implementing and managing security within a relational database using SQL and SQL-related commands. Each major implementation differs on syntax with its security commands, but the overall security for the relational database follows the same basic guidelines discussed in the ANSI standard. You must check your particular implementation for syntax and any special guidelines for security.

The highlights of this hour include

- Database security
- Security versus user management
- Database system privileges
- Database object privileges
- Granting privileges to users
- Revoking privileges from users
- Security features in the database

What Is Database Security?

Database security is the process of simply protecting the data from unauthorized usage. Unauthorized usage includes data access by database users who should have access to part of the database, but not all parts. This protection also includes the act of policing against unauthorized connectivity and distribution of privileges. There are many user levels in a database, from the database creator, individuals responsible for maintaining the database (such as the DBA), database programmers, and end users. End users, although individuals with the most limited access, are the users for which the database exists. Each user has a different level of access to the database and should be limited to the fewest number of privileges needed to perform his or her particular job.

How Does Security Differ from User Management?

You may be wondering what the difference between user management and database security is. After all, the last hour discussed user management, which seems to cover security. Although user management and database security are definitely related, each has its own purpose and work together to achieve a secure database.

A well-planned and maintained user management program goes hand-in-hand with the overall security of a database. Users are assigned user accounts and passwords that give them general access to the database. The user accounts within the database should be stored with information, such as user's actual name, office and department in which the user works, telephone number or extension, and the database name to which the user has access. An initial password for the database user account is assigned by the DBA or security officer and should be changed immediately by the new user.

Security entails more; for instance, if a user no longer requires certain privileges granted to him or her, those privileges should be revoked. If a user no longer requires access to the database, the user account should be dropped from the database.

NEW TERM   Generally, *user management* is the process of creating user accounts, removing user accounts, and keeping track of users' actions within the database. *Database security* is going a step further by granting privileges for specific database access, revoking those privileges from users, and taking measures to protect other parts of the database, such as the underlying database files.

Because this is an SQL book, not a database book, it focuses on database privileges. However, you should keep in mind that there are other aspects to database security, such as the protection of underlying database files, which holds equal importance with the distribution of database privileges. High-level database security can become complex and differs immensely between relational database implementations.

What Are Privileges?

Privileges are authority levels used to access the database itself, access objects within the database, manipulate data in the database, and perform various administrative functions within the database. Privileges are issued via the GRANT command and are taken away via the REVOKE command.

Just because a user can connect to a database does not mean that the user can access data within a database. Access to data within the database is handled through these privileges. There are two types of privileges:

1. System privileges
2. Object privileges

System Privileges

System privileges are those that allow database users to perform administrative actions within the database, such as creating a database, dropping a database, creating user accounts, dropping users, dropping and altering database objects, altering the state of objects, altering the state of the database, and other actions that could result in serious repercussions if not carefully used.

System privileges vary greatly among the different relational database vendors, so you must check your particular implementation for all of the available system privileges and their correct usage.

The following are some common system privileges in Sybase:

```
CREATE DATABASE
CREATE DEFAULT
CREATE PROCEDURE
```

19

```
CREATE RULE
CREATE VIEW
DUMP DATABASE
DUMP TRANSACTION
EXECUTE
```

The following are some common system privileges in Oracle:

```
CREATE TABLE
CREATE ANY TABLE
ALTER ANY TABLE
DROP TABLE
CREATE USER
DROP USER
ALTER USER
ALTER DATABASE
ALTER SYSTEM
BACKUP ANY TABLE
SELECT ANY TABLE
```

Object Privileges

NEW TERM   *Object privileges* are authority levels on objects, meaning you must have been granted the appropriate privileges to perform certain operations on database objects. For example, to select data from another user's table, the user must first grant you access to do so. Object privileges are granted to users in the database by the object's owner. Remember that this owner is also called the schema owner.

The ANSI standard for privileges includes the following object privileges:

USAGE   Authorizes usage of a specific domain

SELECT   Allows access to a specific table

INSERT(column_name)   Allows data insertion to a specific column of a specified table

INSERT   Allows insertion of data into all columns of a specific table

UPDATE(column_name)   Allows a specific column of a specified table to be updated

UPDATE   Allows all columns of a specified table to be updated

REFERENCES(column_name)   Allows a reference to a specified column of a specified table in integrity constraints; this privilege is required for all integrity constraints

REFERENCES   Allows references to all columns of a specified table

> The owner of an object has been automatically granted all privileges that relate to the objects owned. These privileges have also been granted with the GRANT OPTION. The GRANT OPTION is discussed in the "GRANT OPTION," section later this hour, which is a nice feature available in some SQL implementations.

These object-level privileges are those privileges that should be used to grant and restrict access to objects in a schema. These privileges can be used to protect objects in one schema from database users that have access to another schema in the same database.

There are a variety of object privileges available among different implementations not listed in this section. The ability to delete data from another user's object is another common object privilege available in many implementations. Be sure to check your implementation documentation for all of the available object-level privileges.

Who Grants and Revokes Privileges?

The database administrator (DBA) is usually the one who issues the GRANT and REVOKE commands, although a security administrator, if one exists, may have the authority to do so. The authority on what to GRANT or REVOKE would come from management and would hopefully be in writing.

The owner of an object must grant privileges to other users in the database on the object. Even the DBA cannot grant database users privileges on objects that do not belong to the DBA, although there are ways to work around that.

Controlling User Access

User access is primarily controlled by a user account and password, but that is not enough to access the database in most major implementations. The creation of a user account is only the first step in allowing access to the database, as well as controlling that access.

19

After the user account has been created, the database administrator, security officer, or designated individual must be able to assign appropriate system-level privileges to a user for that user to be allowed to perform actual functions within the database, such as creating tables or selecting from tables. What good is it to connect to a database if you cannot do anything? Furthermore, the schema owner usually needs to grant database users access to objects in the schema so that the user can do his or her job.

There are two commands in SQL that allow database access control involving the assignment of privileges and the revocation of privileges. The following are the two commands used to distribute both system and object privileges in a relational database:

GRANT

REVOKE

The GRANT Command

The GRANT command is used to grant both system-level and object-level privileges to an existing database user account.

The syntax is as follows:

```
GRANT PRIVILEGE1 [, PRIVILEGE2 ][ ON OBJECT ]
TO USERNAME [ WITH GRANT OPTION | ADMIN OPTION]
```

Granting one privilege to a user is as follows:

INPUT

```
GRANT SELECT ON EMPLOYEE_TBL TO USER1;
```

OUTPUT

Grant succeeded.

Granting multiple privileges to a user is as follows:

INPUT

```
GRANT SELECT, INSERT ON EMPLOYEE_TBL TO USER1;
```

OUTPUT

Grant succeeded.

Notice that when granting multiple privileges to a user in a single statement, each privilege is separated by a comma.

Granting privileges to multiple users is as follows:

INPUT   `GRANT SELECT, INSERT ON EMPLOYEE_TBL TO USER1, USER2;`

OUTPUT   Grant succeeded.

 Notice the phrase Grant succeeded denoting the successful completion of each grant statement. This is the feedback that you receive when you issue these statements in the implementation used for the book examples (Oracle). Most implementations have some sort of feedback, although the phrase used may vary.

GRANT OPTION

The GRANT OPTION is a very powerful GRANT command option. When an object's owner grants privileges on an object to another user with the GRANT OPTION, the new user can also grant privileges on that object to other users, even though the user does not actually own the object. An example follows:

INPUT   `GRANT SELECT ON EMPLOYEE_TBL TO USER1 WITH GRANT OPTION;`

OUTPUT   Grant succeeded.

ADMIN OPTION

The ADMIN OPTION is similar to the GRANT OPTION in that the user that has been granted the privileges also inherits the ability to grant those privileges to another user. The GRANT OPTION is used for object-level privileges, whereas the ADMIN OPTION is used for system-level privileges. When a user grants system privileges to another user with the ADMIN OPTION, the new user can also grant the system-level privileges to any other user. An example follows:

INPUT   `GRANT CREATE TABLE TO USER1 WITH ADMIN OPTION;`

OUTPUT   Grant succeeded.

19

When a user that has granted privileges using either the GRANT OPTION or the ADMIN OPTION has been dropped from the database, the privileges that the user granted are disassociated with the users to which the privileges were granted.

The REVOKE Command

The REVOKE command removes privileges that have been granted to database users. The REVOKE command has two options—RESTRICT and CASCADE. When the RESTRICT option is used, REVOKE succeeds only if the privileges specified explicitly in the REVOKE statement leave no other users with abandoned privileges. The CASCADE option revokes any privileges that would otherwise be left with other users. In other words, if the owner of an object granted USER1 privileges with the GRANT OPTION, USER1 granted USER2 privileges with the GRANT OPTION, and then the owner revokes USER1's privileges, the CASCADE also removes the privileges from USER2.

NEW TERM   *Abandoned privileges* are privileges that are left with a user who was granted privileges with the GRANT OPTION from a user who has been dropped from the database or had his/her privileges revoked.

The syntax is as follows:

```
REVOKE PRIVILEGE1 [, PRIVILEGE2 ] [ GRANT OPTION FOR ] ON OBJECT
FROM USER { RESTRICT | CASCADE }
```

The following is an example:

INPUT   `REVOKE INSERT ON EMPLOYEE_TBL FROM USER1;`

OUTPUT   Revoke succeeded.

Controlling Access on Individual Columns

Instead of granting object privileges (INSERT, UPDATE, or DELETE) on a table as a whole, you can grant privileges on specific columns in the table to restrict user access, as shown in the following example example:

INPUT   `GRANT UPDATE (NAME) ON EMPLOYEES TO PUBLIC;`

OUTPUT   Grant succeeded.

The PUBLIC Database Account

The PUBLIC database user account is a database account that represents all users in the database. All users are part of the public account. If a privilege is granted to the PUBLIC account, all database users have the privilege. Likewise, if a privilege is revoked from the PUBLIC account, the privilege is revoked from all database users, unless that privilege was explicitly granted to a specific user. The following is an example:

```
GRANT SELECT ON EMPLOYEE_TBL TO PUBLIC;
```

```
Grant succeeded.
```

> Extreme caution should be taken when granting privileges to PUBLIC; all database users acquire the privileges granted.

Groups of Privileges

Some implementations have groups of privileges in the database. These groups of permissions are referred to with different names. Having a group of privileges allows simplicity for granting and revoking common privileges to and from users. For example, if a group consists of ten privileges, the group can be granted to a user instead of all ten privileges.

NEW TERM   SQLBase has groups of privileges called *authority levels*, whereas these groups of privileges in Oracle are called *roles*. SQLBase and Oracle both include the following groups of privileges with their implementations:

CONNECT

RESOURCE

DBA

The CONNECT group allows a user to connect to the database and perform operations on any database objects to which the user has access.

The RESOURCE group allows a user to create objects, drop objects he or she owns, grant privileges to objects he or she owns, and so on.

The DBA group allows a user to perform any function within the database. The user can access any database object and perform any operation with this group.

19

An example for granting a group of privileges to a user follows:

INPUT

```
GRANT DBA TO USER1;
```

OUTPUT

```
Grant succeeded.
```

> Each implementation differs on the use of groups of database privileges. If available, this feature should be used for ease of database security administration.

Controlling Privileges Through Roles

NEW TERM   A *role* is an object created in the database that contains group-like privileges. Roles can reduce security maintenance by not having to grant explicit privileges directly to a user. Group privilege management is much easier to handle with roles. A role's privileges can be changed, and such a change is transparent to the user.

If a user needs SELECT and UPDATE table privileges on a table at a specified time within an application, a role with those privileges can temporarily be assigned until the transaction is complete.

When a role is first created, it has no real value other than being a role within a database. It can be granted to users or other roles. Let's say that a schema named APP01 grants the SELECT table privilege to the RECORDS_CLERK role on the EMPLOYEE_PAY table. Any user or role granted the RECORDS_CLERK role now would have SELECT privileges on the EMPLOYEE_PAY table.

Likewise, if APP01 revoked the SELECT table privilege from the RECORDS_CLERK role on the EMPLOYEE_PAY table, any user or role granted the RECORDS_CLERK role would no longer have SELECT privileges on that table.

The CREATE ROLE Statement

A role is created with the CREATE ROLE statement.

SYNTAX

```
CREATE ROLE role_name;
```

Granting privileges to roles is the same as granting privileges to a user. Study the following example.

INPUT	`CREATE ROLE RECORDS_CLERK;`
OUTPUT	`Role created.`
INPUT	`GRANT SELECT, INSERT, UPDATE, DELETE ON EMPLOYEE_PAY TO RECORDS_CLERK;`
OUTPUT	`Grant succeeded.`
INPUT	`GRANT RECORDS_CLERK TO USER1;`
OUTPUT	`Grant succeeded.`

The DROP ROLE Statement

A role is dropped using the DROP_ROLE statement.

SYNTAX

`DROP ROLE role_name;`

The following is an example:

INPUT	`DROP ROLE RECORDS_CLERK;`
OUTPUT	`Role dropped.`

19

The SET ROLE Statement

A role can be set for a user SQL session using the SET_ROLE statement.

SYNTAX

`SET ROLE role_name;`

The following is an example:

INPUT	`SET ROLE RECORDS_CLERK;`
OUTPUT	`Role set.`

You can set more than one role at once:

INPUT

```
SET ROLE RECORDS_CLERK, ROLE2, ROLE3;
```

OUTPUT

```
Role set.
```

In some implementations, such as Oracle, all roles granted to a user are automatically default roles, which means the roles will be set and available to the user as soon as the user logs in to the database.

Summary

You were shown the basics on implementing security in an SQL database or a relational database. You learned the basics of managing database users. The first step in implementing security at the database level for users is to create the user; after the user has been created, the user must be assigned certain privileges that allow the user access to specific parts of the database, and now ANSI allows the use of roles as discussed during this Hour. Privileges can be granted to users or roles. There are two types of privileges: system and object privileges.

System privileges are those that allow the user to perform various different tasks within the database, such as actually connecting to the database, creating tables, creating users, altering the state of the database, and so on. Object privileges are those that allow a user access to specific objects within the database, such as the ability to select data or manipulate data in a specific table.

There are two commands in SQL that allow a user to grant and revoke privileges to and from other users or roles in the database: GRANT and REVOKE. These two commands are used to control the overall administration of privileges in the database. Although there are many other considerations for implementing security in a relational database, the basics that relate to the language of SQL were discussed during this hour.

Q&A

Q If a user forgets his or her password, what should the user do to gain access to the database again?

A The user should go to his or her immediate management or an available help desk. A help desk should be able to reset a user's password. If not, the DBA or security officer can reset the password. The user should change the password to a password of his or her choosing as soon as the password is reset and the user is notified.

Q **What could I do if I wanted to grant CONNECT to a user, but the user does not need all the privileges that are assigned to the connect role?**

A You would simply not grant CONNECT, but only the privileges required. Should you ever grant CONNECT and the user no longer needs all the privileges that go with it, simply revoke CONNECT from the user and grant the specific privileges required.

Q **Why is it so important for the new user to change the password when received from whomever created the new user?**

A An initial password is assigned upon creation of the user ID. No one, not even the DBA or management, should know a user's password. The password should be kept a secret at all times to prevent another user from logging on to the database under another user's account.

Workshop

The following workshop is composed of a series of quiz questions and practical exercises. The quiz questions are designed to test your overall understanding of the current material. The practical exercises are intended to afford you the opportunity to apply the concepts discussed during the current hour, as well as build upon the knowledge acquired in previous hours of study. Please take time to complete the quiz questions and exercises before continuing. Refer to Appendix C, "Answers to Quizzes and Exercises," for answers.

Quiz

1. What option must a user have to grant another user privileges on an object not owned by the user?

2. When privileges are granted to PUBLIC, do all database users acquire the privileges, or just a listing of specified users?

3. What privilege is required to look at data in a specific table?

4. What type of privilege is SELECT?

Exercises

1. Write a statement to grant select access on a table called EMPLOYEE_TBL, which you own, to a user ID, RPLEW. It should allow RPLEW to grant privileges to another user on the same table.

2. Write the statement that revokes the connect role from both of the users in Exercise 1.

3. Write the statement that allows RPLEW to select, insert, and update the EMPLOYEE_TBL table.

19

PART VII

Summarized Data Structures

Hour

HOUR 20

Creating and Using Views and Synonyms

During this hour, you learn about performance, as well as how to create and drop views, how to use views for security, and how to provide simplicity in data retrieval for end users and reports. You also read a discussion on synonyms.

The highlights of this hour include

- What views are
- How views are used
- Views and security
- Storage of views
- Creating views
- Joining views
- Data manipulation in a view
- What synonyms are
- Managing synonyms
- Creation of synonyms
- Dropping synonyms

What Is a View?

A view is a virtual table. That is, a view looks like a table and acts like a table as far as a user is concerned. A view is actually a composition of a table in the form of a predefined query. For example, a view can be created from the EMPLOYEE_TBL table that contains only the employee's name and address, instead of all columns in the EMPLOYEE_TBL table. A view can contain all rows of a table or select rows from a table. A view can be created from one or many tables.

NEW TERM   A *view* is a predefined query that is stored in the database, has the appearance of an ordinary table, and is accessed like a table, but does not require physical storage.

When a view is created, a SELECT statement is actually run against the database, which defines the view. The SELECT statement used to define the view may simply contain column names from the table, or can be more explicitly written using various functions and calculations to manipulate or summarize the data that the user sees. Study the illustration of a view in Figure 20.1.

FIGURE 20.1

The view.

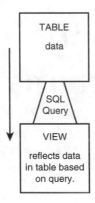

A view is considered a database object, although the view takes up no storage space on its own. The main difference between a view and a table is that data in a table consumes physical storage, whereas a view does not require physical storage because it is actually referring to data from a table.

A view is used in the same manner a table is used in the database, meaning that data can be selected from a view as it is from a table. Data can also be manipulated in a view, although there are some restrictions. The following sections discuss some common uses for views and how views are stored in the database.

If a table that was used to create a view is dropped, the view becomes inaccessible. You receive an error when trying to query against the view.

Views Can Be Utilized as a Form of Security

Views can be utilized as a form of security in the database. Say you have a table called EMPLOYEE_TBL. The EMPLOYEE_TBL includes employee names, addresses, phone numbers, emergency contacts, department, position, and salary or hourly pay. You have some temporary help come in to write some reports; you need a report of employees' names, addresses, and phone numbers. If you give access to the EMPLOYEE_TBL to the temporary help, they can see how much each of your employees receives in compensation—you do not want this to happen. To prevent that, you have created a view containing only the required information: employee name, address, and phone numbers. The temporary help can then be given access to the view to write the report without having access to the compensation columns in the table.

Views can be used to restrict user access to particular columns in a table or to rows in a table that meet specific conditions as defined in the WHERE clause of the view definition.

Views Can Be Utilized to Maintain Summarized Data

If you have a summarized data report in which the data in the table or tables is updated often and the report is created often, a view with summarized data may be an excellent choice.

For example, suppose that you have a table containing information about individuals, such as their city of residence, their sex, their salary, and their age. You could create a view based on the table that shows summarized figures for individuals for each city, such as the average age, average salary, total number of males, and total number of females. After the view is created, to retrieve this information from the base table(s), you can simply query the view instead of composing a SELECT statement that may, in some cases, turn out to be complex.

The only difference between the syntax for creating a view with summarized data and creating a view from a single or multiple tables is the use of aggregate functions. Review Hour 9, "Summarizing Data Results from a Query," for the use of aggregate functions.

20

How Is a View Stored?

A view is stored in memory only. A view takes up no storage space—as do other database objects—other than the space required to store the view definition itself. A view is owned by the view's creator or the schema owner. The view owner automatically has all applicable privileges on that view and can grant privileges on the view to other users, as with tables. The GRANT command's GRANT OPTION privilege works the same as on a table. See Hour 19, "Managing Database Security," for more information.

Creating Views

Views are created using the CREATE VIEW statement. Views can be created from a single table, multiple tables, or another view. To create a view, a user must have the appropriate system privilege according to the specific implementation.

The basic CREATE VIEW syntax is as follows:

```
CREATE [RECURSIVE]VIEW VIEW_NAME
[COLUMN NAME [,COLUMN NAME]]
[OF UDT NAME [UNDER TABLE NAME]
[REF IS COLUMN NAME SYSTEM GENERATED |USER GENERATED | DERIVED]
[COLUMN NAME WITH OPTIONS SCOPE TABLE NAME]]
 AS
{SELECT STATEMENT}
[WITH [CASCADED | LOCAL] CHECK OPTION]
```

The following subsections explore different methods for creating views using the CREATE VIEW statement.

There is no provision for an ALTER VIEW statement in ANSI SQL.

Creating a View from a Single Table

A view can be created from a single table. The WITH CHECK OPTION is discussed later this hour.

The syntax is as follows:

```
CREATE VIEW VIEW_NAME AS
SELECT * | COLUMN1 [, COLUMN2 ]
FROM TABLE_NAME
[ WHERE EXPRESSION1 [, EXPRESSION2 ]]
[ WITH CHECK OPTION ]
[ GROUP BY ]
```

The simplest form for creating a view is one based on the entire contents of a single table, as in the following example:

INPUT
```
CREAT VIEW CUSTOMERS AS
SELECT *
FROM CUSTOMER_TBL;
```

OUTPUT
```
View created.
```

The next example narrows the contents for a view by selecting only specified columns from the base table:

INPUT
```
CREATE VIEW EMP_VIEW AS
SELECT LAST_NAME, FIRST_NAME, MIDDLE_NAME
FROM EMPLOYEE_TBL;
```

OUTPUT
```
View Created.
```

Following is an example of how columns from the BASE TABLE can be combined or manipulated to form a column in a view. The view column is titled NAME by using an alias in the SELECT clause.

INPUT
```
CREATE VIEW NAMES AS
SELECT LAST_NAME || ', ' ||FIRST_NAME || ' ' || MIDDLE_NAME NAME
FROM EMPLOYEE_TBL;
```

OUTPUT
```
View created.
```

Now you select all data from the view that you created, called NAMES.

INPUT
```
SELECT *
FROM NAMES;
NAME
```

OUTPUT
```
----------------
STEPHENS, TINA D
PLEW, LINDA C
GLASS, BRANDON S
GLASS, JACOB
WALLACE, MARIAH
SPURGEON, TIFFANY
6 rows selected.
```

20

The following example shows how to create a view with summarized data from one or more underlying tables:

INPUT
```
CREATE VIEW CITY_PAY AS
SELECT E.CITY, AVG(P PAY_RATE) AVG_PAY
FROM EMPLOYEE_TBL E,
     EMPLOTEE_PAY_TBL P
WHERE E.EMP_ID = P.EMP_ID
GROUP BY E.CITY;
```

OUTPUT   View created.

Now, if you select from your summarized view:

INPUT
```
SELECT *
FROM CITY_PAY;
```

OUTPUT
```
CITY             AVG_PAY
--------------   -------
GREENWOOD
INDIANAPOLIS     13.33333
WHITELAND

3 rows selected.
```

By summarizing a view, SELECTs that may occur in the future are simplified against the underlying table of the view.

Creating a View from Multiple Tables

A view can be created from multiple tables by using a JOIN the SELECT statement. WITH CHECK OPTION is discussed later this hour. The syntax is as follows:

▼ SYNTAX
```
CREATE VIEW VIEW_NAME AS
SELECT * | COLUMN1 [, COLUMN2 ]
FROM TABLE_NAME1, TABLE_NAME2 [, TABLE_NAME3 ]
WHERE TABLE_NAME1 = TABLE_NAME2
[ AND TABLE_NAME1 = TABLE_NAME 3 ]
[ EXPRESSION1 ][, EXPRESSION2 ]
[ WITH CHECK OPTION ]
[ GROUP BY ]
```

The following is an example of creating a view from multiple tables:

INPUT
```
CREATE VIEW EMPLOYEE_SUMMARY AS
SELECT E.EMP_ID, E.LAST_NAME, P.POSITION, P.DATE_HIRE, P.PAY_RATE
FROM EMPLOYEE_TBL E,
     EMPLOYEE PAY_TBL P
WHERE E.EMP_ID = P.EMP_ID;
```

OUTPUT   View created.

Remember that when selecting data from multiple tables, the tables must be joined by common keys in the WHERE clause. A view is nothing more than a SELECT statement itself; therefore, tables are joined in a view definition the same as they are in a regular SELECT statement. Recall the use of table aliases to simplify the readability of a multiple-table query.

Creating a View from a View

SYNTAX

A view can be created from another view using the following format:

```
CREATE VIEW2 AS
SELECT * FROM VIEW1
```

Do Not Create Views too Deep

A view can be created from a view many layers deep (a view of a view of a view, and so on). How deep you can go is implementation-specific. The only problem with creating views based on other views is their manageability. For example, suppose that you create VIEW2 based on VIEW1 and then create VIEW3 based on VIEW2. If VIEW1 is dropped, VIEW2 and VIEW3 are no good. The underlying information that supports these views no longer exists. Therefore, always maintain a good understanding of the views in the database and on which other objects those views rely. See Figure 20.2 on view dependency.

FIGURE 20.2
View dependencies.

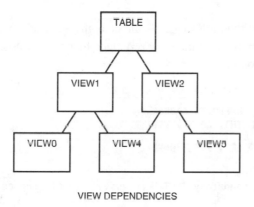

VIEW DEPENDENCIES

If a view is as easy and efficient to create from the base table as from another view, preference should go to the view being created from the BASE TABLE.

20

Figure 20.2 shows the relationship of views that are dependent not only on tables, but on other views. VIEW1 and VIEW2 are dependent on the TABLE. VIEW3 is dependent on VIEW1. VIEW4 is dependent on both VIEW1 and VIEW2. VIEW5 is dependent on VIEW2. Based on these relationships, the following can be concluded:

- If VIEW1 is dropped, VIEW3 and VIEW4 are invalid.
- If VIEW2 is dropped, VIEW4 and VIEW5 are invalid.
- If the TABLE is dropped, none of the views are valid.

The WITH CHECK OPTION

The WITH CHECK OPTION is a CREATE VIEW statement option. The purpose of the WITH CHECK OPTION is to ensure that all UPDATE and INSERTs satisfy the condition(s) in the view definition. If they do not satisfy the condition(s), the UPDATE or INSERT returns an error. The WITH CHECK OPTION has two options of its own: CASCADED and LOCAL. The WITH CHECK OPTION actually enforces referential integrity by checking the view's definition to see that it is not violated.

The following is an example of creating a view with the WITH CHECK OPTION:

INPUT

```
CREATE VIEW EMPLOYEE_PAGERS AS
SELECT LAST_NAME, FIRST_NAME, PAGER
FROM EMPLOYEE_TBL
WHERE PAGER IS NOT NULL
WITH CHECK OPTION;
```

OUTPUT

```
View created.
```

The WITH CHECK OPTION in this case should deny the entry of any NULL values in the view's PAGER column, because the view is defined by data that does not have a NULL value in the PAGER column.

Try to insert a NULL value in the PAGER column:

INPUT

```
INSERT INTO EMPLOYEE PAGERS
VALUES ('SMITH','JOHN',NULL);
```

OUTPUT

```
insert into employee_pagers
            *
ERROR at line 1:
ORA-01400: mandatory (NOT NULL) column is missing or NULL during insert
```

The WITH CHECK OPTION worked.

CASCADED Versus LOCAL

There are two options when choosing to use the WITH CHECK OPTION during creation of a view from a view: CASCADED and LOCAL. CASCADED is the default, assumed if neither is specified. The CASCADED option checks all underlying views, all integrity constraints during an update for the BASE TABLE, and against defining conditions in the second view. The LOCAL option is used to check only integrity constraints against both views and the defining conditions in the second view, not the underlying base table. Therefore, it is safer to create views with the CASCADED option because the base table's referential integrity is preserved.

Updating a View

A view can be updated under certain conditions:

- The view must not involve joins.
- The view must not contain a GROUP BY clause.
- The view cannot contain any reference to the pseudocolumn ROWNUM.
- The view cannot contain any group functions.
- The DISTINCT clause cannot be used.
- The WHERE clause cannot include a nested table expression that includes a reference to the same table as referenced in the FROM clause.

Review Hour 14, "Using Subqueries to Define Unknown Data," for the UPDATE command's syntax.

Inserting Rows into a View

Rows of data can be inserted into a view. The same rules that apply to the UPDATE command also apply to the INSERT command. Review Hour 14 for the syntax of the INSERT command.

Deleting Rows from a View

Rows of data can be deleted from a view. The same rules that apply to the UPDATE and INSERT commands apply to the DELETE command. Review Hour 14 for the syntax of the DELETE command.

Joining Views with Tables and Other Views

A view can be joined with tables and with other views. The same principles apply to joining views with tables and other views that apply to joining tables to other tables. Review Hour 13, "Joining Tables in Queries," on the joining of tables.

Creating a Table from a View

A table can be created from a view, just as a table can be created from another table (or a view from another view).

The syntax is as follows:

```
CREATE TABLE TABLE_NAME AS
SELECT {* | COLUMN1 [, COLUMN2 ]
FROM VIEW_NAME
[ WHERE CONDITION1 [, CONDITION2 ]
[ ORDER BY ]
```

20

SYNTAX

First, create a view based on two tables:

INPUT
```
CREATE VIEW ACTIVE_CUSTOMERS AS
SELECT C.*
FROM CUSTOMER_TBL C,
     ORDERS_TBL O
WHERE C.CUST_ID = O.CUST_ID;
```

OUTPUT
```
View created.
```

Next, create a table based on the previously created view:

INPUT
```
CREATE TABLE SUCTOMER_ROSTER_TBL AS
SELECT CUST_ID, CUST_NAME
FROM ACTIVE_CUSTOMERS;
```

OUTPUT
```
Table created.
```

Finally, select data from the table, the same as any other table:

INPUT
```
SELECT *
FROM CUSTOMER_ROSTER_TBL;
```

OUTPUT
```
CUST_ID      CUST_NAME
..........   ...................
232          LESLIE GLEASON
12           MARYS GIFT SHOP
43           SCHYLERS NOVELTIES
090          WENDY WOLF
287          GAVINS PLACE
432          SCOTTYS MARKET
6 rows selected.
```

Remember that the main difference between a table and a view is that a table contains actual data and consumes physical storage, whereas a view contains no data and requires no storage other than to store the view definition (the query).

Views and the ORDER BY Clause

The ORDER BY clause cannot be used in the CREATE VIEW statement; however, the GROUP BY clause when used in the CREATE VIEW statement has the same effect as an ORDER BY clause.

Using the ORDER BY clause in the SELECT statement that is querying the view is better and simpler than using the GROUP BY clause in the CREATE VIEW statement.

The following is an example of a GROUP BY clause in a CREATE VIEW statement:

INPUT
```
CREATE VIEW NAMES2 AS
SELECT LAST_NAME || ', ' || FIRST_NAME || ' ' ||MIDDLE_NAME NAME
FROM EMPLOYEE_TBL
GROUP BY LAST_NAME || ', ' || FIRST_NAME || ' ' || MIDDLE_NAME;
```

OUTPUT
```
View created.
```

If you select all data from the view, the data is in alphabetical order (because you grouped by NAME).

INPUT
```
SELECT *
FROM NAMES2;
NAME
```

OUTPUT
```
----------------
GLASS, BRANDON S
GLASS, JACOB
PLEW, LINDA C
SPURGEON, TIFFANY
STEPHENS, TINA D
WALLACE, MARIAH
6 rows selected.
```

Dropping a View

The DROP VIEW command is used to drop a view from the database. There are two options to the DROP VIEW command: RESTRICT and CASCADE. If a view is dropped with the RESTRICT option, when any other views are referenced in a constraint, the DROP VIEW errs. If the CASCADE option is used and another view or constraint is referenced, the DROP VIEW succeeds and the underlying view or constraint is also dropped. An example follows:

INPUT
```
DROP VIEW NAMES2;
```

OUTPUT
```
View dropped.
```

20

What Is a Synonym?

NEW TERM   A *synonym* is merely another name for a table or a view. Synonyms are usually created so that a user can avoid having to qualify another user's table or view to access the table or view. Synonyms can be created as PUBLIC or PRIVATE. A PUBLIC synonym can be used by any user of the database; a PRIVATE synonym can be used only by the owner and any users that have been granted privileges.

Synonyms are used by several major implementations. Synonyms are not ANSI SQL standard; however, because synonyms are used by major implementations, it is best to discuss them briefly. You must check your particular implementation for the exact use of synonyms, if available.

Managing Synonyms

Synonyms are either managed by the database administrator (or another designated individual) or by individual users. Because there are two types of synonyms, PUBLIC and PRIVATE, different system-level privileges may be required to create one or the other. All users can generally create a PRIVATE synonym. Typically, only a DBA or privileged database user can create a PUBLIC synonym. Refer to your specific implementation for required privileges when creating synonyms.

Creating Synonyms

SYNTAX

The general syntax to create a synonym is as follows:

CREATE [PUBLIC|PRIVATE] SYNONYM *SYNONYM_NAME* FOR TABLE|VIEW

You create a synonym called CUST, short for CUSTOMER_TBL, in the following example. This frees you from having to spell out the full table name.

INPUT

```
CREATE SYNONYM CUST FOR CUSTOMER_TBL;
```

OUTPUT

```
Synonym created.
```

INPUT

```
SELECT CUST_NAME
FROM CUST;
```

OUTPUT

```
CUST_NAME
----------------------------
LESLIE GLEASON
NANCY BUNKER
ANGELA DOBKO
WENDY WOLF
MARYS GIFT SHOP
SCOTTYS MARKET
JASONS AND DALLAS GOODIES
MORGANS CANDIES AND TREATS
SCHYLERS NOVELTIES
GAVINS PLACE
HOLLYS GAMEARAMA
HEATHERS FEATHERS AND THINGS
```

```
RAGANS HOBBIES INC
ANDYS CANDIES
RYANS STUFF
15 rows selected.
```

It is also a common practice for a table owner to create a synonym for the table to which you have been granted access so that you do not have to qualify the table name by the name of the owner:

```
CREATE SYNONYM PRODUCTS_TBL FOR USER1.PRODUCTS_TBL;
```

OUTPUT

```
Synonym created.
```

Dropping Synonyms

Dropping synonyms is like dropping most any database object. The general syntax to drop a synonym is as follows:

```
DROP [PUBLIC|PRIVATE] SYNONYM SYNONYM_NAME
```

The following is an example:

INPUT

```
DROP SYNONYM CUST;
```

OUTPUT

```
Synonym dropped.
```

Summary

Views and synonyms, two important features in SQL, were discussed this hour. In many cases, these things are not used when they could aid in the overall functionality of relational database users. Views were defined as virtual tables—objects that look and act like tables, but do not take physical space like tables. Views are actually defined by queries against tables and possible other views in the database. Views are typically used to restrict data that a user sees and to simplify and summarize data. Views can be created from views, but care must be taken not to embed views too deeply, to avoid losing control over their management. There are various options when creating views, some implementation-specific.

Synonyms, objects in the database that represent other objects, were also discussed. Synonyms are used to simplify the name of another object in the database, either by creating a synonym with a short name for an object with a long name or by creating a synonym on an object owned by another user to which you have access. There are two types of synonyms: PUBLIC and PRIVATE. A PUBLIC synonym is one that is accessible to all database users, whereas a PRIVATE synonym is accessible to a single user. A DBA typically creates a PUBLIC synonym, while each individual user normally creates his or her own PRIVATE synonyms.

Q&A

Q How can a view contain data but take no storage space?

A A view does not contain data. A view is a virtual table or a stored query. The only space required for a view is for the actual view creation statement, called the *view definition*.

Q What happens to the view if a table from which a view was created is dropped?

A The view is invalid because the underlying data for the view no longer exists.

Q What are limits on naming the synonym when creating synonyms?

A This is implementation-specific. However, the naming convention for synonyms in most major implementations follows the same rules that apply to the tables and other objects in the database.

Workshop

The following workshop is composed of a series of quiz questions and practical exercises. The quiz questions are designed to test your overall understanding of the current material. The practical exercises are intended to afford you the opportunity to apply the concepts discussed during the current hour, as well as build upon the knowledge acquired in previous hours of study. Please take time to complete the quiz questions and exercises before continuing. Refer to Appendix C, "Answers to Quizzes and Exercises," for answers.

Quiz

1. Can a row of data be deleted from a view that was created from multiple tables?
2. When creating a table, the owner is automatically granted the appropriate privileges on that table. Is this true when creating a view?
3. What clause is used to order data when creating a view?
4. What option can be used when creating a view from a view, to check integrity constraints?
5. You try to drop a view and receive an error because there are one or more underlying views. What must you do to drop the view?

Exercises

1. Write a statement to create a view based on the total contents of the EMPLOYEE_TBL table.

2. Write a statement that creates a summarized view containing the average pay rate and average salary for each city in the EMPLOYEE_TBL table.

3. Write statements that drop the two views that you created in Exercises 1 and 2.

20

Hour 21

Working with the System Catalog

During this hour, you learn about the system catalog, commonly referred to as the data dictionary in some relational database implementations. By the end of this hour, you will understand the purpose and contents of the system catalog and will be able to query the system catalog to find information about the database based on commands that you have learned in previous hours. Each major implementation has some form of a system catalog that stores information about the database itself. This hour shows examples of the elements contained in a few different system catalogs.

The highlights of this hour include

- What the system catalog is
- How the system catalog is created
- What data is contained in the system catalog
- Examples of system catalog tables
- Querying the system catalog
- Updating the system catalog

What Is the System Catalog?

The *system catalog* is a collection of tables and views that contain important information about a database. A system catalog is available for each database. Information in the system catalog defines the structure of the database. For example, the DDL (data dictionary language) for all tables in the database is stored in the system catalog. See Figure 21.1 for an illustration of the system catalog within the database.

FIGURE 21.1

The system catalog.

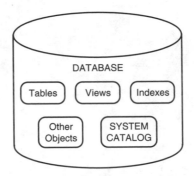

As you can see in Figure 21.1, the system catalog for a database is actually part of the database. Within the database are objects, such as tables, indexes, and views. The system catalog is basically a group of objects that contain information that defines other objects in the database, the structure of the database itself, and various other significant information.

The system catalog for your implementation may be divided into logical groups of objects to provide tables that are accessible by not only the database administrator, but any other database user as well. For example, a user may need to view the particular database privileges that he or she has been granted, but has no need to know about the internal structure or processes of the database. A user typically queries the system catalog to acquire information on the user's own objects and privileges, whereas the DBA needs to be able to inquire about any structure or event within the database. In some implementations, there are system catalog objects that are accessible only to the database administrator.

The system catalog is crucial to the database administrator or any other database user who needs to know about the database's structure and nature. The system catalog allows order to be kept, not only by the database administrator and users, but by the database server itself.

Each implementation has its own naming conventions for the system catalog's tables and views. The naming is not of importance; learning what the
system catalog does is important, as is what it contains and how and where
to retrieve the information.

How Is the System Catalog Created?

The system catalog is either created automatically with the creation of the database, or
by the database administrator immediately following the creation of the database. For
example, a set of predefined, vendor-provided SQL scripts in Oracle are executed, which
builds all the database tables and views in the system catalog that are accessible to a
database user. The system catalog tables and views are system-owned and not specific to
any one schema. In Oracle, for example, the system catalog owner is a user account
called SYS, which has full authority in the database. In Sybase, the system catalog for the
SQL server is located in the MASTER database.

What Is Contained in the System Catalog?

The system catalog contains a variety of information accessible to many users and is
sometimes used for different specific purposes by each of those users.

The system catalog contains information such as the following:

- User accounts and default settings
- Privileges and other security information
- Performance statistics
- Object sizing
- Object growth
- Table structure and storage
- Index structure and storage
- Information on other database objects, such as views, synonyms, triggers, and
  stored procedures
- Table constraints and referential integrity information
- User sessions
- Auditing information
- Internal database settings
- Locations of database files

21

The system catalog is maintained by the database server. For example, when a table is created, the database server inserts the data into the appropriate system catalog table or view. When a table's structure is modified, appropriate objects in the data dictionary are also updated. The following sections describe, by category, the types of data that are contained in the system catalog.

User Data

All information about individual users is stored in the system catalog: the system and object privileges a user has been granted, the objects a user owns, and the objects not owned by the user to which the user has access. The user tables or views are accessible to the individual to query for information. See your implementation documentation on the system catalog objects.

Security Information

The system catalog also stores security information, such as user identifications, encrypted passwords, and various privileges and groups of privileges database users utilize to access the data. Audit tables exist in some implementations for tracking actions that occur within the database, as well as by whom, when, and so on. Database user sessions also can be closely monitored through the use of the system catalog in many implementations.

Database Design Information

The system catalog contains information regarding the actual database. That information includes the database's creation date, name, objects sizing, size and location of data files, referential integrity information, indexes that exist in the database, and specific column information and column attributes for each table in the database.

Performance Statistics

Performance statistics are typically maintained in the system catalog as well. Performance statistics include information concerning the performance of SQL statements, both elapsed time and the execution method of a SQL statement taken by the optimizer. Other information for performance concerns memory allocation and usage, free space in the database, and information that allows table and index fragmentation to be controlled within the database. This performance information can be used to properly tune the database, rearrange SQL queries, or redesign methods of access to data to achieve better overall performance and SQL query response time.

Examples of System Catalog Tables by Implementation

Each implementation has several tables and views that compose the system catalog, some of which are categorized by user level, system level, and DBA level. For your particular implementation, you should query these tables and read your implementation's documentation for more information on system catalog tables. See Table 21.1 for a few examples of five major implementations.

TABLE 21.1 Major Implementations' System Catalog Objects

Microsoft SQL Server

Table Name	Description
SYSUSERS	Information on database users
SYSSEGMENTS	Information on all database segments
OYOINDEXES	Information on all indexes
SYSCONSTRAINTS	Information on all constraints

dBase

Table Name	Description
SYSVIEWS	Information on all views
SYSTABLS	Information on all tables
SYSIDXS	Information on all indexes
SYSCOLS	Information on columns of tables

Microsoft Access

Table Name	Description
MSysColumns	Information on columns in tables
MSysIndexes	Information on indexes in tables
MSysMacros	Information on macros created
MSysObjects	Information on all database objects
MSysQueries	Information on queries created
MSysRelationships	Information on table relationships

21

Sybase

Table Name	Description
SYSMESSAGES	Lists all server error messages
SYSKEYS	Primary and foreign key information
SYSTABLES	Information on all tables and views
SYSVIEWS	Text of all views
SYSCOLUMNS	Information on table columns
SYSINDEXES	Information on indexes
SYSOBJECTS	Information on tables, triggers, views, and the like
SYSDATABASES	Information on all databases on server
SYSPROCEDURES	Information on views, triggers, and stored procedures

Oracle

Table Name	Description
ALL_TABLES	Information on tables accessible by a user
USER_TABLES	Information on tables owned by a user
DBA_TABLES	Information on all tables in the database
DBA_SEGMENTS	Information about segment storage
DBA_INDEXES	Information on all indexes
DBA_USERS	Information on all users of the database
DBA_ROLE_PRIVS	Information about roles granted
DBA_ROLES	Information about roles in the database
DBA_SYS_PRIVS	Information about system privileges granted
DBA_FREE_SPACE	Information about database free space
V$DATABASE	Information about the creation of the database
V$SESSION	Information on current sessions

These are just a few of the system catalog objects from a few various relational database implementations. Many of the system catalog objects that are similar between implementations are shown here, but this hour strives to provide some variety. Overall, each implementation is very specific to the organization of the system catalog's contents.

Querying the System Catalog

The system catalog tables or views are queried as any other table or view in the database using SQL. A user can usually query the user-related tables, but may be denied access to various system tables that can be accessed only by privileged database user accounts, such as the database administrator.

You create an SQL query to retrieve data from the system catalog just as you create a query to access any other table in the database.

For example, the following query returns all rows of data from the Sybase table SYSTABLES:

```
SELECT * FROM SYSTABLES
GO
```

The following section displays a few examples of querying system catalog tables and some of the information that you may stumble across.

Examples of System Catalog Queries

The following examples use Oracle's system catalog. Oracle is chosen for no particular reason other than that is the implementation with which this book's authors are most familiar.

The following query lists all user accounts in the database:

```
SELECT USERNAME
FROM ALL_USERS;
```

```
USERNAME
- - - - - - - - - - - - - - -
SYS
SYSTEM
RYAN
SCOTT
DEMO
RON
USER1
USER2
8 rows selected.
```

21

The following query lists all tables owned by a user:

INPUT
```
SELECT TABLE_NAME
FROM USER_TABLES;
```

OUTPUT
```
TABLE_NAME
- - - - - - - - - - - - - - - -
CANDY_TBL
CUSTOMER_TBL
EMPLOYEE_PAY_TBL
EMPLOYEE_TBL
PRODUCTS_TBL
ORDERS_TBL
6 rows selected.
```

The next query returns all the system privileges that have been granted to the database user BRANDON:

INPUT
```
SELECT GRANTEE, PRIVILEGE
FROM SYS.DBA_SYS_PRIVS
WHERE GRANTEE = 'BRANDON';
```

OUTPUT
```
GRANTEE                          PRIVILEGE
- - - - - - - - - - - - - - - - - - - - -   - - - - - - - - - - - - - - - - - - - -
BRANDON                          ALTER ANY TABLE
BRANDON                          ALTER USER
BRANDON                          CREATE USER
BRANDON                          DROP ANY TABLE
BRANDON                          SELECT ANY TABLE
BRANDON                          UNLIMITED TABLESPACE
6 rows selected.
```

The following is an example from MS Access:

INPUT
```
SELECT NAME
FROM MSYSOBJECTS
WHERE NAME = 'MSYSOBJECTS'
```

OUTPUT
```
NAME
- - - - - - - - - - -
MSYSOBJECTS
```

> The examples shown in this section are a drop in the bucket compared to the information that you can retrieve from any system catalog. Please refer to your implementation documentation for specific system catalog tables and columns within those available tables.

Updating System Catalog Objects

The system catalog is used only for query operations—even when being used by the database administrator. Updates to the system catalog are accomplished automatically by the database server. For example, a table is created in the database when a CREATE TABLE statement is issued by a database user. The database server then places the DDL that was used to create the table in the system catalog under the appropriate system catalog table. There is never a need to manually update any table in the system catalog. The database server for each implementation performs these updates according to actions that occur within the database, as shown in Figure 21.2.

Figure 21.2

Updates to the system catalog.

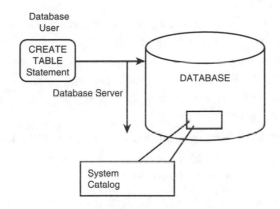

Never directly manipulate tables in the system catalog in any way. Doing so may compromise the database's integrity. Remember that information concerning the structure of the database, as well as all objects in the database, are maintained in the system catalog. The system catalog is typically isolated from all other data in the database.

Summary

You have learned about the system catalog for a relational database. The system catalog is, in a sense, a database within a database. The system catalog is essentially a database that contains all information about the database in which it resides. It is a way of maintaining the database's overall structure, tracking events and changes that occur within the database, and providing a vast pool of information necessary for overall database management. The system catalog is only used for query operations. No database user should

21

ever make changes directly to system tables. However, changes are implicitly made each time a change is made to the database structure itself, such as the creation of a table. These entries in the system catalog are made automatically by the database server.

Q&A

Q **As a database user, I realize I can find information about my objects. How can I find information about other users' objects?**

A There are sets of tables and/or views that users can use to query in most system catalogs. One set of these tables and views includes information on what objects to which you have access.

Q **If a user forgets his or her password, is there a table that the database administrator can query to get the password?**

A Yes and no. The password is maintained in a system table, but is typically encrypted, so that even the database administrator cannot read the password. The password will have to be reset if the user forgets it, which the database administrator can easily accomplish.

Q **How can I tell what columns are in a system catalog table?**

A The system catalog tables can be queried as any other table. Simply query the table that holds that particular information.

Workshop

The following workshop is composed of a series of quiz questions and practical exercises. The quiz questions are designed to test your overall understanding of the current material. The practical exercises are intended to afford you the opportunity to apply the concepts discussed during the current hour, as well as build upon the knowledge acquired in previous hours of study. Please take time to complete the quiz questions and exercises before continuing. Refer to Appendix C, "Answers to Quizzes and Exercises," for answers.

Quiz

1. The system catalog is also known as what in some implementations?
2. Can a regular user update the system catalog?
3. What Sybase system table is used to retrieve information about views that exist in the database?
4. Who owns the system catalog?

5. What is the difference between the Oracle system objects ALL_TABLES and DBA_TABLES?

6. Who makes modifications to the system tables?

Exercises

1. Try querying the system catalog tables for your implementation. You can start with the tables that hold information about your user database user account.

2. Query the system catalog to list all tables to which you have access.

3. Query the tables that contain system and object privileges that you have been granted.

4. If you have the DBA or SELECT privilege on the database administrator tables, query these tables. If you do not have these privileges, take a look at a hard copy of the tables, which should be located in your implementation documentation set.

21

PART VIII

Applying SQL Fundamentals in Today's World

Hour

Hour **22**

Advanced SQL Topics

During this hour, you are introduced to some advanced SQL topics. By the end of the hour you should understand the concepts behind cursors, stored procedures, triggers, dynamic SQL, direct versus embedded SQL, and SQL generated from SQL.

The highlights of this hour include

- What cursors are
- Using stored procedures
- What triggers are
- Basics of dynamic SQL
- Using SQL to generate SQL
- Direct SQL versus embedded SQL
- Call-level interface

Advanced Topics

The advanced SQL topics discussed this hour are those that extend beyond the basic operations that you have learned so far, such as querying data from the database, building database structures, and manipulating data within the database. These advanced topics are features available in many implementations, all of which provide enhancements to the parts of SQL discussed so far.

> Not all topics are ANSI SQL, so you must check your particular implementation for variations in syntax and rules. A few major vendors' syntax is shown here for comparison.

Cursors

NEW TERM To most people, a cursor is commonly known as a blinking dot or square that appears on the monitor and indicates where you are in a file or application. That is not the same type of cursor discussed here. An SQL *cursor* is an area in database memory where the last SQL statement is stored. If the current SQL statement is a database query, a row from the query is also stored in memory. This row is the cursor's *current value* or *current row*. The area in memory is named and is available to programs.

A cursor is typically used to retrieve a subset of data from the database. Thereby, each row in the cursor can be evaluated by a program, one row at a time. Cursors are normally used in SQL that is embedded in procedural-type programs. Some cursors are created implicitly by the database server, whereas others are defined by the SQL programmer. Each SQL implementation may define the use of cursors differently.

This section shows syntax examples from two popular implementations: Microsoft SQL Server and Oracle.

The syntax to declare a cursor for Microsoft SQL Server is as follows:

SYNTAX
```
DECLARE CURSOR_NAME CURSOR
FOR SELECT_STATEMENT
[ FOR [READ ONLY | UPDATE [ COLUMN_LIST ]}]
```

The syntax for Oracle is as follows:

SYNTAX
```
DECLARE CURSOR CURSOR_NAME
IS {SELECT_STATEMENT}
```

The following cursor contains the result subset of all records from the EMPLOYEE_TBL table:

```
DECLARE CURSOR EMP_CURSOR IS
SELECT * FROM EMPLOYEE_TBL
{ OTHER PROGRAM STATEMENTS }
```

According to the ANSI standard, the following operations are used to access a cursor once it has been defined:

OPEN	Opens a defined cursor
FETCH	Fetches rows from a cursor into a program variable
CLOSE	Closes the cursor when operations against the cursor are complete

Opening a Cursor

When a cursor is opened, the specified cursor's SELECT statement is executed and the results of the query are stored in a staging area in memory.

SYNTAX

The syntax to open a cursor in dBase is as follows:

```
OPEN CURSOR_NAME
```

The syntax in Oracle is as follows:

```
OPEN CURSOR_NAME [ PARAMETER1 [, PARAMETER2 ]]
```

SYNTAX

To open the EMP_CURSOR:

```
OPEN EMP_CURSOR
```

Fetching Data from a Cursor

The contents of the cursor (results from the query) can be retrieved through the use of the FETCH statement once a cursor has been opened.

SYNTAX

The syntax for the FETCH statement in Microsoft SQL Server is as follows:

```
FETCH CURSOR_NAME [ INTO FETCH_LIST ]
```

SYNTAX

The syntax for Oracle is as follows:

```
FETCH CURSOR_NAME {INTO : HOST_VARIABLE
[[ INDICATOR ] : INDICATOR_VARIABLE ]
[, : HOST_VARIABLE
[[ INDICATOR ] : INDICATOR_VARIABLE ]]
| USING DESCRIPTOR DESCRIPTOR ]
```

SYNTAX

The syntax for dBase is as follows:

```
FETCH CURSOR_NAME INTO MEMORY_VARIABLES
```

To fetch the contents of EMP_CURSOR into a variable called EMP_RECORD, your FETCH statement may appear as follows:

```
FETCH EMP_CURSOR INTO EMP_RECORD
```

Closing a Cursor

You can obviously close a cursor if you can open a cursor. Closing a cursor is quite simple. After it's closed, it is no longer available to user programs.

> Closing a cursor does not necessarily free the memory associated with the cursor. In some implementations, the memory used by a cursor must be deallocated by using the `deallocate` statement. When the cursor is deallocated, the memory associated is freed and the name of the cursor can then be reused. In other implementations, memory is implicitly deallocated when the cursor is closed. Memory is available for other operations, such as opening another cursor, when space used by a cursor is reclaimed.

SYNTAX

The Microsoft SQL Server syntax for the closing of a cursor and the deallocation of a cursor is as follows:

```
CLOSE CURSOR_NAME

DEALLOCATE CURSOR CURSOR_NAME
```

SYNTAX

When the cursor is closed in Oracle, the resources and name are released without the `DEALLOCATE` statement. The syntax for Oracle is as follows:

```
CLOSE CURSOR_NAME
```

SYNTAX

To release the resources in dBase, the table must be closed and reopened before the resources are released and the name can be reused. The syntax for dBase is as follows:

```
CLOSE CURSOR_NAME
```

> As you can see from the previous examples, variations among the implementations are extensive, especially with advanced features of and extensions to SQL, which are covered during Hour 24, "Extensions to Standard SQL." You must check your particular implementation for the exact usage of a cursor.

Stored Procedures and Functions

Stored procedures are groupings of related SQL statements—commonly referred to as *functions* and *subprograms*—that allow ease and flexibility for a programmer. This ease and flexibility is derived from the fact that a stored procedure is often easier to execute than a number of individual SQL statements. Stored procedures can be nested within other stored procedures. That is, a stored procedure can call another stored procedure, which can call another stored procedure, and so on.

Stored procedures allow for procedural programming. The basic SQL DDL, DML, and DQL statements (CREATE TABLE, INSERT, UPDATE, SELECT, and so on) allow you the opportunity to tell the database what needs to be done, but not how to do it. By coding stored procedures, you tell the database engine how to go about processing the data.

NEW TERM   A *stored procedure* is a group of one or more SQL statements or functions that are stored in the database and compiled and are ready to be executed by a database user. A *stored function* is the same as a stored procedure, but a function is used to return a value.

Functions are called by procedures. When a function is called by a procedure, parameters can be passed into a function like a procedure, a value is computed, and then the value is passed back to the calling procedure for further processing.

When a stored procedure is created, the various subprograms and functions (that use SQL) that compose the stored procedure are actually stored in the database. These stored procedures are pre-parsed, and are immediately ready to execute when invoked by the user.

The Microsoft SQL Server syntax for creating a stored procedure is as follows:

▼ SYNTAX

```
CREATE PROCEDURE PROCEDURE_NAME
[ [(] @PARAMETER_NAME
DATATYPE [(LENGTH) | (PRECISION] [, SCALE ])
[ = DEFAULT ][ OUTPUT ]]
[, @PARAMETER_NAME
DATATYPE [(LENGTH) | (PRECISION [, SCALE ])
[ = DEFAULT ][ OUTPUT ]] [)]]
[ WITH RECOMPILE ]
AS SQL_STATEMENTS
```

▲

The syntax for Oracle is as follows:

SYNTAX

```
CREATE [ OR REPLACE ] PROCEDURE PROCEDURE_NAME
[ (ARGUMENT [{IN | OUT | IN OUT} ] TYPE,
ARGUMENT [{IN | OUT | IN OUT} ] TYPE) ] {IS | AS}
PROCEDURE_BODY
```

An example of a very simple stored procedure is as follows:

INPUT

```
CREATE PROCEDURE NEW_PRODUCT
(PROD_ID IN VARCHAR2, PROD_DESC IN VARCHAR2, COST IN NUMBER)
AS
BEGIN
    INSERT INTO PRODUCTS_TBL
    VALUES (PROD_ID, PROD_DESC, COST);
    COMMIT;
END;
```

OUTPUT

```
Procedure created.
```

This procedure is used to insert new rows into the PRODUCTS_TBL table.

The syntax for executing a stored procedure in Microsoft SQL Server is as follows:

```
EXECUTE [ @RETURN_STATUS = ]
PROCEDURE_NAME
[[@PARAMETER_NAME = ] VALUE |
[@PARAMETER_NAME = ] @VARIABLE [ OUTPUT ]]
[WITH RECOMPLIE]
```

The syntax for Oracle is as follows:

```
EXECUTE [ @RETURN STATUS =] PROCEDURE NAME
[[ @PARAMETER NAME = ] VALUE | [ @PARAMETER NAME = ] @VARIABLE [ OUTPUT ]]]
[ WITH RECOMPLIE ]
```

Now execute the procedure you have created:

INPUT

```
EXECUTE NEW_PRODUCT ('9999','INDIAN CORN',1.99);
```

OUTPUT

```
PL/SQL procedure successfully completed.
```

> You may find that there are distinct differences between the allowed syntax used to code procedures in different implementations of SQL. The basic SQL commands should be the same, but the programming constructs (variables, conditional statements, cursors, loops) may vary drastically among implementations.

Advantages of Stored Procedures and Functions

Stored procedures pose several distinct advantages over individual SQL statements executed in the database. Some of these advantages include the following:

22

- The statements are already stored in the database.
- The statements are already parsed and in an executable format.
- Stored procedures support modular programming.
- Stored procedures can call other procedures and functions.
- Stored procedures can be called by other types of programs.
- Overall response time is typically better with stored procedures.
- Overall ease of use.

Triggers

NEW TERM   A *trigger* is a compiled SQL procedure in the database used to perform actions based on other actions that occur within the database. A trigger is a form of a stored procedure that is executed when a specified (Data Manipulation Language) action is performed on a table. The trigger can be executed before or after an INSERT, DELETE, or UPDATE. Triggers can also be used to check data integrity before and INSERT, DELETE, or UPDATE. Triggers can roll back transactions, and they can modify data in one table and read from another table in another database.

Triggers, for the most part, are very good functions to use; they can, however, cause more I/O overhead. Triggers should not be used when a stored procedure or a program can accomplish the same results with less overhead.

The CREATE TRIGGER Statement

A trigger can be created using the CREATE TRIGGER statement.

The ANSI standard syntax is:

SYNTAX
```
CREATE TRIGGER TRIGGER NAME
[[BEFORE | AFTER] TRIGGER EVENT ON TABLE NAME]
[REFERENCING VALUES ALIAS LIST]
[TRIGGERED ACTION
TRIGGER EVENT::=
INSERT | UPDATE | DELETE [OF TRIGGER COLUMN LIST]
TRIGGER COLUMN LIST ::= COLUMN NAME [,COLUMN NAME]
VALUES ALIAS LIST ::=
VALUES ALIAS LIST ::=
OLD [ROW] [AS] OLD VALUES CORRELATION NAME |
NEW [ROW] [AS] NEW VALUES CORRELATION NAME |
OLD TABLE [AS] OLD VALUES TABLE ALIAS |
NEW TABLE [AS] NEW VALUES TABLE ALIAS
OLD VALUES TABLE ALIAS ::= IDENTIFIER
NEW VALUES TABLE ALIAS ::= IDENTIFIER
TRIGGERED ACTION ::=
```

```
▼ [FOR EACH [ROW | STATEMENT] [WHEN SEARCH CONDITION]]
  TRIGGERED SQL STATEMENT
  TRIGGERED SQL STATEMENT ::=
  SQL STATEMENT | BEGIN ATOMIC [SQL STATEMENT;]
▲ END
```

The Microsoft SQL Server syntax to create a trigger is as follows:

SYNTAX

```
CREATE TRIGGER TRIGGER_NAME
ON TABLE_NAME
FOR { INSERT | UPDATE | DELETE [, ..]}
AS
SQL_STATEMENTS
[ RETURN ]
```

The basic syntax for Oracle is as follows:

SYNTAX

```
CREATE [ OR REPLACE ] TRIGGER TRIGGER_NAME
[ BEFORE | AFTER]
[ DELETE | INSERT | UPDATE]
ON [ USER.TABLE_NAME ]
[ FOR EACH ROW ]
[ WHEN CONDITION ]
[ PL/SQL BLOCK ]
```

The following is an example trigger:

INPUT

```
CREATE TRIGGER EMP_PAY_TRIG
AFTER UPDATE ON EMPLOYEE_PAY_TBL
FOR EACH ROW
BEGIN
  INSERT INTO EMPLOYEE_PAY_HISTORY
  (EMP_ID, PREV_PAY_RATE, PAY_RATE, DATE_LAST_RAISE,
   TRANSACTION_TYPE)
  VALUES
  (:NEW.EMP_ID, :OLD.PAY_RATE, :NEW.PAY_RATE,
   :NEW.DATE_LAST_RAISE, 'PAY CHANGE');
END;
/
```

OUTPUT

```
Trigger created.
```

This example shows the creation of a trigger called EMP_PAY_TRIG. This trigger inserts a row into the EMPLOYEE_PAY_HISTORY table, reflecting the changes made every time a row of data is updated in the EMPLOYEE_PAY_TBL table.

> The body of a trigger cannot be altered. You must either replace or re-create the trigger. Some implementations allow a trigger to be replaced (if the trigger with the same name already exists) as part of the CREATE TRIGGER statement.

The DROP TRIGGER Statement

A trigger can be dropped using the DROP TRIGGER statement. The syntax for dropping a trigger is as follows:

```
DROP TRIGGER TRIGGER_NAME
```

22

Dynamic SQL

Dynamic SQL allows a programmer or end user to create an SQL statement's specifics at runtime and pass the statement to the database. The database then returns data into the program variables, which are bound at SQL runtime.

To comprehend dynamic SQL, review static SQL. Static SQL is what this book has discussed thus far. A *static SQL statement* is written and not meant to be changed. Although static SQL statements can be stored as files ready to be executed later or as stored procedures in the database, static SQL does not quite offer the flexibility that is allowed with dynamic SQL.

The problem with static SQL is that even though numerous queries may be available to the end user, there is a good chance that none of these "canned queries" will satisfy the users' needs on every occasion. Dynamic SQL is often used by ad hoc query tools, which allow an SQL statement to be created on-the-fly by a user to satisfy the particular query requirements for that particular situation. After the statement is customized according to the user's needs, the statement is sent to the database, checked for syntax errors and privileges required to execute the statement, and is compiled in the database where the statement is carried out by the database server. Dynamic SQL can be created by using call-level interface, which is explained in the next section.

> Although dynamic SQL provides more flexibility for the end user's query needs, the performance may not compare to that of a stored procedure, whose code has already been analyzed by the SQL optimizer.

Call-Level Interface

NEW TERM   *Call-level interface* is used to embed SQL code in a host program, such as ANSI C. Application programmers should be very familiar with the concept of call-level interface. It is one of the methods that allows a programmer to embed SQL in different procedural programming languages. When using call-level interface (CLI), you simply pass the text of an SQL statement into a variable using the rules of the host programming language. You can execute the SQL statement in the host program through the use of the variable into which you passed the SQL text.

`EXEC SQL` is a common host programming language command that allows you to call an SQL statement (CLI) from within the program.

EXEC SQL

The following are examples of programming languages that support CLI:

- COBOL
- ANSI C
- Pascal
- Fortran
- Ada

 Refer to the syntax of the host programming language with which you are using call-level interface options.

Using SQL to Generate SQL

Using SQL to generate SQL is very valuable time-budgeting when writing SQL statements. Assume you have 100 users in the database already. A new role, `ENABLE` (a user-defined object that is granted privileges), has been created and must be granted to those 100 users. Instead of manually creating 100 `GRANT` statements, the following SQL statement generates each of those statements for you:

```
SELECT 'GRANT ENABLE TO '|| USERNAME||';'
FROM SYS.DBA_USERS;
```

This example uses Oracle's system catalog view (which contains information for users).

Notice the use of single quotation marks around the `GRANT ENABLE TO`. The use of single quotation marks allows whatever is between the marks to be literal. Remember that literal values can be selected from tables, the same as columns from a table. `USERNAME` is the column in the system catalog table `SYS.DBA_USERS`. The double pipe signs (`||`) are used to concatenate the columns. The use of double pipes followed by `';'` concatenates the semicolon to the end of the username, thus completing the statement.

The results of the SQL statement look like the following:

```
GRANT ENABLE TO RRPLEW;
GRANT ENABLE TO RKSTEP;
```

These results should be spooled to a file, which can be sent to the database. The database, in turn, executes each SQL statement in the file, saving you many keystrokes and much time. The GRANT ENABLE TO USERNAME; statement is repeated once for every user in the database.

Next time you are writing SQL statements and have repeated the same statement several times, allow your imagination to take hold and let SQL do the work for you.

Direct Versus Embedded SQL

Direct SQL is where an SQL statement is executed from some form of an interactive terminal. The SQL results are returned directly to the terminal that issued the statement. Most of this book has focused on direct SQL. Direct SQL is also referred to as *interactive invocation* or *direct invocation*.

NEW TERM *Embedded SQL* is SQL code used within other programs, such as Pascal, Fortran, COBOL, and C. SQL code is actually embedded in a host programming language, as discussed previously, with call-level interface. Embedded SQL statements in host programming language code are commonly preceded by EXEC SQL and terminated by a semicolon in many cases. Other termination characters include END-EXEC and the right parenthesis.

The following is an example of embedded SQL in a host program, such as the ANSI C language:

```
{host programming commands}
EXEC SQL {SQL statement};
{more host programming commands}
```

Summary

Some advanced SQL concepts are discussed this hour. Although this hour does not go into a lot of detail, it does provide you with a basic understanding of how you can apply the basic concepts that you have learned up to this point. You start with cursors, which are used to pass a data set selected by a query into a location in memory. After a cursor is declared in a program, it must first be opened for accessibility. Then the contents of the cursor are fetched into a variable, at which time the data can be used for program processing. The result set for the cursor is contained in memory until the cursor is closed and the memory deallocated.

Stored procedures and triggers are covered next. Stored procedures are basically SQL statements that are stored together in the database. These statements, along with other implementation-specific commands, are compiled in the database and are ready to be executed by a database user at any given time. A trigger is also a type of stored procedure—one that allows actions to be automatically performed based on other actions that occur within the database. Stored procedures typically provide better performance benefits than individual SQL statements.

Dynamic SQL, using SQL to generate other SQL statements, and the differences between direct SQL and embedded SQL were the last subjects discussed. Dynamic SQL is SQL code dynamically created during runtime by a user, unlike static SQL. Using SQL code to generate other SQL statements is a great time-saver. It is a way of automating the creation of numerous, tedious SQL statements using features available with your implementation, such as concatenation and the selection of literal values. Finally, the main difference between direct SQL and embedded SQL is that the user issues direct SQL statements from some terminal, whereas embedded SQL is actually embedded within a host program to help process data.

The concepts of some of the advanced topics discussed during this hour are used to illustrate the application of SQL in an enterprise, covered in Hour 23, "Extending SQL to the Enterprise, the Internet, and the Intranet."

Q&A

Q Can a stored procedure call another stored procedure?

A Yes. The stored procedure being called is referred to as being nested.

Q How do I execute a cursor?

A Simply use the OPEN CURSOR statement. This sends the results of the cursor to a staging area.

Workshop

The following workshop is composed of a series of quiz questions and practical exercises. The quiz questions are designed to test your overall understanding of the current material. The practical exercises are intended to afford you the opportunity to apply the concepts discussed during the current hour, as well as build upon the knowledge acquired in previous hours of study. Please take time to complete the quiz questions and exercises before continuing. Refer to Appendix C, "Answers to Quizzes and Exercises," for answers.

Quiz

1. Can a trigger be altered?
2. When a cursor is closed, can you reuse the name?
3. What command is used to retrieve the results after a cursor has been opened?
4. Are triggers executed before or after an INSERT, DELETE, or UPDATE?

Exercises

1. Using your implementation's system catalog tables, write the SQL that creates the following SQL statements. Substitute the name of an actual object for the object names.

   a.
   ```
   GRANT SELECT ON TABLE_NAME TO USERNAME;
   ```
   b.
   ```
   GRANT, CONNECT, RESOURCE TO USERNAME;
   ```
   c.
   ```
   SELECT COUNT(*) FROM TABLE_NAME;
   ```

2. Write a statement to create a stored procedure that deletes an entry from the PRODUCTS_TBL table; it should be similar to the example used in this hour to insert a new product.

3. Write the statement that executes the stored procedure that you created in Exercise 2 to delete the row for PROD_ID '9999'.

Hour **23**

Extending SQL to the Enterprise, the Internet, and the Intranet

During this hour, you learn how SQL is actually used in an enterprise and a company's intranet and how it has been extended to the Internet.

The highlights of this hour include

- SQL and the enterprise
- Front-end and back-end applications
- Accessing a remote database
- SQL and the Internet
- SQL and the intranet

SQL and the Enterprise

NEW TERM   The previous hour covered some advanced SQL topics. These topics built on earlier hours in the book and began to show you practical applications for the SQL
you have learned. During this hour, you focus on the concepts behind extending SQL to
the enterprise, which involve SQL applications and making data available to all appropriate members of a company for daily use. Many commercial enterprises have specific data
available to other enterprises, customers, and vendors. For example, the enterprise may
have detailed information on its products available for customers' access in hopes of
acquiring more purchases. Enterprise employee needs are included as well. For example,
employee-specific data can also be made available, such as for timesheet logs, vacation
schedules, training schedules, company policies, and so on. A database can be created,
and customers and employees can be allowed easy access to an enterprise's important
data via SQL and an Internet language.

The Back End

NEW TERM   The heart of any application is the back-end application. This is where things happen behind the scenes, transparent to the database end user. The *back-end application* includes the actual database server, data sources, and the appropriate middleware used
to connect an application to the Web or a remote database on the local network.

NEW TERM   As a review, some of the major database servers include Oracle, Informix,
Sybase, Microsoft SQL Server, and Borland InterBase. This is typically the
first step in porting any application, either to the enterprise through a local area network
(LAN), to the enterprise's own intranet, or to the Internet. *Porting* describes the process
of implementing an application in an environment that is available to users. The database
server should be established by an onsite database administrator who understands the
company's needs and the application's requirements.

The middleware for the application includes a Web server and a tool capable of connecting the Web server to the database server. The main objective is to have an application on
the Web that can communicate with a corporate database.

The Front-End Application

NEW TERM   The *front-end application* is the part of an application with which an end user
interacts. The front-end application is either a commercial, off-the-shelf software
product that a company purchases, or an application that is developed in-house using
other third-party tools. Third-party tools are those described in the following paragraphs.

Before the rise of many of the new front-end tools available today, users had to know
how to program in languages such as C++, HTML, or one of many other procedural

programming languages that develop Web-based applications. Other languages, such as ANSI C, COBOL, FORTRAN, and Pascal, have been used to develop front-end, onsite corporate applications, which were mainly character-based. Today, most newly developed front-end applications are GUI—they have a graphical user interface.

The tools available today are user-friendly and object-oriented, by way of icons, wizards, and dragging and dropping with the mouse. Some of the popular tools to port applications to the Web include C++Builder and IntraBuilder by Borland and Microsoft's Visual J++ and C++. Other popular applications used to develop corporate-based applications on a LAN include PowerBuilder by Powersoft, Developer/2000 by Oracle Corporation, Visual Basic by Microsoft, and Delphi by Borland.

23

The front-end application promotes simplicity for the database end user. The underlying database, code, and events that occur within the database are transparent to the user. The front-end application is developed to relieve the end user from guesswork and confusion, which may otherwise be caused by having to be too intuitive to the system itself. The new technologies allow the applications to be more intuitive, enabling the end users to focus on the true aspects of their particular jobs, thereby increasing overall productivity.

Figure 23.1 illustrates the back-end and front-end components of a database application. The back end resides on the host server, where the database resides. Back-end users include developers, programmers, database administrators, system administrators, and system analysts. The front-end application resides on the client machine, which is typically each end user's PC. End users are the vast audience for the front-end component of an application, which can include users such as data entry clerks and accountants. The end user is able to access the back-end database through a network connection—either a local area network (LAN) or a wide area network (WAN). Some type of middleware (such as an ODBC driver) is used to provide a connection between the front and back ends through the network.

Accessing a Remote Database

NEW TERM   Sometimes the database you are accessing is a local database, one to which you are directly connected. For the most part, you will probably access some form of a remote database. A *remote database* is one that is nonlocal, located on a server other than the server to which you are currently connected, meaning that you must utilize the network and some network protocol in order to interface with the database.

FIGURE 23.1
A database application.

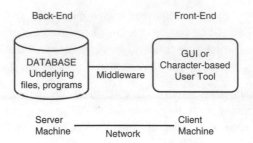

There are several ways to access a remote database. From a broad perspective, a remote database is accessed via the network or Internet connection using a middleware product (ODBC, a standard middleware, is discussed in the next section). Figure 23.2 shows three scenarios for accessing a remote database.

FIGURE 23.2
Accessing a remote database.

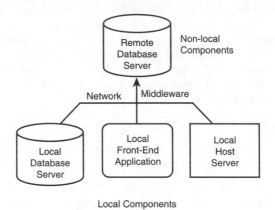

This figure shows access to a remote server from another local database server, a local front-end application, and a local host server. The local database server and local host server are often the same because the database normally resides on a local host server. However, you can usually connect to a remote database from a local server without a current local database connection. For the end user, the front-end application is the most typical method of remote database access. All methods must route their database requests through the network.

ODBC

NEW TERM   Open Database Connectivity (ODBC) allows connections to remote databases through a library driver. An *ODBC driver* is used by a front-end application to interface with a back-end database. A network driver may also be required for a connection to a remote database. An application calls the ODBC functions, and a driver manager loads the ODBC driver. The ODBC driver processes the call, submits the SQL request, and returns the results from the database. ODBC is now a standard and is used by several products, such as Sybase's PowerBuilder, FoxPro, Visual C++, Visual Basic, Borland's Delphi, Microsoft Access, and many more.

As a part of ODBC, all the RDBMS vendors have an Application Programmatic Interface (API) with their database. Oracle's Open Call Interface (OCI) and Centura's SQLGateway and SQLRouter are some of the available products.

Vendor Connectivity Products

In addition to an ODBC driver, many vendors have their own products that allow a user to connect to a remote database. Each of these vendor products is specific to the particular vendor implementation and may not be portable to other types of database servers.

Oracle Corporation has a product called Net8, which allows for remote database connectivity. Net8 can be used with almost all the major network products such as TCP/IP, OSI, SPX/IPX, and more. In addition, Net8 runs on most of the major operating systems.

Sybase, Incorporated has a product called Open Client/C Developers Kit, which supports other vendor products such as Oracle's Net8.

Accessing a Remote Database Through a Web Interface

Accessing a remote database through a Web interface is very similar to accessing one through a local network. The main difference is that all requests to the database from the user are routed through the Web server (see Figure 23.3).

You can see in Figure 23.3 that an end user accesses a database through a Web interface by first invoking a Web browser. The Web browser is used to connect to a particular URL or Internet IP address, determined by the location of the Web server. The Web server authenticates user access and sends the user request, perhaps a query, to the remote database, which may also verify user authenticity. The database server then returns the results to the Web server, which displays the results on the user's Web browser. Unauthorized access to a particular server can be controlled by using a firewall.

NEW TERM   A *firewall* is a security mechanism that ensures against unauthorized connections to a server. One or multiple firewalls can be enabled to patrol access to a database or server.

FIGURE 23.3

A Web interface to a remote database.

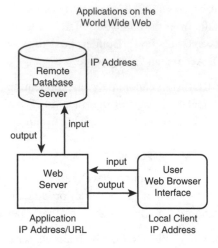

Be careful what information you make available on the Web. Always ensure that precautions are taken to properly implement security at all appropriate levels; that may include the Web server, the host server, and the remote database. Privacy act data, such as individuals' Social Security numbers, should always be protected and should not be broadcast over the Web.

SQL and the Internet

SQL can be embedded or used in conjunction with programming languages such as C or COBOL. SQL can also be embedded in Internet programming languages, such as Java. Text from HTML, another Internet language, can be translated into SQL to send a query to a remote database from a Web front-end. After the database resolves the query, the output is translated back into HTML and displayed on the Web browser of the individual executing the query. The following sections discuss the use of SQL on the Internet.

Making Data Available to Customers Worldwide

With the advent of the Internet, data became available to customers and vendors worldwide. The data is normally available for read-only access through a front-end tool.

The data that is available to customers can contain general customer information, product information, invoice information, current orders, back orders, and other pertinent information. Private information, such as corporate strategies and employee information, should not be available.

Home Web pages on the Internet have become nearly a necessity for companies that want to keep pace with their competition. A Web page is a very powerful tool that can tell surfers all about a company—its services, products, and other information—with very little overhead.

Making Data Available to Employees and Privileged Customers

A database can be made accessible through the Internet or a company's intranet, to employees or its customers. Using Internet technologies is a valuable communication asset for keeping employees informed about company policies, benefits, training, and so on.

Front-End Web Tools Using SQL

There are several tools that can access databases. Many have a graphical user interface, where a user does not necessarily have to understand SQL to query a database. These front-end tools allow users to point and click with the mouse, to select objects that represent tables, manipulate data within objects, specify criteria on data to be returned, and so on. These tools are often developed and customized to meet a company's database needs.

SQL and the Intranet

IBM originally created SQL for use between databases located on mainframe computers and the users on client machines. The users were connected to the mainframes via a local area network. SQL was adopted as the standard language of communication between databases and users. An intranet is basically a small Internet. The main difference is that an *intranet* is for a single organization's use, whereas the Internet is accessible to the general public. The user (client) interface in an intranet remains the same as that in a client/server environment. SQL requests are routed through the Web server and languages (such as HTML) before being directed to the database for evaluation.

> Database security is much more stable than security on the Internet. Always be sure to use the security features available to you through your database server.

Summary

Some concepts behind deploying SQL and database applications to the Internet were discussed as you near your last hour of study in this book. It is very important, in this day and age, for companies to remain competitive. To keep up with the rest of the world, it has proven beneficial—almost mandatory—to obtain a presence on the World Wide Web. In accomplishing this presence, applications must be developed and even migrated from client/server systems to the Internet on a Web server. One of the greatest concerns when publishing any kind or any amount of corporate data on the Web is security. Security must be considered, adhered to, and strictly enforced.

Accessing remote databases across local networks as well as over the Internet was discussed. Each major method for accessing any type of a remote database requires the use of the network and protocol adapters used to translate requests to the database. This has been a broad overview of the application of SQL over local networks, company intranets, and the Internet. After the digestion of a few quiz and exercise questions, you should be ready to venture into the last hour of your journey through SQL.

Q&A

Q **What is the difference between the Internet and an intranet?**

A The Internet provides connections for the public to information reservoirs by using a Web interface. An intranet also uses a Web interface, but only internal access is allowed, such as to company employees and privileged customers.

Q **Is a back-end database for a Web application any different than a back-end database for a client/server system?**

A The back-end database itself for a Web application is not necessarily any different than that of a client/server system. However, there are other requirements that must be met to implement a Web-based application. For example, a Web server is used to access the database with a Web application. With a Web application, end users do not typically connect directly to the database.

Workshop

The following workshop is composed of a series of quiz questions and practical exercises. The quiz questions are designed to test your overall understanding of the current material. The practical exercises are intended to afford you the opportunity to apply the concepts discussed during the current hour, as well as build upon the knowledge acquired in previous hours of study. Please take time to complete the quiz questions and exercises before continuing. Refer to Appendix C, "Answers to Quizzes and Exercises," for answers.

Quiz

1. Can a database on a server be accessed from another server?
2. What can a company use to disseminate information to its own employees?
3. Products that allow connections to databases are called what?
4. Can SQL be embedded into Internet programming languages?
5. How is a remote database accessed through a Web application?

Exercises

1. Connect to the Internet and take a look at various companies' home pages. If your own company has a home page, compare it to the competition's home pages. Ask yourself these questions about the pages:

   a. Does the page come up quickly or is it bogged down with too many graphics?

   b. Is the page interesting to read?

   c. Do you know anything about the company, services, or products after reading the available information?

   d. If applicable, has access to the database been easy?

   e. Do there appear to be any security mechanisms on the Web page?

2. If your company has an intranet, sign on and take a look at what information is available about the company. Is there a database available? If so, who is the vendor? What type of front-end tools are available?

23

HOUR **24**

Extensions to Standard SQL

This hour covers extensions to ANSI-standard SQL. Although most implementations conform to the standard for the most part, many vendors have provided extensions to standard SQL through various enhancements.

The highlights of this hour include

- Various implementations
- Differences between implementations
- Compliance with ANSI SQL
- Interactive SQL statements
- Using variables
- Using parameters

Various Implementations

There are numerous SQL implementations that are released by various vendors. All of the relational database vendors could not possibly be mentioned;

a few of the leading implementations, however, are discussed. The implementations discussed here are Sybase, dBase, Microsoft SQL Server, and Oracle. Other popular vendors providing database products other than those mentioned previously include Borland, IBM, Informix, Progress, CA-Ingres, and many more.

Differences Between Implementations

Although the implementations listed here are relational database products, there are specific differences between each. These differences stem from the design of the product and the way data is handled by the database engine; however, this book concentrates on the SQL aspect of the differences. All implementations use SQL as the language for communicating with the database, as directed by ANSI. Many have some sort of extension to SQL that is unique to that particular implementation.

> Differences in SQL have been adopted by various vendors to enhance ANSI SQL for performance considerations and ease of use. Vendors also strive to make enhancements that provide them with advantages over other vendors, making their implementation more attractive to the customer.

Now that you know SQL, you should have little problem adjusting to the differences in SQL among the various vendors. In other words, if you can write SQL in a Sybase implementation, you should be able to write SQL in Oracle. Besides, knowing SQL for various vendors accomplishes nothing less than improving your résumé.

The following sections compare the SELECT statement's syntax from a few major vendors to the ANSI standard.

The following is the ANSI standard:

```
SELECT [DISTINCT ] [* | COLUMN1 [, COLUMN2 ]

FROM TABLE1 [, TABLE2 ]
[ WHERE SEARCH_ CONDITION ]
GROUP BY [ TABLE_ALIAS | COLUMN1 [, COLUMN2 ]
[ HAVING SEARCH_CONDITION ]]
[{UNION | INTERSECT | EXCEPT}][ ALL ]
[ CORRESPONDING [ BY (COLUMN1 [, COLUMN2 ]) ]
QUERY_SPEC | SELECT * FROM TABLE | TABLE_CONSTRUCTOR ]
[ORDER BY SORT_LIST ]
```

▼ SYNTAX
▲

The following is the syntax for SQLBase:

```
SELECT  [ ALL | DISTINCT ] COLUMN1 [, COLUMN2 ]
FROM TABLE1 [, TABLE2 ]
[ WHERE SEARCH_CONDITION ]
[ GROUP BY COLUMN1 [, COLUMN2 ]
[ HAVING SEARCH_CONDITION ]]
[ UNION [ ALL ]]
[ ORDER BY SORT_LIST ]
[ FOR UPDATE OF COLUMN1 [, COLUMN2 ]]
```

The following is the syntax for Oracle:

```
SELECT [ ALL | DISTINCT ] COLUMN1 [, COLUMN2 ]
FROM TABLE1 [, TABLE2 ]
[ WHERE SEARCH_CONDITION ]
[[ START WITH SEARCH_CONDITION ]
CONNECT BY SEARCH_CONDITION ]
[ GROUP BY COLUMN1 [, COLUMN2 ]
[ HAVING SEARCH_CONDITION ]]
[{UNION [ ALL ] | INTERSECT | MINUS} QUERY_SPEC ]
[ ORDER BY COLUMN1 [, COLUMN2 ]]
[ NOWAIT ]
```

24

The following is the syntax for Informix:

```
SELECT [ ALL  | DISTINCT | UNIQUE ] COLUMN1 [, COLUMN2 ]
FROM TABLE1 [, TABLE2 ]
[ WHERE SEARCH_CONDITION ]
[ GROUP BY {COLUMN1 [, COLUMN2 ] | INTEGER}
[ HAVING SEARCH_CONDITION ]]
[ UNION QUERY_SPEC ]
[ ORDER BY COLUMN1 [, COLUMN2 ]
[ INTO TEMP TABLE [ WITH NO LOG ]]
```

As you can see by comparing the syntax examples, the basics are there. All have the SELECT, FROM, WHERE, GROUP BY, HAVING, UNION, and ORDER BY clauses. Each of these clauses works conceptually the same, but some have additional options that may not be found in other implementations. These options are called *enhancements*.

Compliance with ANSI SQL

Vendors do strive to comply with ANSI SQL; however, none are 100 percent ANSI SQL-standard. Some vendors have added commands or functions to ANSI SQL, and many of these new commands or functions have been adopted by ANSI SQL. It is beneficial for a vendor to comply with the standard for many reasons. One obvious benefit to standard compliance is that the vendor's implementation will be easy to learn, and the SQL code used is portable to other implementations. Portability is definitely a factor when a database is being migrated from one implementation to another. Why would a company spend uncountable dollars on a conversion to another implementation that was not compliant to the standard? It probably wouldn't if too many changes would have to be made to the application and the new implementation were difficult to learn. Therefore, ANSI SQL compliance is not a problem in most cases.

Extensions to SQL

Practically all the major vendors have an extension to SQL. A SQL extension is unique to a particular implementation and is generally not portable between implementations. However, popular standard extensions are reviewed by ANSI and are sometimes implemented as a part of the new standard.

PL/SQL, which is a product of Oracle Corporation, and Transact-SQL, which is used by both Sybase and Microsoft SQL Server, are two examples of standard SQL extensions. Both extensions are discussed in relative detail for the examples during this hour.

Examples of Extensions from Some Implementations

Both PL/SQL and Transact-SQL are considered fourth-generation programming languages. Both are procedural languages versus SQL, which is a non-procedural language. We will also briefly discuss another implementation of SQL called MySQL, which can be downloaded from the Internet.

The non-procedural language SQL includes statements such as the following:

- INSERT
- UPDATE
- DELETE
- SELECT
- COMMIT
- ROLLBACK

An SQL extension considered a procedural language includes all of the preceding statements, commands, and functions of standard SQL. In addition, extensions include statements such as:

- Variable declarations
- Cursor declarations
- Conditional statements

- Loops
- Error handling
- Variable incrementing
- Date conversions
- Wildcard operators
- Triggers
- Stored procedures

These statements allow the programmer to have more control over the way data is handled in a procedural language.

> Standard SQL is primarily a *non-procedural language*, which means that you issue statements to the database server. The database server decides how to optimally execute the statement. *Procedural languages* allow the programmer not only to request the data to be retrieved or manipulated, but to tell the database server exactly how to carry out the request.

Transact-SQL

Transact-SQL is a procedural language, which means you tell the database the hows and wheres of finding and manipulating data; SQL is non-procedural, and the database decides the hows and wheres of selecting and manipulating data. Some highlights of Transact-SQL's capabilities include declaring local and global variables, cursors, error handling, triggers, stored procedures, loops, wildcard operators, date conversions, and summarized reports.

An example Transact-SQL statement follows:

```
IF (SELECT AVG(COST) FROM PRODUCTS_TBL) > 50
BEGIN
  PRINT "LOWER ALL COSTS BY 10 PERCENT."
END
ELSE
  PRINT "COSTS ARE REASONABLE."
END
```

ANALYSIS This is a very simple Transact-SQL statement. It states that if the average cost in the PRODUCTS_TBL table is greater than 50, the text "LOWER ALL COSTS BY 10 PERCENT" will be printed. If the average cost is less-than or equal to 50, the text "COSTS ARE REASONABLE" will be printed.

24

Notice the use of the IF...ELSE statement to evaluate conditions of data values. The PRINT command is also a new command. These additional options are not even a drop in the bucket of Transact-SQL capabilities.

PL/SQL

PL/SQL is Oracle's extension to SQL. Like Transact-SQL, PL/SQL is a procedural language. PL/SQL is structured in logical blocks of code. There are three sections to a PL/SQL block, two of which are optional. The first section is the DECLARE section and is optional. The DECLARE section contains variables, cursors, and constants. The second section is called the PROCEDURE section. The PROCEDURE section contains the conditional commands and SQL statements. This section is where the block is controlled. The PROCEDURE section is mandatory. The third section is called the EXCEPTION section. The EXCEPTION section defines how the program should handle errors and user-defined exceptions. The EXCEPTION section is optional. Highlights of PL/SQL include the use of variables, constants, cursors, attributes, loops, handling exceptions, displaying output to the programmer, transactional control, stored procedures, triggers, and packages.

An example PL/SQL statement follows:

```
DECLARE
  CURSOR EMP_CURSOR IS SELECT EMP_ID, LAST_NAME, FIRST_NAME, MID_INIT
                       FROM EMPLOYEE_TBL;
  EMP_REC EMP_CURSOR%ROWTYPE;
BEGIN
  OPEN EMP_CURSOR;
  LOOP
    FETCH EMP_CURSOR INTO EMP_REC;
    EXIT WHEN EMP_CURSOR%NOTFOUND;
    IF (EMP_REC.MID_INIT IS NULL) THEN
      UPDATE EMPLOYEE_TBL
      SET MID_INIT = 'X'
      WHERE EMP_ID = EMP_REC.EMP_ID;
      COMMIT;
    END IF;
  END LOOP;
  CLOSE EMP_CURSOR;
END;
```

ANALYSIS There are two out of three sections being used in this example: the DECLARE section and the PROCEDURE section. First, a cursor called EMP_CURSOR is defined by a query. Second, a variable called EMP_REC is declared, whose values have the same data type (%ROWTYPE) as each column in the defined cursor. The first step in the PROCEDURE section (after BEGIN) is to open the cursor. After the cursor is opened, you use the LOOP command to scroll through each record of the cursor, which is eventually terminated by END LOOP. The EMPLOYEE_TBL table should be updated for all rows in the cursor—if the middle initial of an employee is NULL. The update sets the middle initial to 'X'. Changes are committed and the cursor is eventually closed.

MySQL

MySQL is a multi-user, multi-threaded SQL database client/server implementation. MySQL consists of a server daemon, a terminal monitor client program, and several client programs and libraries. The main goals of MySQL are speed, robustness, and ease of use. MySQL was originally designed to provide faster access to very large databases.

MySQL can be downloaded from http://www.mysql.com. To install a MySQL binary distribution, you need GNU gunzip to uncompress the distribution and a reasonable TAR to unpack the distribution. The binary distribution file will be named mysql-VERSION-OS.tar.gz, where VERSION is the version ID of MySQL, and OS is the name of the operating system.

An example query from a MySQL database follows:

INPUT

```
mysql> SELECT CURRENT_DATE(),VERSION();
```

OUTPUT

```
+----------------+----------+
| current_date() | version() |
+----------------+----------+
| 1999-08-09     | 3.22.23b |
+----------------+----------+

1 row in set (0.00 sec)
mysql>
```

24

Interactive SQL Statements

Interactive SQL statements are SQL statements that ask you for a variable, parameter, or some form of data before fully executing. Say you have a SQL statement that is interactive. The statement is used to create users into a database. The SQL statement could prompt you for information such as user ID, name of user, and phone number. The statement could be for one or many users, and would be executed only once. Otherwise, each user would have to be entered individually with the CREATE USER statement. The SQL statement could also prompt you for privileges. Not all vendors have interactive SQL statements; you must check your particular implementation. The following sections show some examples of interactive SQL using Oracle.

Using Parameters

NEW TERM *Parameters* are variables that are written in SQL and reside within an application. Parameters can be passed into an SQL statement during runtime, allowing more flexibility for the user executing the statement. Many of the major implementations allow use of these parameters. The following sections show examples of passing parameters for Oracle and Sybase.

Oracle

Parameters in Oracle can be passed into an otherwise static SQL statement.

```
SELECT EMP_ID, LAST_NAME, FIRST_NAME
FROM EMPLOYEE_TBL
WHERE EMP_ID = '&EMP_ID'
```

The preceding SQL statement returns the EMP_ID, LAST_NAME, and FIRST_NAME for whatever EMP_ID you enter at the prompt.

```
SELECT *
FROM EMPLOYEE_TBL
WHERE CITY = '&CITY'
AND STATE = '&STATE'
```

The preceding statement prompts you for the city and the state. The query returns all data for those employees living in the city and state that you entered.

Sybase

Parameters in Sybase can be passed into a stored procedure.

```
CREATE PROC EMP_SEARCH
(@EMP_ID)
AS
SELECT LAST_NAME, FIRST_NAME
FROM EMPLOYEE_TBL
WHERE EMP_ID = @EMP_ID
```

Type the following to execute the stored procedure and pass a parameter:

```
SP_EMP_SEARCH "443679012"
```

Summary

This hour discussed extensions to standard SQL among vendors' implementations and their compliance with the ANSI standard. Once you learn SQL, you can easily apply your knowledge—and your code—to other implementations of SQL. SQL is portable between vendors, being that most SQL code can be utilized among most implementations with a few minor modifications.

The last part of this hour was spent showing two specific extensions used by three implementations. Transact-SQL is used by Microsoft SQL Server and Sybase, and PL/SQL is used by Oracle. You should have seen some similarities between Transact-SQL and PL/SQL. One thing to note is that these two implementations have first sought their compliance with the standard, and then added enhancements to their implementations for better overall functionality and efficiency. Also discussed was MySQL, which was designed to increase performance for large database queries. This hour intended to make you aware that many SQL extensions do exist and to teach the importance of a vendor's compliance to the ANSI SQL standard.

If you take what you have learned in this book and apply it (build your code, test it, and build upon your knowledge), you are well on your way to mastering SQL. Companies have data and cannot function without databases. Relational databases are everywhere—and because SQL is the standard language with which to communicate and administer a relational database, you have made an excellent decision by learning SQL. Good luck!

Q&A

Q Why do variations in SQL exist?

A Variations in SQL exist between the various implementations because of the way data is stored, the various vendors' ambition for trying to get an advantage over competition, and new ideas that surface.

Q After learning basic SQL, will I be able to use SQL in different implementations?

A Yes. However, remember that there are differences and variations between the implementations. The basic framework for SQL is the same among most implementations.

Workshop

The following workshop is composed of a series of quiz questions and practical exercises. The quiz questions are designed to test your overall understanding of the current material. The practical exercises are intended to afford you the opportunity to apply the concepts discussed during the current hour, as well as build upon the knowledge acquired in previous hours of study. Please take time to complete the quiz questions and exercises before continuing. Refer to Appendix C, "Answers to Quizzes and Exercises," for answers.

Quiz

1. Is SQL a procedural or non-procedural language?
2. What are some of the reasons differences in SQL exist?
3. What are the three basic operations of a cursor, outside of declaring the cursor?
4. Procedural or non-procedural: With which does the database engine decide how to evaluate and execute SQL statements?

Exercises

1. Try some research about the SQL variations among the various vendors. Go to a library or bookstore and look for vendor-specific books on SQL. Compare various SQL statements, such as Data Manipulation Language (DML). Compare the INSERTs, DELETEs, and UPDATEs for the differences. You might also look for an ANSI SQL book in which to make comparisons.

2. Using the EMPLOYEE_TBL (see Appendix D, "CREATE TABLE Statements for Book Examples"), write the interactive SQL statement that returns the name of all employees who have a ZIP code of 46234.

PART IX
Appendixes

APPENDIX A

Common SQL Commands

SQL Statements

ALTER TABLE

```
ALTER TABLE TABLE_NAME
[MODIFY | ADD | DROP]
  [COLUMN COLUMN_NAME][DATATYPE|NULL NOT NULL] [RESTRICT|CASCADE]
[ADD | DROP]  CONSTRAINT CONSTRAINT_NAME]
```

Description: Alters a table's columns.

COMMIT

```
COMMIT [ TRANSACTION ]
```

Description: Saves a transaction to the database.

CREATE DOMAIN

```
CREATE DOMAIN DOMAIN_NAME AS DATA_TYPE [ NULL | NOT NULL]
```

Description: Creates a domain—an object that is associated with a data type and constraints.

CREATE INDEX

```
CREATE INDEX INDEX_NAME
ON TABLE_NAME (COLUMN_NAME)
```

Description: Creates an index on a table.

CREATE ROLE

```
CREATE ROLE ROLE NAME
[ WITH ADMIN [CURRENT_USER | CURRENT_ROLE]]
```

Description: Creates a database role to which system and object privileges can be granted.

CREATE TABLE

```
CREATE TABLE TABLE_NAME
( COLUMN1     DATA_TYPE     [NULL|NOT NULL],
  COLUMN2     DATA_TYPE     [NULL|NOT NULL]É)
```

Description: Creates a database table.

CREATE TABLE AS

```
CREATE TABLE TABLE_NAME AS
SELECT COLUMN1, COLUMN2,...
FROM TABLE_NAME
[ WHERE CONDITIONS ]
[ GROUP BY COLUMN1, COLUMN2,...]
[ HAVING CONDITIONS ]
```

Description: Creates a database table based on another table.

CREATE TYPE

```
CREATE TYPE typename AS OBJECT
( COLUMN1     DATA_TYPE     [NULL|NOT NULL],
  COLUMN2     DATA_TYPE     [NULL|NOT NULL]É)
```

Description: Creates a user-defined type that can be used to define columns in a table.

CREATE VIEW

```
CREATE VIEW AS
SELECT COLUMN1, COLUMN2,...
FROM TABLE_NAME
[ WHERE CONDITIONS ]
[ GROUP BY COLUMN1, COLUMN2,... ]
[ HAVING CONDITIONS ]
```

Description: Creates a view of a table.

DELETE

```
DELETE
FROM TABLE_NAME
[ WHERE CONDITIONS ]
```

Description: Deletes rows of data from a table.

DROP INDEX

```
DROP INDEX INDEX_NAME
```

Description: Drops an index on a table.

DROP TABLE

```
DROP TABLE TABLE_NAME
```

Description: Drops a table from the database.

DROP VIEW

```
DROP VIEW VIEW_NAME
```

Description: Drops a view of a table.

GRANT

```
GRANT PRIVILEGE1, PRIVILEGE2, ... TO USER_NAME
```

Description: Grants privileges to a user.

INSERT

```
INSERT INTO TABLE_NAME [ (COLUMN1, COLUMN2,...]
VALUES ('VALUE1','VALUE2',...)
```

Description: Inserts new rows of data into a table.

INSERT...SELECT

```
INSERT INTO TABLE_NAME
SELECT COLUMN1, COLUMN2
FROM TABLE_NAME
[ WHERE CONDITIONS ]
```

Description: Inserts new rows of data into a table based on data in another table.

REVOKE

```
REVOKE PRIVILEGE1, PRIVILEGE2, ... FROM USER_NAME
```

Description: Revokes privileges from a user.

A

ROLLBACK

```
ROLLBACK [ TO SAVEPOINT_NAME ]
```

Description: Undoes a database transaction.

SAVEPOINT

```
SAVEPOINT SAVEPOINT_NAME
```

Description: Creates transaction SAVEPOINTs in which to ROLLBACK if necessary.

SELECT

```
SELECT [ DISTINCT ] COLUMN1, COLUMN2,...
FROM TABLE1, TABLE2,...
[ WHERE CONDITIONS ]
[ GROUP BY COLUMN1, COLUMN2,...]
[ HAVING CONDITIONS ]
[ ORDER BY COLUMN1, COLUMN2,...]
```

Description: Returns data from one or more database tables; used to create queries.

UPDATE

```
UPDATE TABLE_NAME
SET COLUMN1 = 'VALUE1',
    COLUMN2 = 'VALUE2',...
[ WHERE CONDITIONS ]
```

Description: Updates existing data in a table.

SQL Clauses

SELECT

```
SELECT *
```

```
SELECT COLUMN1, COLUMN2,...
```

```
SELECT DISTINCT (COLUMN1)
```

```
SELECT COUNT(*)
```

Description: Defines columns to display as part of query output.

FROM

```
FROM TABLE1, TABLE2, TABLE3,...
```

Description: Defines tables from which to retrieve data.

WHERE

```
WHERE COLUMN1 = 'VALUE1'
  AND COLUMN2 = 'VALUE2'
...

WHERE COLUMN1 = 'VALUE1'
   OR COLUMN2 = 'VALUE2'
...
WHERE COLUMN IN ('VALUE1' [, 'VALUE2'] )
```

Description: Defines conditions (criteria) placed on a query for data to be returned.

GROUP BY

```
GROUP BY GROUP_COLUMN1, GROUP_COLUMN2,...
```

Description: A form of a sorting operation; used to divide output into logical groups.

HAVING

```
HAVING GROUP_COLUMN1 - 'VALUE1'
   AND GROUP_COLUMN2 = 'VALUE2'
...
```

Description: Similar to the WHERE clause; used to place conditions on the GROUP BY clause.

ORDER BY

```
ORDER BY COLUMN1, COLUMN2,...

ORDER BY 1,2,...
```

Description: Used to sort a query's results.

A

APPENDIX B

ASCII Table

Dec X_{10}	Hex X_{16}	Binary X_2	ASCII	Dec X_{10}	Hex X_{16}	Binary X_2	ASCII
000	00	0000 0000	null	026	1A	0001 1010	→
001	01	0000 0001	☺	027	1B	0001 1011	←
002	02	0000 0010	☻	028	1C	0001 1100	∟
003	03	0000 0011	♥	029	1D	0001 1101	↔
004	04	0000 0100	♦	030	1E	0001 1110	▲
005	05	0000 0101	♣	031	1F	0001 1111	▼
006	06	0000 0110	♠	032	20	0010 0000	space
007	07	0000 0111	•	033	21	0010 0001	!
008	08	0000 1000	◘	034	22	0010 0010	"
009	09	0000 1001	○	035	23	0010 0011	#
010	0A	0000 1010	◙	036	24	0010 0100	$
011	0B	0000 1011	♂	037	25	0010 0101	%
012	0C	0000 1100	♀	038	26	0010 0110	&
013	0D	0000 1101	♪	039	27	0010 0111	'
014	0E	0000 1110	♫	040	28	0010 1000	(
015	0F	0000 1111	☼	041	29	0010 1001	)
016	10	0001 0000	►	042	2A	0010 1010	*
017	11	0001 0001	◄	043	2B	0010 1011	+
018	12	0001 0010	↕	044	2C	0010 1100	,
019	13	0001 0011	‼	045	2D	0010 1101	-
020	14	0001 0100	¶	046	2E	0010 1110	.
021	15	0001 0101	§	047	2F	0010 1111	/
022	16	0001 0110	▬	048	30	0011 0000	0
023	17	0001 0111	↨	049	31	0011 0001	1
024	18	0001 1000	↑	050	32	0011 0010	2
025	19	0001 1001	↓	051	33	0011 0011	3

Dec X_{10}	Hex X_{16}	Binary X_2	ASCII	Dec X_{10}	Hex X_{16}	Binary X_2	ASCII
052	34	0011 0100	4	078	4E	0100 1110	N
053	35	0011 0101	5	079	4F	0100 1111	O
054	36	0011 0110	6	080	50	0101 0000	P
055	37	0011 0111	7	081	51	0101 0001	Q
056	38	0011 1000	8	082	52	0101 0010	R
057	39	0011 1001	9	083	53	0101 0011	S
058	3A	0011 1010	:	084	54	0101 0100	T
059	3B	0011 1011	;	085	55	0101 0101	U
060	3C	0011 1100	<	086	56	0101 0110	V
061	3D	0011 1101	=	087	57	0101 0111	W
062	3E	0011 1110	>	088	58	0101 1000	X
063	3F	0011 1111	?	089	59	0101 1001	Y
064	40	0100 0000	@	090	5A	0101 1010	Z
065	41	0100 0001	A	091	5B	0101 1011	[
066	42	0100 0010	B	092	5C	0101 1100	\
067	43	0100 0011	C	093	5D	0101 1101	]
068	44	0100 0100	D	094	5E	0101 1110	^
069	45	0100 0101	E	095	5F	0101 1111	–
070	46	0100 0110	F	096	60	0110 0000	`
071	47	0100 0111	G	097	61	0110 0001	a
072	48	0100 1000	H	098	62	0110 0010	b
073	49	0100 1001	I	099	63	0110 0011	c
074	4A	0100 1010	J	100	64	0110 0100	d
075	4B	0100 1011	K	101	65	0110 0101	e
076	4C	0100 1100	L	102	66	0110 0110	f
077	4D	0100 1101	M	103	67	0110 0111	g

B

Dec X_{10}	Hex X_{16}	Binary X_2	ASCII	Dec X_{10}	Hex X_{16}	Binary X_2	ASCII
104	68	0110 1000	h	130	82	1000 0010	é
105	69	0110 1001	i	131	83	1000 0011	â
106	6A	0110 1010	j	132	84	1000 0100	ä
107	6B	0110 1011	k	133	85	1000 0101	à
108	6C	0110 1100	l	134	86	1000 0110	å
109	6D	0110 1101	m	135	87	1000 0111	ç
110	6E	0110 1110	n	136	88	1000 1000	ê
111	6F	0110 1111	o	137	89	1000 1001	ë
112	70	0111 0000	p	138	8A	1000 1010	è
113	71	0111 0001	q	139	8B	1000 1011	ï
114	72	0111 0010	r	140	8C	1000 1100	î
115	73	0111 0011	s	141	8D	1000 1101	ì
116	74	0111 0100	t	142	8E	1000 1110	Ä
117	75	0111 0101	u	143	8F	1000 1111	Å
118	76	0111 0110	v	144	90	1001 0000	É
119	77	0111 0111	w	145	91	1001 0001	æ
120	78	0111 1000	x	146	92	1001 0010	Æ
121	79	0111 1001	y	147	93	1001 0011	ô
122	7A	0111 1010	z	148	94	1001 0100	ö
123	7B	0111 1011	{	149	95	1001 0101	ò
124	7C	0111 1100	¦	150	96	1001 0110	û
125	7D	0111 1101	}	151	97	1001 0111	ù
126	7E	0111 1110	~	152	98	1001 1000	ÿ
127	7F	0111 1111	Δ	153	99	1001 1001	Ö
128	80	1000 0000	Ç	154	9A	1001 1010	Ü
129	81	1000 0001	ü	155	9B	1001 1011	¢

Dec X_{10}	Hex X_{16}	Binary X_2	ASCII	Dec X_{10}	Hex X_{16}	Binary X_2	ASCII
156	9C	1001 1100	£	182	B6	1011 0110	╢
157	9D	1001 1101	¥	183	B7	1011 0111	╖
158	9E	1001 1110	₧	184	B8	1011 1000	╕
159	9F	1001 1111	ƒ	185	B9	1011 1001	╣
160	A0	1010 0000	á	186	BA	1011 1010	║
161	A1	1010 0001	í	187	BB	1011 1011	╗
162	A2	1010 0010	ó	188	BC	1011 1100	╝
163	A3	1010 0011	ú	189	BD	1011 1101	╜
164	A4	1010 0100	ñ	190	BE	1011 1110	╛
165	A5	1010 0101	Ñ	191	BF	1011 1111	┐
166	A6	1010 0110	ª	192	C0	1100 0000	└
167	A7	1010 0111	º	193	C1	1100 0001	┴
168	A8	1010 1000	¿	194	C2	1100 0010	┬
169	A9	1010 1001	⌐	195	C3	1100 0011	├
170	AA	1010 1010	¬	196	C4	1100 0100	─
171	AB	1010 1011	½	197	C5	1100 0101	┼
172	AC	1010 1100	¼	198	C6	1100 0110	╞
173	AD	1010 1101	¡	199	C7	1100 0111	╟
174	AE	1010 1110	«	200	C8	1100 1000	╚
175	AF	1010 1111	»	201	C9	1100 1001	╔
176	B0	1011 0000	■	202	CA	1100 1010	╩
177	B1	1011 0001	■	203	CB	1100 1011	╦
178	B2	1011 0010	■	204	CC	1100 1100	╠
179	B3	1011 0011	│	205	CD	1100 1101	═
180	B4	1011 0100	┤	206	CE	1100 1110	╬
181	B5	1011 0101	╡	207	CF	1100 1111	╧

B

Dec X_{10}	Hex X_{16}	Binary X_2	ASCII	Dec X_{10}	Hex X_{16}	Binary X_2	ASCII
208	D0	1101 0000	⊥⊥	234	EA	1110 1010	Ω
209	D1	1101 0001	⊤	235	EB	1110 1011	δ
210	D2	1101 0010	∏	236	EC	1110 1100	∞
211	D3	1101 0011	⊩	237	ED	1110 1101	ø
212	D4	1101 0100	⊢	238	EE	1110 1110	∈
213	D5	1101 0101	F	239	EF	1110 1111	∩
214	D6	1101 0110	∏	240	F0	1110 0000	≡
215	D7	1101 0111	∦	241	F1	1111 0001	±
216	D8	1101 1000	╪	242	F2	1111 0010	≥
217	D9	1101 1001	⌐	243	F3	1111 0011	≤
218	DA	1101 1010	Γ	244	F4	1111 0100	⌠
219	DB	1101 1011	■	245	F5	1111 0101	⌡
220	DC	1101 1100	■	246	F6	1111 0110	÷
221	DD	1101 1101	▌	247	F7	1111 0111	≈
222	DE	1101 1110	▐	248	F8	1111 1000	°
223	DF	1101 1111	▬	249	F9	1111 1001	•
224	E0	1110 0000	α	250	FA	1111 1010	·
225	E1	1110 0001	β	251	FB	1111 1011	√
226	E2	1110 0010	Γ	252	FC	1111 1100	ⁿ
227	E3	1110 0011	π	253	FD	1111 1101	²
228	E4	1110 0100	Σ	254	FE	1111 1110	■
229	E5	1110 0101	σ	255	FF	1111 1111	
230	E6	1110 0110	μ				
231	E7	1110 0111	γ				
232	E8	1110 1000	Φ				
233	E9	1110 1001	θ				

APPENDIX C

Answers to Quizzes and Exercises

Hour 1, "Welcome to the World of SQL"

Quiz Answers

1. What does the acronym SQL stand for?

    A SQL stands for Structured Query Language.

2. What are the six main categories of SQL commands?

    A Data Definition Language (DDL)

    Data Manipulation Language (DML)

    Data Query Language (DQL)

    Data Control Language (DCL)

    Data Administration Commands (DAC)

    Transactional Control Commands (TCC)

3. What are the four transactional control commands?

   A COMMIT

   ROLLBACK

   SAVEPOINT

   SET TRANSACTIONS

4. What is the main difference between client/server technologies and the mainframe?

   A The mainframe is a centralized computer linked to the user through a dumb terminal. In the client/server environment, the user is linked to the server via a network and the user typically has a personal computer versus a dumb terminal.

5. If a field is defined as NULL, does that mean that something has to be entered into that field?

   A No. If a column is defined as NULL, nothing has to be in the column. If a column is defined as NOT NULL, then something has to be entered.

Exercise Answers

1. Identify in what categories the following SQL commands fall.

   CREATE TABLE
   DELETE
   SELECT
   INSERT
   ALTER TABLE
   UPDATE

   A CREATE TABLE DDL, Data Definition Language

   DELETE DML, Data Manipulation Language

   SELECT DQL, Data Query Language

   INSERT DML, Data Manipulation Language

   ALTER TABLE DDL, Data Definition Language

   UPDATE DML, Data Manipulation Language

Hour 2, "Defining Data Structures"

Quiz Answers

1. True or false: An individual's Social Security number can be any of the following data types: constant length character, varying length character, numeric.

   A True, as long as the precision is the correct length.

2. True or false: The scale of a numeric value is the total length allowed for values.

   A False. The precision is the total length, where the scale represents the number of places reserved to the right of a decimal point.

3. Do all implementations use the same data types?

   A No. Most implementations differ in their use of data types. The data types prescribed by ANSI are adhered to, but may differ between implementations according to storage precautions taken by each vendor.

4. What is the precision and scale of the following:

   a. DECIMAL(4,2)

      a. precision = 4, scale = 2

   b. DECIMAL(10,2)

      b. precision = 10, scale = 2

   c. DECIMAL(14,1)

      c. precision = 14, scale = 1

5. Which numbers could be inserted into a DECIMAL(4,1)?

   a. 16.2

   b. 116.2

   c. 16.21

   d. 1116.2

   e. 1116.21

   The first three fit, although 16.21 is rounded off. The numbers 1116.2 and 1116.21 exceed the maximum precision, which was set at 4.

Exercise Answers

1. Take the following column titles, assign them to a data type, and decide on the proper length.

   a. SSN   constant-length character

   b. CITY   varying-length character

   c. STATE   varying-length character

   d. ZIP   constant-length character

   e. PHONE_NUMBER   constant-length character

   f. LAST_NAME   varying-length character

   g. FIRST_NAME   varying-length character

C

h. MIDDLE_NAME   varying-length character

i. SALARY   numeric data type

j. HOURLY_PAY_RATE   decimal

k. DATE_HIRED   date

2. Take the same column titles and decide if they should be NULL or NOT NULL.

a. SSN   NOT NULL

b. STATE   NOT NULL

c. CITY   NOT NULL

d. PHONE_NUMBER   NULL

e. ZIP   NOT NULL

f. LAST_NAME   NOT NULL

g. FIRST_NAME   NOT NULL

h. MIDDLE_NAME   NULL

i. SALARY   NULL

j. HOURLY_PAY_RATE   NULL

k. DATE_HIRED   NOT NULL

Every individual may not have a phone (however rare that may be) and not everyone has a middle name, so these columns should allow NULL values. In addition, not all employees are paid an hourly rate.

Hour 3, "Managing Database Objects"

Quiz Answers

1. Will the following CREATE TABLE statement work? If not, what needs to be done to correct the problem(s)?

```
CREATE TABLE EMPLOYEE_TABLE AS:
( SSN          NUMBER(9)     NOT NULL,
  LAST_NAME    VARCHAR2(20)    NOT NULL
  FIRST_NAME    VARCHAR2(20)     NOT NULL,
  MIDDLE_NAME    VARCHAR2(20)      NOT NULL,
  ST ADDRESS    VARCHAR2(30)      NOT NULL,
  CITY         CHAR(20)     NOT NULL,
  STATE        CHAR2)         NOT NULL,
  ZIP         NUMBER(4)     NOT NULL,
  DATE HIRED    DATE)
  STORAGE
  (INITIAL       3K,
  next            1k);
```

A The CREATE TABLE statement will not work because there are several errors in the syntax. The corrected statement follows. A listing of what was incorrect follows a corrected statement.

```
CREATE TABLE EMPLOYEE_TABLE
 ( SSN            NUMBER()     NOT NULL,
 LAST_NAME      VARCHAR2(20)    NOT NULL,
 FIRST_NAME     VARCHAR2(20)    NOT NULL,
 MIDDLE_NAME     VARCHAR2(20),
 ST_ADDRESS     VARCHAR2(30)    NOT NULL,
 CITY          VARCHAR2(20)    NOT NULL,
 STATE         CHAR(2)        NOT NULL,
 ZIP          NUMBER(5)    NOT NULL,
 DATE_HIRED     DATE )
 STORAGE
 (INITIAL       3k
 NEXT                1k);
```

The following needs to be done:

1. The as: should not be in this CREATE TABLE statement.

2. Missing a comma after the NOT NULL for the LAST_NAME column.

3. The MIDDLE_NAME column should be NULL because not everyone has a middle name.

4. The column ST ADDRESS should be ST_ADDRESS. Being two words, the database looked at ST as being the column name, which would make the database look for a valid data type, where it would find the word ADDRESS.

5. The city column works, although it would be better to use the VARCHAR2 data type. If all city names were constant length, CHAR would be okay.

6. The STATE column is missing a left parenthesis.

7. The ZIP column length should be (5), not (4).

8. The DATE HIRED column should be DATE_HIRED with an underscore to make the column name one continuous string.

9. The comma after 3k in the STORAGE clause should not be there.

2. Can I drop a column from a table?

A Yes. However, even though it is an ANSI standard, you must check your particular implementation to see if it has been accepted.

3. What happens if I do not include the STORAGE clause in the CREATE TABLE statement?

A The CREATE TABLE statement should process, barring any syntax errors of course; however, most implementations have a default sizing. Check your particular implementation for the sizing.

C

Hour 4, "The Normalization Process"

Quiz Answers

1. True or false: Normalization is the process of grouping data into logical related groups.

   A True.

2. True or false: Having no duplicate or redundant data in a database and having everything in the database normalized is always the best way to go.

   A False. Not always; normalization can and does slow performance because more tables must be joined which results in more I/O and CPU time.

3. True or false: If data is in the third normal form, it is automatically in the first and second normal forms.

   A True.

4. What is a major advantage of a denormalized database versus a normalized database?

   A Improved performance.

5. What are some major disadvantages of denormalization?

   A Having redundant and duplicate data takes up valuable space; it is harder to code, and much more data maintenance is required.

Exercise Answers

1. Employees:

   Angela Smith, secretary, 317-545-6789, RR 1 Box 73, Greensburg, Indiana, 47890, $9.50 hour, date started January 22, 1996, SSN is 323149669.

   Jack Lee Nelson, salesman, 3334 N Main St, Brownsburg, IN, 45687, 317-852-9901, salary of $35,000.00 year, SSN is 312567342, date started 10/28/95.

   Customers:

   Robert's Games and Things, 5612 Lafayette Rd, Indianapolis, IN, 46224, 317-291-7888, customer ID is 432A.

   Reed's Dairy Bar, 4556 W 10th St, Indianapolis, IN, 46245, 317-271-9823, customer ID is 117A.

   Customer Orders:

   Customer ID is 117A, date of last order is February 20, 1999, product ordered was napkins, and the product ID is 661.

A

Employees	Customers	Orders
SSN	CUSTOMER ID	CUSTOMER ID
NAME	NAME	PRODUCT ID
STREET ADDRESS	STREET ADDRESS	PRODUCT
CITY	CITY	DATE ORDERED
STATE	STATE	
ZIP	ZIP	
PHONE NUMBER	PHONE NUMBER	
SALARY		
HOURLY PAY		
START DATE		
POSITION		

Hour 5, "Manipulating Data"

Quiz Answers

1. Using the EMPLOYEE_TBL with the structure:

COLUMN	DATA TYPE	(NOT)NULL
LAST_NAME	VARCHAR2(20)	NOT NULL
FIRST_NAME	VARCHAR2(20)	NOT NULL
SSN	CHAR(9)	NOT NULL
PHONE	NUMBER(10)	NULL

LAST_NAME	FIRST_NAME	SSN	PHONE
SMITH	JOHN	312456788	3174549923
ROBERTS	LISA	232118857	3175452321
SMITH	SUE	443221989	3178398712
PIERCE	BILLY	310239856	3176763990

C

What would happen if the following statements were run?

a.
```
INSERT INTO EMPLOYEE_TBL
(''JACKSON', 'STEVE', '313546078', '3178523443');
```

A   The INSERT statement would not run because the key word VALUES is missing in the syntax.

b.
```
INSERT INTO EMPLOYEE_TBL VALUES
('JACKSON', 'STEVE', '313546078', '3178523443');
```

A   One row would be inserted into the EMPLOYEE_TBL.

c.
```
INSERT INTO EMPLOYEE_TBL VALUES
('MILLER', 'DANIEL', '230980012', NULL);
```

A   One row would be inserted into the EMPLOYEE_TBL, with a NULL value in the PHONE column.

d.
```
INSERT INTO EMPLOYEE_TBL VALUES
('TAYLOR', NULL, '445761212', '3179221331');
```

A   The INSERT statement would not process because the FIRST_NAME column is NOT NULL.

e.
```
DELETE FROM RMPLOYEE_TBL;
```

A   All rows in the EMPLOYEE_TBL would be deleted.

f.
```
DELETE FROM EMPLOYEE_TBL
WHERE LAST_NAME = 'SMITH';
```

A   All employees with the last name of SMITH would be deleted from the EMPLOYEE_TBL.

g.
```
DELETE FROM EMPLOYEE_TBL
WHERE LAST_NAME = 'SMITH'
AND FIRST_NAME = 'JOHN';
```

A   Only JOHN SMITH would be deleted from the EMPLOYEE_TBL.

h.
```
UPDATE EMPLOYEE_TBL
SET LAST_NAME - 'CONRAD';
```

A All last names would be changed to CONRAD.

i.
```
UPDATE EMPLOYEE_TBL
SET LAST_NAME = 'CONRAD'
WHERE LAST_NAME = 'SMITH';
```

A Both JOHN and SUE SMITH would now be JOHN and SUE CONRAD.

j.
```
UPDATE EMPLOYEE_TBL
SET LAST_NAME = 'CONRAD',
FIRST_NAME = 'LARRY';
```

A All employees are now LARRY CONRAD.

k.
```
UPDATE EMPLOYEE_TBL
SET LAST_NAME = 'CONRAD',
FIRST_NAME = 'LARRY'
WHERE SSN = '312456788';
```

A JOHN SMITH is now LARRY CONRAD.

Exercise Answers

2. Using the EMPLOYEE_TBL with the following structure:

COLUMN	DATA TYPE	(NOT)NULL
LAST_NAME	VARCHAR2(20)	NOT NULL
FIRST_NAME	VARCHAR2(20)	NOT NULL
SSN	CHAR(9)	NOT NULL
PHONE	NUMBER(10)	NULL

LAST_NAME	FIRST_NAME	SSN	PHONE
SMITH	JOHN	312456788	3174549923
ROBERTS	LISA	232118857	3175452321
SMITH	SUE	443221989	3178398712
PIERCE	BILLY	310239856	3176763990

Write DML to accomplish the following:

a. Change Billy Pierce's SSN to 310239857.

C

A

```
UPDATE EMPLOYEE_TBL
SET SSN = '310239857'
WHERE SSN = '310239856';
```

b. Add Ben Moore to the EMPLOYEE_TBL, PHONE_NUMBER is 317-564-9880, SSN = 313456789.

A

```
INSERT INTO EMPLOYEE_TBL VALUES
('MOORE', 'BEN', '313456789',
'3175649880');
```

c. John Smith quit; remove his record.

A

```
DELETE FROM EMPLOYEE_TBL
WHERE SSN = '312456788';
```

Hour 6, "Managing Database Transactions"

Quiz Answers

1. True or false: If you have committed several transactions and have several more transactions that have not been committed and you issue a rollback command, all your transactions for the same session will be undone.

   A False. When a transaction is committed, the transaction cannot be rolled back.

2. True or false: A SAVEPOINT actually saves transactions after a specified amount of transactions have executed.

   A False. A SAVEPOINT is only used as a point for a rollback to return to.

3. Briefly describe the purpose of each one of the following commands: COMMIT, ROLLBACK, and SAVEPOINT.

   A The COMMIT saves changes made by a transaction. The ROLLBACK undoes changes made by a transaction. The SAVEPOINT creates logical points in a transaction in which to roll back.

Exercise Answers

1. Take the following transactions and create savepoints after every three transactions; then commit the transactions.

```
SAVEPOINT SAVEPOINT1
TRANSACTION1;
TRANSACTION2;
TRANSACTION3;
```

```
SAVEPOINT SAVEPOINT2
TRANSACTION4;
TRANSACTION5;
TRANSACTION6;
SAVEPOINT SAVEPOINT3
TRANSACTION7;
TRANSACTION8;
TRANSACTION9;
SAVEPOINT SAVEPOINT4
TRANSACTION10;
TRANSACTION11;
TRANSACTION12;
COMMIT;
```

Hour 7, "Introduction to the Database Query"

Quiz Answers

1. Name the required parts for any SELECT statement.

   A The SELECT and FROM keywords, also called clauses, are required for all SELECT statements.

2. In the WHERE clause, are single quotation marks required for all the data?

   A No. Single quotation marks are required when selecting alphanumeric data types. Number data types do not require single quotation marks.

3. Under what part of the SQL language does the SELECT statement (database query) fall?

   A The SELECT statement is considered Data Query Language.

4. Can multiple conditions be used in the WHERE clause?

   A Yes. Multiple conditions can be specified in the WHERE clause of SELECT, INSERT, UPDATE, and DELETE statements. Multiple conditions are used with the operators AND and OR, which are thoroughly discussed next hour.

Exercise Answers

1. Look over the following SELECT statements. Determine whether the syntax is correct. If the syntax is not correct, what would correct the syntax? A table called EMPLOYEE_TBL is used.

   a.
   ```
   SELECT EMP_ID, LAST_NAME, FIRST_NAME,
   FROM EMPLOYEE_TBL;
   ```

b.
```
SELECT EMP_ID, LAST_NAME
ORDER BY EMP_ID
FROM EMPLOYEE_TBL;
```

c.
```
SELECT EMP_ID, LAST_NAME, FIRST_NAME
FROM EMPLOYEE_TBL
WHERE EMP_ID = '333333333'
ORDER BY EMP_ID;
```

d.
```
SELECT EMPE_ID SSN, LAST_NAME
FROM EMPLOYEE_TBL
WHERE EMP_ID = '333333333'
ORDER BY 1;
```

e.
```
SELECT EMP_ID, LAST_NAME, FIRST_NAME
FROM EMPLOYEE_TBL
WHERE EMP_ID = '333333333'
ORDER BY 3, 1, 2;
```

A

a. This SELECT statement does not work because there is a comma after the
   FIRST_NAME column that does not belong there. The correct syntax follows:
```
SELECT EMPLOYEE_ID, LAST_NAME, FIRST_NAME,
    FROM EMPLOYEE_TBL;
```

b. This SELECT statement does not work because the FROM and ORDER BY clauses
   are in the incorrect order. The correct syntax follows:
```
SELECT EMP_ID, LAST_NAME
FROM EMPLOYEE_TBL
ORDER BY EM_ID;
```

c. The syntax for this SELECT statement is correct.

d. The syntax for this SELECT statement is correct. Notice that the employee_id
   column is renamed SSN.

e. Yes. The syntax is correct for this SELECT statement. Notice the order of the
   columns in the ORDER BY. This SELECT statement returns records from the database that are sorted by FIRST_NAME, and then by EMPLOYEE_ID, and finally
   by LAST_NAME.

Hour 8, "Using Operators to Categorize Data"

Quiz Answers

1. True or false: Both conditions when using the OR operator must be TRUE.

   A False. Only one of the conditions must be TRUE.

2. True or false: All specified values must match when using the IN operator.

   A False. Only one of the values must match.

3. True or false: The AND operator can be used in the SELECT and the WHERE clauses.

   A False. The AND can only be used in the WHERE clause.

4. What, if anything, is wrong with the following SELECT statements?

   a.

   ```
   SELECT SALARY
   FROM EMPLOYEE_PAY_TBL
   WHERE SALARY BETWEEN 20000, 30000;
   ```

   A The AND is missing between 20000, 30000. The correct syntax is:

   ```
   SELECT SALARY
   FROM EMPLOYEE_PAY_TBL
   WHERE SALARY BETWEEN 20000 AND 30000;
   ```

   b.

   ```
   SELECT SALARY + DATE_HIRE
   FROM EMPLOYEE_PAY_TBL;
   ```

   A The DATE_HIRE column is a DATE data type and is in the incorrect format for arithmetic functions.

   c.

   ```
   SELECT SALARY, BONUS
   FROM EMPLOYEE_PAY_TBL
   WHERE DATE_HIRE BETWEEN 22-SEP-97
   AND 23-NOV-97
   AND POSITION = 'SALES'
   OR POSITION = 'MARKETING'
   AND EMPLOYEE_ID LIKE '%55%;
   ```

   A The syntax is correct.

C

Exercise Answers

1. Using the following CUSTOMER_TBL:

```
DESCRIBE CUSTOMER_TBL
Name                               Null?     Type
------------------------------- -------- ------------
CUST_ID                         NOT NULL VARCHAR2(10)
 CUST_NAME                      NOT NULL VARCHAR2(30)
 CUST_ADDRESS                   NOT NULL VARCHAR2(20)
 CUST_CITY                      NOT NULL VARCHAR2(12)
 CUST_STATE                     NOT NULL CHAR(2)
 CUST_ZIP                       NOT NULL CHAR(5)
 CUST_PHONE                              NUMBER(10)
 CUST_FAX                                NUMBER(10)
```

Write a SELECT statement that returns customer IDs and customer names (alpha order) for customers who live in Indiana, Ohio, Michigan, and Illinois, with names that begin with the letters A or B.

A

```
SELECT CUST_ID, CUST_NAME, CUST_STATE
FROM CUSTOMER_TBL
WHERE CUST_STATE IN ('IN', 'OH', 'MI', 'IL')
AND CUST_NAME LIKE 'A%'
OR CUST_NAME LIKE 'B%'
ORDER BY CUST_NAME
```

2. Using the following PRODUCTS_TBL:

```
DESCRIBE PRODUCTS_TBL
Name                               Null?     Type
------------------------------- -------- ------------
PROD_ID                         NOT NULL VARCHAR2(10)
PROD_DESC                       NOT NULL VARCHAR2(25)
COST                            NOT NULL NUMBER(6,2)
```

Write a SELECT statement that returns the product ID, PROD_DESC, and the product cost. Limit the product cost to range from $1.00 to $12.50.

A

```
SELECT *
FROM PRODUCTS_TBL
WHERE COST BETWEEN 1.00 AND 12.50
```

Hour 9, "Summarizing Data Results from a Query"

Quiz Answers

1. The AVG function returns an average of all rows from a select column including any NULL values.

   A False. The NULLs are not considered.

2. The SUM function is used to add column totals.

   A False. The SUM function is used to return a total for a group of rows.

3. The COUNT(*) function counts all rows in a table.

   A True.

4. Will the following SELECT statements work? If not, what will fix the statements?

   a.
   ```
   SELECT COUNT *
   FROM EMPLOYEE_PAY_TBL;
   ```

   A This statement will not work because the left and right parentheses are missing around the asterisk. The correct syntax is
   ```
   SELECT COUNT(*)
   FROM EMPLOYEE_PAY_TBL;
   ```

   b.
   ```
   SELECT COUNT(EMPLOYEE_ID), SALARY
   FROM EMPLOYEE_PAY_TBL;
   ```

   A Yes, this statement will work.

   c.
   ```
   SELECT MIN(BONUS), MAX(SALARY)
   FROM EMPLOYEE_PAY_TBL
   WHERE SALARY > 20000;
   ```

   A Yes, this statement will work.

Exercise Answers

1. Using the following EMPLOYEE_PAY_TBL:

   ```
   EMP_ID      POSITION      DATE_HIRE PAY_RATE DATE_LAST   SALARY     BONUS
   ---------   ------------  --------- -------- ----------  ---------  ---------
   311549902 MARKETING      23-MAY-89           01-MAY-99   300002000
   442346889 TEAM LEADER    17-JUN-90  14.75    01-JUN-99
   213764555 SALES MANAGER 14-AUG-94            01-AUG-99   40000      3000
   ```

C

```
313782439 SALESMAN      28-JUN-97                           20000      1000
220984332 SHIPPER       22-JUL-96       11 01-JUL-99
443679012 SHIPPER       14-JAN-91       15 01-JAN-99
```

6 rows selected.

Construct SQL statements to find:

a. The average salary.

A The average salary is $30,000.00. The SQL statement to return the data is

```
SELECT AVG(SALARY)
FROM EMPLOYEE_PAY_TBL;
```

b. The maximum bonus.

A The maximum bonus is $3000.00. The SQL statement to return the data is

```
SELECT MAX(BONUS)
FROM EMPLOYEE_PAY_TBL;
```

c. The total salaries.

A The sum of all the salaries is $60,000.00. The SQL statement to return the data is

```
SELECT SUM(SALARY)
FROM EMPLOYEE_PAY_TBL;
```

d. The minimum pay rate.

A The minimum pay rate is $11.00 an hour. The SQL statement to return the data is

```
SELECT MIN(PAY_RATE)
FROM EMPLOYEE_PAY_TBL;
```

e. The total rows in the table.

A The total row count of the table is six. The SQL statement to return the data is

```
SELECT COUNT(*)
FROM EMPLOYEE_PAY_TBL;
```

Hour 10, "Sorting and Grouping Data"

Quiz Answers

1. Will the following SQL statements work?

   a.
   ```
   SELECT SUM(SALARY), EMP_ID
   FROM EMPLOYEE_PAY_TBL
   GROUP BY 1 and 2;
   ```

A No, this statement does not work. The and in the GROUP BY clause does not belong there, and you cannot use an integer in the GROUP BY clause. The correct syntax is

```
SELECT SUM(SALARY), EMP_ID
FROM EMPLOYEE_PAY_TBL
GROUP BY SALARY, EMP_ID;
```

b.

```
SELECT EMP_ID, MAX(SALARY)
FROM EMPLOYEE_PAY_TBL
GROUP BY SALARY, EMP_ID;
```

A Yes, this statement will work.

c.

```
SELECT EMP_ID, COUNT(SALARY)
FROM EMPLOYEE_PAY_TBL
ORDER BY EMP_ID
GROUP BY SALARY;
```

A No, this statement will not work. The ORDER BY clause and the GROUP BY clause are not in the correct sequence. Also, the EMP_ID column is required in the GROUP BY clause The correct syntax is

```
SELECT EMP_ID, COUNT(SALARY)
FROM EMPLOYEE_PAY_TBL
GROUP BY EMP_ID
ORDER BY EMP_ID;
```

2. True or false: You must also use the GROUP BY clause whenever using the HAVING clause.

   A False. The HAVING clause can be used without a GROUP BY clause.

3. True or false: The following SQL statement returns a total of the salaries by groups.

```
SELECT SUM(SALARY)
FROM EMPLOYEE_PAY_TBL;
```

   A False. The statement cannot return a total of the salaries by groups because there is no GROUP BY clause.

4. True or false: The columns selected must appear in the GROUP BY clause in the same order.

   A False. The order of the columns in the SELECT clause can be in a different order in the GROUP BY clause.

5. The HAVING clause tells the GROUP BY which groups to include.

   A True.

Exercise Answers

1. Write an SQL statement that returns the employee ID, employee name, and city from the EMPLOYEE_TBL. Group by the city column first.

   A

   ```
   SELECT EMP_ID, LAST_NAME, FIRST_NAME, CITY
   FROM EMPLOYEE_TBL
   GROUP BY CITY, EMP_ID, LAST)NAME, FIRST_NAME;
   ```

2. Write an SQL statement that returns the city and a count of all employees per city from EMPLOYEE_TBL. Add a HAVING clause to display only those cities that have a count of more than two employees.

   A

   ```
   SELECT CITY, COUNT(EMP_ID)
   FROM EMPLOYEE_TBL
   GROUP BY CITY
   HAVING COUNT(EMP_ID) > 2;
   ```

Hour 11, "Restructuring the Appearance of Data"

Quiz Answers

Match the Descriptions with the possible Functions.

DESCRIPTIONS	ANSWERS
a. Used to select a portion of a character string.	SUBSTR
b. Used to trim characters from either the right or left of a string.	LTRIM/RTRIM
c. Used to change all letters to lowercase.	LOWER
d. Used to find the length of a string.	LENGTH
e. Used to combine strings. (CONCATENATION is the same as ||.)	CONCATENATION

2. True or false: The SOUNDEX function is used to compare strings that may sound alike.

   A True.

3. The outermost function is always resolved first when functions are embedded within other functions in a query.

   A False. The innermost function is always resolved first when embedding functions within one another.

Exercise Answers

1. Use the appropriate function to convert the string hello to all uppercase letters.

   A

   ```
   SELECT UPPER('hello') FROM TABLE_NAME
   ```

2. Use the appropriate function to print only the first four characters of the string JOHNSON.

   A

   ```
   SELECT SUBSTR('JOHNSON',1,4) FROM TABLE_NAME
   ```

3. Use an appropriate function to concatenate the strings JOHN and SON.

   A Oracle

   ```
   SELECT 'JOHN' || 'SON' FROM TABLE_NAME
   ```

   or

   A SQL Server

   ```
   SELECT 'JOHN' + 'SON' FROM TABLE_NAME
   ```

Hour 12, "Understanding Dates and Time"

Quiz Answers

1. From where are the system date and time normally derived?

   A The system date is derived from the current date and time of the operating system on the host machine.

2. List the standard internal elements of a DATETIME value.

   A YEAR, MONTH, DAY, HOUR, MINUTE, and SECOND.

3. What could be a major factor concerning the representation and comparison of date and time values if your company is an international organization?

   A The awareness of time zones may be a concern.

4. Can a character string date value be compared to a date value defined as a valid DATETIME data type?

   A A DATETIME data type cannot be accurately compared to a date value defined as a character string. The character string must first be converted to the DATETIME data type.

Exercise Answers

1. Provide SQL code for the exercises given the following information:

   Use SYSDATE to represent the current date and time.

   Use the table called DATES.

   Use the TO_CHAR function to convert dates to character strings with the following syntax:

   TO_CHAR('EXPRESSION','DATE_PICTURE')

   Use the TO_DATE function to convert character strings to dates with the following syntax:

   TO_DATE('EXPRESSION','DATE_PICTURE')

Date picture information:

DATE PICTURE	MEANING
MONTH	Month spelled out
DAY	Day spelled out
DD	Day of month, number
MM	Month of year, number
YY	Two-digit year
YYYY	Four-digit year
MI	Minutes of the hour
SS	Seconds of the minute

1. Assuming today is 1999-12-31, convert the current date to the format December 31 1999.

   A
   ```
   SELECT TO_CHAR(SYSDATE,'MONTH DD YYYY')
   FROM DATES;
   ```

2. Convert the following string to DATE format:

   'DECEMBER 31 1999'

A

```
SELECT TO_DATE('DECEMBER 31 1999','MONTH DD YYYY')
FROM DATES;
```

3. Write the code to return the day of the week on which New Year's Eve of 1999 falls. Assume that the date is stored in the format 31-DEC-99, which is a valid DATETIME data type.

A

```
SELECT TO_CHAR('31-DEC-99','DAY')
FROM DATES;
```

Hour 13, "Joining Tables in Queries"

Quiz Answers

1. What type of join would you use to return records from one table, regardless of the existence of associated records in the related table?

   A You would use an OUTER JOIN.

2. The JOIN conditions are located in what part of the SQL statement?

   A The JOIN conditions are located in the WHERE clause.

3. What type of JOIN do you use to evaluate equality among rows of related tables?

   A You would use an EQUIJOIN.

4. What happens if you select from two different tables but fail to join the tables?

   A You receive a Cartesian Product by not joining the tables (this is also called a cross join).

5. Use the following tables:

ORD_NUM	VARCHAR2(10)	NOT NULL	PRIMARY KEY
CUST_ID	VARCHAR2(10)	NOT NULL	
PROD_ID	VARCHAR2(10)	NOT NULL	
QTY	NUMBER(6)	NOT NULL	
ORD_DATE	DATE		

PRODUCTS_TBL

PROD_ID	VARCHAR2(10)	NOT NULL	PRIMARY KEY
PROD_DESC	VARCHAR2(40)	NOT NULL	
COST	NUMBER(6,2)	NOT NULL	

C

Is the following syntax correct for using an OUTER JOIN?

```
SELECT C.CUST_ID, C.CUST_NAME, O.ORD_NUM
FROM CUSTOMER_TBL C, ORDERS_TBL O
WHERE C.CUST_ID(+) = O.CUST_ID(+)
```

A No, the syntax is not correct. The (+) operator should only follow the O.CUST_ID column in the WHERE clause. The correct syntax is

```
SELECT C.CUST_ID, C.CUST_NAME, O.ORD_NUM
FROM CUSTOMER_TBL C, ORDERS_TBL O
WHERE C.CUST_ID = O.CUST_ID(+);
```

Exercise Answers

1. Perform the exercises using the following tables:

EMPLOYEE_TBL

EMP_ID	VARCHAR2(9)	NOT NULL	PRIMARY KEY
LAST_NAME	VARCHAR2(15)	NOT NULL	
FIRST_NAME	VARCHAR2(15)	NOT NULL	
MIDDLE_NAME	VARCHAR2(15)		
ADDRESS	VARCHAR2(30)	NOT NULL	
CITY	VARCHAR2(15)	NOT NULL	
STATE	CHAR(2)	NOT NULL	
ZIP	NUMBER(5)	NOT NULL	
PHONE	CHAR(10)		
PAGER	CHAR(10)		

EMPLOYEE_PAY_TBL

EMP_ID	VARCHAR2(9)	NOT NULL	PRIMARY KEY
POSITION	VARCHAR2(15)	NOT NULL	
DATE_HIRE	DATE		
PAY_RATE	NUMBER(4,2)	NOT NULL	
DATE_LAST-RAISE	DATE		
SALARY	NUMBER(6,2)		
BONUS	NUMBER(4,2)		

```
CONSTRAINT EMP_FK FOREIGN KEY  (EMP_ID) REFERENCED
    EMPLOYEE_TBL (EMP_ID)
```

<u>CUSTOMER_TBL</u>

CUST_ID	VARCHAR2(10)	NOT NULL	PRIMARY KEY
CUST_NAME	VARCHAR2(30)	NOT NULL	
CUST_ADDRESS	VARCHAR2(20)	NOT NULL	
CUST_CITY	VARCHAR2(15)	NOT NULL	
CUST_STATE	CHAR(2)	NOT NULL	
CUST_ZIP	NUMBER(5)	NOT NULL	
CUST_PHONE	NUMBER(10)		
CUST_FAX	NUMBER(10)		

<u>ORDERS_TBL</u>

ORD_NUM	VARCHAR2(10)	NOT NULL	PRIMARY KEY
CUST_ID	VARCHAR2(10)	NOT NULL	
PROD_ID	VARCHAR2(10)	NOT NULL	
QTY	NUMBER(6)	NOT NULL	
ORD_DATE	DATE		

<u>PRODUCTS_TBL</u>

PROD_ID	VARCHAR2(10)	NOT NULL	PRIMARY KEY
PROD_DESC	VARCHAR2(40)	NOT NULL	
COST	NUMBER(6,2)	NOT NULL	

1. Write an SQL statement to return the EMP_ID, LAST_NAME, and FIRST_NAME from the EMPLOYEE_TBL and SALARY, BONUS from the EMPLOYEE_PAY_TBL.

   A

   ```
   SELECT E.EMP_ID, E.LAST_NAME, E.FIRST_NAME
   EP.SALARY, EP.BONUS
   FROM EMPLOYEE_TBL E,
   EMPLOYE_PAY_TBL EP
   WHERE E.EMP_ID = EP.EMP_ID
   ```

2. Select from the CUSTOMERS_TBL the columns: CUST_ID, CUST_NAME. Select from the PRODUCTS_TBL the columns: PROD_ID, COST. Select from the ORDERS_TBL the columns: ORD_NUM, QTY. Join all three of the tables into one SQL statement.

   A

   ```
   SELECT C.CUST_ID, C.CUST_NAME, P.PROD_ID, P.COST,
   O.ORD_NUM, O.QTY
   ```

C

```
FROM CUSTOMER_TBL C,
PRODUCT_TBL P,
ORDERS_TBL O
WHERE C.CUST_ID = O.CUST_ID
AND P.PROD_ID = O.PROD_ID
```

Hour 14, "Using Subqueries to Define Unknown Data"

Quiz Answers

1. What is the function of a subquery when used with a SELECT statement?

   A The main function of a subquery when used with a SELECT statement is to return data that the main query can use to resolve the query.

2. Can you update more than one column when using the UPDATE statement in conjunction with a subquery?

   A Yes, you can update more than one column using the same UPDATE and subquery statement.

3. Are the following syntaxes correct? If not, what is the correct syntax?

   a.
```
SELECT CUST_ID, CUST_NAME
       FROM CUSTOMER_TBL
       WHERE CUST_ID =
                    (SELECT CUST_ID
                     FROM ORDERS_TBL
                     WHERE ORD_NUM = '16C17')
```

   A Yes, this syntax is correct.

   b.
```
SELECT EMP_ID, SALARY
       FROM EMPLOYEE_PAY_TBL
       WHERE SALARY BETWEEN '20000'
                    AND (SELECT SALARY
                         FROM EMPLOYEE_ID
                         WHERE SALARY = '40000')
```

   A No. The BETWEEN operator cannot be used in this format.

   c.
```
UPDATE PRODUCTS_TBL
   SET COST = 1.15
   WHERE CUST_ID =
                  (SELECT CUST_ID
                   FROM ORDERS_TBL
                   WHERE ORD_NUM = '32A132')
```

A Yes, this syntax is correct.

4. What would happen if the following statement were run?

```
DELETE FROM EMPLOYEE_TBL
WHERE EMP_ID IN
            (SELECT EMP_ID
             FROM EMPLOYEE_PAY_TBL)
```

A All rows that were retrieved from the EMPLOYEE_PAY_TBL would be used by the DELETE to remove them from the EMPLOYEE_TBL. A WHERE clause in the subquery is highly advised.

Exercise Answers

1. Use the following tables:

EMPLOYEE_TBL

EMP_ID	VARCHAR2(9)	NOT NULL	PRIMARY KEY
LAST_NAME	VARCHAR2(15)	NOT NULL	
FIRST_NAME	VARCHAR2(15)	NOT NULL	
MIDDLE NAME	VARCHAR2(15)		
ADDRESS	VARCHAR2(30)	NOT NULL	
CITY	VARCHAR2(15)	NOT NULL	
STATE	CHAR(2)	NOT NULL	
ZIP	NUMBER(5)	NOT NULL	
PHONE	CHAR(10)		
PAGER	CHAR(10)		

EMPLOYEE_PAY_TBL

EMP_ID	VARCHAR2(9)	NOT NULL	PRIMARY KEY
POSITION	VARCHAR2(15)	NOT NULL	
DATE_HIRE	DATE		
PAY_RATE	NYMBER(4,2)	NOT NULL	
DATE_LAST_RAISE	DATE		

```
CONSTRAINT EMP_FK FOREIGN KEY  (EMP_ID_ REFERENCES
    EMPLOYEE_TBL (EMP_ID)
```

C

CUSTOMER_TBL			
CUST_ID	VARCHAR2(10)	NOT NULL	PRIMARY KEY
CUST_NAME	VARCHAR2(30)	NOT NULL	
CUST_ADDRESS	VARCHAR2(20)	NOT NULL	
CUST_CITY	VARCHAR2(15)	NOT NULL	
CUST_STATE	CHAR(2)	NOT NULL	
CUST_ZIP	NUMBER(5)	NOT NULL	
CUST_PHONE	NUMBER(10)		
CUST_FAX	NUMBER(10)		

ORDERS_TBL			
ORD_NUM	VARCHAR2(10)	NOT NULL	PRIMARY KEY
CUST_ID	VARCHAR2(10)	NOT NULL	
PROD_ID	VARCHAR2(10)	NOT NULL	
QTY	NUMBER(6)	NOT NULL	
ORD_DATE	DATE		

PRODUCTS_TBL			
PROD_ID	VARCHAR2(10)	NOT NULL	PRIMARY KEY
PROD_DESC	VARCHAR2(40)	NOT NULL	
COST	NUMBER(6,2)	NOT NULL	

2. Using a subquery, write an SQL statement to update the CUSTOMER_TBL table, changing the customer name to DAVIDS MARKET, with order number 23E934.

A
```
UPDATE CUSTOMER_TBL
   SET CUST_NAME = 'DAVIDS MARKET'
   WHERE CUST_ID =
                (SELECT CUST_ID
                 FROM ORDERS_TBL
                 WHERE ORD_NUM = '23E934');
```

3. Using a subquery, write a query that returns the names of all employees who have a pay rate greater than JOHN DOE, who's employee identification number is 343559876.

A
```
SELECT E.LAST_NAME, E.FIRST_NAME, E.MIDDLE_NAME
   FROM EMPLOYEE_TBL E,
        EMPLOYEE_PAY_TBL P
```

```
        WHERE P.PAY_RATE > (SELECT PAY_RATE
                            FROM EMPLOYEE_PAY_TBL
                            WHERE EMP_ID = '343559876');
```

4. Using a subquery, write a query that lists all products that cost more than the average cost of all products.

   A

```
SELECT PROD_DESC
  FROM PRODUCTS_TBL
  WHERE COST > (SELECT AVG(COST)
               FROM PRODUCTS_TBL);
```

Hour 15, "Combining Multiple Queries into One"

Quiz Answers

1. Is the syntax correct for the following compound queries? If not, what would correct the syntax? Use the EMPLOYEE_TBL and the EMPLOYEE_PAY_TBL shown as follows:

   EMPLOYEE_TBL

EMP_ID	VARCHAR2(9)	NOT NULL
LAST_NAME	VARCHAR2(15)	NOT NULL
FIRST_NAME	VARCHAR2(15)	NOT NULL
MIDDLE_NAME	VARCHAR2(15)	
ADDRESS	VARCHAR2(30)	NOT NULL
CITY	VARCHAR2(15)	NOT NULL
STATE	CHAR(2)	NOT NULL
ZIP	NUMBER(5)	NOT NULL
PHONE	CHAR(10)	
PAGER	CHAR(10)	

C

EMPLOYEE_PAY_TBL			
EMP_ID	VARCHAR2(9)	NOT NULL	PRIMARY KEY
POSITION	VARCHAR2(15)	NOT NULL	
DATE_HIRE	DATE		
PAY_RATE	NUMBER(4,2)	NOT NULL	
DATE_LAST_RAISE	DATE		
SALARY	NUMBER(8,2)		
BONUS	NUMBER(6,2)		

a.
```
SELECT EMP_ID, LAST_NAME, FIRST_NAME
FROM EMPLOYEE_TBL
UNION
SELECT EMP_ID, POSITION, DATE_HIRE
FROM EMPLOYEE_PAY_TBL
```

A This compound query does not work because the data types do not match. The EMP_ID columns match, but the LAST_NAME and FIRST_NAME data types do not match the POSITION and DATE_HIRE data types.

b.
```
SELECT EMP_ID FROM EMPLOYEE_TBL
UNION ALL
SELECT EMP_ID FROM EMPLOYEE_PAY_TBL
ORDER BY EMP_ID
```

A Yes, the statement is correct.

c.
```
SELECT EMP_ID FROM EMPLOYEE_PAY_TBL
INTERSECT
SELECT EMP_ID FROM EMPLOYEE_TBL
ORDER BY 1
```

A Yes, this compound query works.

2. Match the correct operator to the following statements:

STATEMENT	OPERATOR
a. Show duplicates.	**A** UNION ALL
b. Return only rows from the first query that match those in the second query.	**A** INTERSECT

c. Return no duplicates.   **A** UNION

d. Return only rows from
   the first query not
   returned by the second.   **A** EXCEPT

Exercise Answers

1. Using the CUSTOMER_TBL and the ORDERS_TBL as listed:

   CUSTOMER_TBL

CUST_IN	VARCHAR2(10)	NOT NULL	PRIMARY KEY
CUST_NAME	VARCHAR2(30)	NOT NULL	
CUST_ADDRESS	VARCHAR2(20)	NOT NULL	
CUST_CITY	VARCHAR2(15)	NOT NULL	
CUST_STATE	CHAR(2)	NOT NULL	
CUST_ZIP	NUMBER(5)	NOT NULL	
CUST_PHONE	NUMBER(10)		
CUST_FAX	NUMBER(10)		

   ORDERS_TBL

ORD_NUM	VARCHAR2(10)	NOT NULL	PRIMARY KEY
CUST_ID	VARCHAR2(10)	NOT NULL	
PROD_ID	VARCHAR2(10)	NOT NULL	
QTY	NUMBER(6)	NOT NULL	
ORD_DATE	DATE		

a. Write a compound query to find the customers who have placed an order.

   A

   ```
   SELECT CUST_ID FROM CUSTOMER_TBL
   INTERSECT
   SELECT CUST_ID FROM ORDERS_TBL;
   ```

b. Write a compound query to find the customers who have not placed an order.

   A

   ```
   SELECT CUST_ID FROM CUSTOMER_TBL
   EXCEPT
   SELECT CUST_ID FROM ORDERS_TBL;
   ```

C

Hour 16, "Using Indexes to Improve Performance"

Quiz Answers

1. What are some major disadvantages of using indexes?

   A Major disadvantages of an index include slowing batch jobs, storage space on the disk, and maintenance upkeep on the index.

2. Why is the order of columns in a composite important?

   A Because query performance is improved by putting the column with the most restrictive values first.

3. Should a column with a large percentage of NULLs be indexed?

   A No. A column with a large percentage of NULLs should not be indexed, because the speed of accessing these rows degrades when the value of a large percentage of rows is the same.

4. Is the main purpose of an index to stop duplicate values in a table?

   A No. The main purpose of an index is to enhance data retrieval speed, although a unique index stops duplicate values in a table.

5. True or false: The main reason for a composite index is for aggregate function usage in an index.

   A False. The main reason for composite indexes is for two or more columns in the same table to be indexed.

Exercise Answers

1. Decide whether an index should be used in the following situations, and if so, what type of index should be used.

   a. Several columns, but a rather small table.

   A Being a very small table, no index needed.

   b. Medium-sized table, no duplicates should be allowed.

   A A unique index could be used.

   c. Several columns, very large table, several columns are used as filters in the WHERE clause.

   A A composite index on the columns used as filter in the WHERE clause should be the choice.

   d. Large table, many columns, lots of data manipulation.

A A choice of a single-column or composite index should be considered, depending on filtering, ordering, and grouping. For the large amount of data manipulation, the index could be dropped and re-created after the INSERT, UPDATE, or DELETE jobs were done.

Hour 17, "Improving Database Performance"

Quiz Answers

1. Would the use of a unique index on a small table be of any benefit?

   A The index may not be of any use for performance issues; but, the unique index would keep referential integrity intact. Referential integrity is discussed in Hour 3, "Managing Database Objects."

2. What happens when the optimizer chooses not to use an index on a table when a query has been executed?

   A A full table scan occurs.

3. Should the most restrictive clause(s) be evaluated before or after the join condition(s) in the WHERE clause?

   A The most restrictive clause(s) should be evaluated before the join condition(s) because join conditions normally return a large number of rows.

Exercise Answers

1. Rewrite the following SQL statements to improve their performance. Use the EMPLOYEE_TBL and the EMPLOYEE_PAY_TBL as described here:

EMPLOYEE_TBL

EMP_ID	VARCHAR2(9)	NOT NULL	PRIMARY KEY
LAST_NAME	VARCHAR2(15)	NOT NULL	
FIRST_NAME	VARCHAR2(15)	NOT NULL	
MIDDLE_NAME	VARCHAR2(15)		
ADDRESS	VARCHAR2(30)	NOT NULL	
CITY	VARCHAR2(15)	NOT NULL	
STATE	CHAR(2)	NOT NULL	
ZIP	NUMBER(5)	NOT NULL	
PHONE	CHAR(10)		
PAGER	CHAR(10)		

C

EMPLOYEE_PAY_TBL

EMP_ID	VARCHAR2(9)	NOT NULL	PRIMARY KEY
POSITION	VARCHAR2(15)	NOT NULL	
DATE_HIRE	DATE		
PAY_RATE	NUMBER(4,2)	NOT NULL	
DATE_LAST_RAISE	DATE		
SALARY	NUMBER(8,2)		
BONUS	NUMBER(8,2)		

a.
```
SELECT EMP_ID, LAST_NAME, FIRST_NAME,
          PHONE
   FROM EMPLOYEE_TBL
   WHERE SUBSTR(PHONE, 1, 3) = '317' OR
         SUBSTR(PHONE, 1, 3) = '812' OR
         SUBSTR(PHONE, 1, 3) = '765';
```

A
```
SELECT EMP_ID, LAST_NAME, FIRST_NAME, PHONE
   FROM EMPLOYEE_TBL
   WHERE SUBSTR(PHONE, 1, 3) IN ('317', '812', '765');
```

b.
```
SELECT LAST_NAME, FIRST_NAME
   FROM EMPLOYEE_TBL
   WHERE LAST_NAME LIKE '%ALL%';
```

A
```
SELECT LAST_NAME, FIRST_NAME
 FROM EMPLOYEE_TBL
 WHERE LAST_NAME LIKE 'WAL%';
```

c.
```
SELECT E.EMP_ID, E.LAST_NAME, E.FIRST_NAME,
          EP.SALARY
   FROM EMPLOYEE_TBL E,
   EMPLOYEE_PAY_TBL EP
   WHERE LAST_NAME LIKE 'S%'
   AND E.EMP_ID = EP.EMP_ID;
```

A
```
SELECT E.EMP_ID, E.LAST_NAME, E.FIRST_NAME,
          EP.SALARY
   FROM EMPLOYEE_PAY_TBL EP,
        EMPLOYEE_TBL E
   WHERE E.EMP_ID = EP.EMP_ID
   AND LAST_NAME LIKE 'S';
```

Hour 18, "Managing Database Users"

Quiz Answers

1. What command is used to establish a session?

   A The CONNECT TO statement.

2. Which option must be used to drop a schema that still contains database objects?

   A The CASCADE option allows the schema to be dropped if there are still objects under that schema.

3. What statement is used to remove a database privilege?

   A The REVOKE statement is used to remove database privileges.

4. What command creates a grouping or collection of tables, views, and privileges?

   A The CREATE SCHEMA statement.

Exercise Answers

1. Describe or list the steps that allow a new employee database access.

   A The immediate supervisor should instigate the request process by completing a user ID request form, which contains all the information necessary to add the user to the database. The form should then be forwarded to the security officer. The user request is then routed to either the database administrator or the individual designated to assist the database administrator with security, so that the user can be added to the database. This is a general process that should be followed and modified accordingly for each company.

Hour 19, "Managing Database Security"

Quiz Answers

1. What option must a user have to grant another user privileges to an object not owned by the user?

   A The GRANT OPTION.

2. When privileges are granted to PUBLIC, do all users of the database acquire the privileges, or just a listing of chosen users?

   A All users of the database will be granted the privileges.

3. What privilege is required to look at data in a specific table?

   A The SELECT privilege.

C

4. What type of privilege is the SELECT privilege?

   A An object-level privilege.

Exercise Answers

1. Write a statement to grant select access on a table called EMPLOYEE_TBL, which you own, to a user ID, RPLEW. It should allow RPLEW to grant privileges to another user on the same table.

   A

   ```
   GRANT SELECT ON EMPLOYEE_TBL TO RPLEW WITH GRANT OPTION;
   ```

2. Write a statement that revokes the connect role from both of the users in Exercise 1.

   A

   ```
   REVOKE CONNECT ON EMPLOYEE_TBL FROM RPLEW;
   ```

3. Write a statement that allows RPLEW to select, insert, and update the EMPLOYEE_TBL table.

   A

   ```
   GRANT SELECT, INSERT, UPDATE ON EMPLOYEE_TBL TO RPLEW;
   ```

Hour 20, "Creating and Using Views and Synonyms"

Quiz Answers

1. Can a row of data be deleted from a view that was created from multiple tables?

   A No. The DELETE, INSERT, and UPDATE commands can only be used on views created from a single table.

2. When creating a table, the owner is automatically granted the appropriate privileges on that table. Is this true when creating a view?

   A Yes. The owner of a view is automatically granted the appropriate privileges on the view.

3. What clause is used to order data when creating a view?

   A The GROUP BY clause functions in a view much as the ORDER BY clause (or GROUP BY clause) does in a regular query.

4. What option can be used, when creating a view from a view, to check integrity constraints?

   A The WITH CHECK OPTION.

5. You try to drop a view and receive an error because there are one or more underlying views. What must you do to drop the view?

   A Re-execute your DROP statement with the CASCADE option. This allows the DROP statement to succeed by also dropping all underlying views.

Exercise Answers

1. Write a statement to create a view based on the total contents of the EMPLOYEE_TBL table.

   A
```
CREATE VIEW EMP_VIEW AS
SELECT * FROM EMPLOYEE_TBL;
```

2. Write a statement that creates a summarized view containing the average pay rate and average salary for each city in the EMPLOYEE_TBL table.

   A
```
CREATE VIEW AVG_PAY_VIEW AS
SELECT E.CITY, AVG(P.PAY_RATE), AVG(P.SALARY)
FROM EMPLOYEE_PAY_TBL P,
EMPLOYEE_TBL E
WHERE P.EMP_ID - E.EMP_ID
GROUP BY E.CITY;
```

3. Write statements that drop the two views that you created in Exercises 1 and 2.

   A
```
DROP VIEW EMP_VIEW
DROP VIEW AVG_PAY_VIEW;
```

Hour 21, "Working with the System Catalog"

Quiz Answers

1. The system catalog is also known as what?

   A The system catalog is also known as the data dictionary.

2. Can a regular user update the system catalog?

   A Not directly; however, when a user creates an object such as a table, the System Catalog is automatically updated.

3. What Sybase system table would be used to retrieve information about views that exist in the database?

   A SYSVIEWS

C

4. Who owns the system catalog?

   A The owner of the system catalog is often a privileged database user account called SYS or SYSTEM. The system catalog can also be owned by the owner of the database, but is not ordinarily owned by a particular schema in the database.

5. What is the difference between the Oracle system objects ALL_TABLES and DBA_TABLES?

   A ALL_TABLES shows all tables that are accessible by a particular user, while DBA_TABLES shows all tables that exist in the database.

6. Who makes modifications to the system tables?

   A The database server itself.

Hour 22, "Advanced SQL Topics"

Quiz Answers

1. Can a trigger be altered?

   A No, the trigger must be replaced or re-created.

2. When a cursor is closed, can you reuse the name?

   A This is implementation-specific. In some implementations, the closing of the cursor will allow you to reuse the name and even free the memory, while for other implementations you must use the DEALLOCATE statement before the name can be reused.

3. What command is used to retrieve the results after a Cursor has been opened?

   A The FETCH command.

4. Are triggers executed before or after an INSERT, DELETE, or UPDATE?

   A Triggers can be executed before or after an INSERT, DELETE, or UPDATE. There are many different types of triggers that can be created.

Exercise Answers

1. Using your implementation's system catalog tables, write the SQL that creates the following SQL statements. Substitute the name of an actual object for the object names.

   a.

   ```
   GRANT SELECT ON TABLE_NAME TO USERNAME;
   ```

A

```
SELECT 'GRANT SELECT ON '||TABLE_NAME|| ' TO '||
USERNAME||';'
FROM SYSTEM CATALOG TABLE_NAME;
```

b.

```
GRANT, CONNECT, RESOURCE TO USERNAME;
```

A

```
SELECT 'GRANT, CONNECT, RESOURCE TO '
||USERNAME||';'
FROM SYSTEM CATALOG TABLE_NAME;
```

c.

```
SELECT COUNT(*) FROM TABLE_NAME;
```

A

```
SELECT 'SELECT COUNT(*) FROM '||TABLE_NAME||';'
FROM SYSTEM CATALOG TABLE_NAME;
```

2. Write a statement to create a stored procedure that deletes an entry from the PRODUCTS_TBL table; it should be similar to the example used in this hour to insert a new product.

   A

   ```
   CREATE PROCEDURE DELETE_PRODUCT
   (OLD_PROD_ID IN VARCHAR2)
   AS
   BEGIN
       DELETE FROM PRODUCTS_TBL
       WHERE PROD_ID = OLD_PROD_ID;
       COMMIT;
   END;
   /
   ```

3. Write a statement that executes the stored procedure that you created in Exercise 2 to delete the row for PROD_ID '9999'.

   A

   ```
   EXECUTE DELETE_PRODUCT ('9999');
   ```

C

Hour 23, "Extending SQL to the Enterprise, the Internet, and the Intranet"

Quiz Answers

1. Can a database on a server be accessed from another server?

   A Yes; by using a middleware product. This is called accessing a remote database.

2. What can a company use to disseminate information to its own employees?

   A An intranet.

3. Products that allow connections to databases are called what?

   A Middleware.

4. Can SQL be embedded into Internet programming languages?

   A Yes. SQL can be embedded in Internet programming languages, such as Java.

5. How is a remote database accessed through a Web application?

   A Via a Web server.

Hour 24, "Extensions to Standard SQL

Quiz Answers

1. Is SQL a procedural or non-procedural language?

   A SQL is non-procedural, meaning that the database decides how to execute the SQL statement. The extensions discussed during this hour were procedural.

2. What are some of the reasons differences in SQL exist?

   A Differences exist in SQL among the vendors because of storage requirements, advantages over competitors, ease of use, and performance considerations.

3. What are the three basic operations of a cursor outside of declaring the cursor?

   A OPEN, FETCH, and CLOSE.

4. Procedural or non-procedural: With which does the database engine decide how to evaluate and execute SQL statements?

   A Non-procedural.

Exercise Answers

1. No specific answer.
2. Using the EMPLOYEE_TBL (see Appendix D), write an interactive SQL statement that returns the name of all employees who have a ZIP code of 46234. (Hint: Refer to the Oracle example in this hour for parameter passing.)

Name	Null	Type
EMP_ID	NOT NULL	VARCHAR2(9)
LAST_NAME	NOT NULL	VARCHAR2(8)
FIRST_NAME	NOT NULL	VARCHAR2(8)
MID_INIT		CHAR(1)
ADDRESS	NOT NULL	VARCHAR2(15)
CITY	NOT NULL	VARCHAR2(12)
STATE	NOT NULL	CHAR(2)
ZIP	NOT NULL	CHAR(5)
PHONE		CHAR(10)
PAGER		CHAR(10)

A

```
SELECT LAST_NAME, FIRST_NAME
FROM EMPLOYEE_TBL
WHERE ZIP = '&ZIP';

Enter value for zip: 46234
old   3: WHERE ZIP = '&ZIP'
new   3: WHERE ZIP = '46234'

Results of Query


LAST_NAM FIRST_NA
_____ _____
SPURGEON TIFFANY

1 row selected.
```

C

3. Be sure to mention your knowledge of SQL in your resume, or in an interview. Knowledge of SQL is usually a plus for many IT positions today. Also, try to practice as much as possible, consistently, to extend your knowledge of SQL and relational databases.

APPENDIX D

CREATE TABLE Statements for Book Examples

This appendix is very useful. The CREATE TABLE statements used in the examples are listed. You can use these statements to create your own tables to query.

EMPLOYEE_TBL

```
CREATE TABLE EMPLOYEE_TBL
{
EMP_ID              VARCHAR2(9)      NOT NULL,
LAST_NAME           VARCHAR2(15)     NOT NULL,
FIRST_NAME          VARCHAR2(15)     NOT NULL,
MIDDLE_NAME         VARCHAR2(15),
ADDRESS             VARCHAR2(30)     NOT NULL,
CITY                VARCHAR2(15)     NOT NULL,
STATE               CHAR(2)          NOT NULL,
ZIP                 NUMBER(5)        NOT NULL,
PHONE               CHAR(10),
PAGER               CHAR(10),
CONSTRAINT EMP_PK PRIMARY KEY (EMP_ID)
}
/
```

EMPLOYEE_PAY_TBL

```
CREATE TABLE EMPLOYEE_PAY_TBL
{
EMP_ID              VARCHAR2(9)      NOT NULL    PRIMARY KEY,
POSITION            VARCHAR2(15)     NOT NULL,
DATE_HIRE           DATE,
PAY_RATE            NUMBER(4,2),
DATE_LAST_RAISE     DATE,
SALARY              NUMBER(8,2),
BONUS               NUMBER(6,2),
CONSTRAINT EMP_FK FOREIGN KEY  (EMP_ID) REFERENCES EMPLOYEE_TBL (EMP_ID)
}
/
```

CUSTOMER_TBL

```
CREATE TABLE CUSTOMER_TBL
}
CUST_ID             VARCHAR2(10)     NOT NULL    PRIMARY KEY,
CUST_NAME           VARCHAR2(30)     NOT NULL,
CUST_ADDRESS        VARCHAR2(20)     NOT NULL,
CUST_CITY           VARCHAR2(15)     NOT NULL,
CUST_STATE          CHAR(2)          NOT NULL,
CUST_ZIP            NUMBER(5)        NOT NULL,
CUST_PHONE          NUMBER(10),
CUST_FAX            NUMBER(10),
}
/
```

ORDERS_TBL

```
CREATE TABLE ORDERS_TBL
{
ORD_NUM             VARCHAR2(10)     NOT NULL    PRIMARY KEY,
CUST_ID             VARCHAR2(10)     NOT NULL,
PROD_ID             VARCHAR2(10)     NOT NULL,
QTY                 NUMBER(6)        NOT NULL,
ORD_DATE            DATE,
}
/
```

PRODUCTS_TBL

```
CREATE TABLE PRODUCTS_TBL
}
PROD_ID             VARCHAR2(10)     NOT NULL    PRIMARY KEY,
PROD_DESC           VARCHAR2(40)     NOT NULL,
COST                NUMBER(6,2)      NOT NULL,
}
/
```

APPENDIX E

INSERT Statements for Data in Book Examples

This appendix contains the INSERT statements that were used to populate the tables that are listed in Appendix D, "CREATE TABLE Statements for Book Examples." These INSERT statements can be used to populate the tables after you create them.

INSERT Statements

EMPLOYEE_TBL

```
INSERT INTO EMPLOYEE_TBL VALUES
('311549902', 'STEPHENS', 'TINA', 'DAWN',  'RR 3 BOX 17A', 'GREENWOOD',
'IN', '47890', '3178784465',  NULL)
/

INSERT INTO EMPLOYEE_TBL VALUES
('442346889', 'PLEW', 'LINDA', 'CAROL', '3301 BEACON', 'INDIANAPOLIS',
'IN', '46224', '3172978990', NULL)
/
```

```
INSERT INTO EMPLOYEE_TBL VALUES
('213764555', 'GLASS', 'BRANDON', 'SCOTT', '1710 MAIN ST', 'WHITELAND',
'IN', '47885', '3178984321', '3175709980')
/

INSERT INTO EMPLOYEE_TBL VALUES
('313782439', 'GLASS', 'JACOB', NULL, '3789 WHITE RIVER BLVD',
'INDIANAPOLIS', 'IN', '45734', '3175457676', '8887345678')
/

INSERT INTO EMPLOYEE_TBL VALUES
('220984332', 'WALLACE', 'MARIAH', NULL, '7889 KEYSTONE AVE',
'INDIANAPOLIS', 'IN', '46741', '3173325986', NULL)
/

INSERT INTO EMPLOYEE_TBL VALUES
('443679012', 'SPURGEON', 'TIFFANY', NULL, '5 GEORGE COURT',
'INDIANAPOLIS', 'IN', '46234', '3175679007', NULL)
/
```

EMPLOYEE_PAY_TBL

```
INSERT INTO EMPLOYEE_PAY_TBL VALUES
('311549902', 'MARKETING', '23-MAY-89', NULL, '01-MAY-99', '40000', NULL)
/

INSERT INTO EMPLOYEE_PAY_TBL VALUES
('442346889', 'TEAM LEADER', '17-JUN-90', '14.75', '01-JUN-99', NULL, NULL)
/

INSERT INTO EMPLOYEE_PAY_TBL VALUES
('213764555', 'SALES MANAGER', '14-AUG-94', NULL, '01-AUG-99', '30000', '2000')
/

INSERT INTO EMPLOYEE_PAY_TBL VALUES
('313782439', 'SALESMAN', '28-JUN-97', NULL, NULL, '20000', '1000')
/

INSERT INTO EMPLOYEE_PAY_TBL VALUES
('220984332', 'SHIPPER', '22-JUL-96', '11.00', '01-JUL-99', NULL, NULL)
/

INSERT INTO EMPLOYEE_PAY_TBL VALUES
('443679012', 'SHIPPER', '14-JAN-91', '15.00', '01-JAN-99', NULL, NULL)
/
```

CUSTOMER_TBL

```
INSERT INTO CUSTOMER_TBL VALUES
('232', 'LESLIE GLEASON', '798 HARDAWAY DR', 'INDIANAPOLIS',
'IN', '47856', '3175457690', NULL)
/
```

```
INSERT INTO CUSTOMER_TBL VALUES
('109', 'NANCY BUNKER', 'APT A 4556 WATERWAY', 'BROAD RIPPLE',
'IN', '47950', '3174262323', NULL)
/

INSERT INTO CUSTOMER_TBL VALUES
('345', 'ANGELA DOBKO', 'RR3 BOX 76', 'LEBANON', 'IN', '49967',
'7658970090', NULL)
/

INSERT INTO CUSTOMER_TBL VALUES
('090', 'WENDY WOLF', '3345 GATEWAY DR', 'INDIANAPOLIS', 'IN',
'46224', '3172913421', NULL)
/

INSERT INTO CUSTOMER_TBL VALUES
('12', 'MARYS GIFT SHOP', '435 MAIN ST', 'DANVILLE', 'IL', '47978',
'3178567221', 3178523434')
/

INSERT INTO CUSTOMER_TBL VALUES
('432', 'SCOTTYS MARKET', 'RR2 BOX 173', 'BROWNSBURG', 'IN',
'45687', '3178529835', '3178529836')
/

INSERT INTO CUSTOMER_TBL VALUES
('333', 'JASONS AND DALLAS GOODIES', 'LAFAYETTE SQ MALL',
'INDIANAPOLIS', 'IN', '46222', '3172978886', '3172978887')
/

INSERT INTO CUSTOMER_TBL VALUES
('21', 'MORGANS CANDIES AND TREATS', '5657 W TENTH ST',
'INDIANAPOLIS', 'IN', '46234', 3172714398', NULL)
/

INSERT INTO CUSTOMER_TBL VALUES
('43', 'SCHYLERS NOVELTIES', '17 MAPLE ST', 'LEBANON', 'IN',
'48990', '3174346758', NULL)
/

INSERT INTO CUSTOMER_TBL VALUES
('287', 'GAVINS PLACE', '9880 ROCKVILLE RD', 'INDIANAPOLIS',
'IN', '46244', '3172719991', 3172719992')
/

INSERT INTO CUSTOMER_TBL VALUES
('288', 'HOLLYS GAMEARAMA', '567 US 31 SOUTH', 'WHITELAND',
'IN', '49980', '3178879023', NULL)
/

INSERT INTO CUSTOMER_TBL VALUES
('590', 'HEATHERS FEATHERS AND THINGS', '4090 N SHADELAND AVE',
'INDIANAPOLIS', 'IN', '43278', '3175456768', NULL)
/
```

```
INSERT INTO CUSTOMER_TBL VALUES
('610', 'RAGANS HOBBIES INC', '451 GREEN ST', 'PLAINFIELD', 'IN',
'46818', '3178393441', 3178399090')
/

INSERT INTO CUSTOMER_TBL VALUES
('560', 'ANDYS CANDIES', 'RR 1 BOX 34', 'NASHVILLE', 'IN',
'48756', '8123239871', NULL)
/

INSERT INTO CUSTOMER_TBL VALUES
('221', 'RYANS STUFF', '2337 S SHELBY ST', 'INDIANAPOLIS', 'IN',
'47834', '3175634402', NULL) .
/
```

ORDERS_TBL

```
INSERT INTO ORDERS_TBL VALUES
('56A901', '232', '11235', '1', '22-OCT-99')
/

INSERT INTO ORDERS_TBL VALUES
('56A917', '12', '907', '100', '30-SEP-99')
/

INSERT INTO ORDERS_TBL VALUES
('32A132', '43', '222', '25', '10-OCT-99')
/

INSERT INTO ORDERS_TBL VALUES
('16C17', '090', '222', '2', '17-OCT-99')
/

INSERT INTO ORDERS_TBL VALUES
('18D778', '287', '90', '10', '17-OCT-99')
/

INSERT INTO ORDERS_TBL VALUES
('23E934', '432', '13', '20', '15-OCT-99')
/
```

PRODUCTS_TBL

```
INSERT INTO PRODUCTS_TBL VALUES
('11235', 'WITCHES COSTUME', '29.99')
/

INSERT INTO PRODUCTS_TBL VALUES
('222', 'PLASTIC PUMPKIN 18 INCH', '7.75')
/

INSERT INTO PRODUCTS_TBL VALUES
('13', 'FALSE PARAFFIN TEETH', '1.10')
/
```

```
INSERT INTO PRODUCTS_TBL VALUES
('90', 'LIGHTED LANTERNS', '14.50')
/

INSERT INTO PRODUCTS_TBL VALUES
('15', 'ASSORTED COSTUMES', '10.00')
/

INSERT INTO PRODUCTS_TBL VALUES
('9', 'CANDY CORN', '1.35')
/

INSERT INTO PRODUCTS_TBL VALUES
('6', 'PUMPKIN CANDY', '1.45')
/

INSERT INTO PRODUCTS_TBL VALUES
('87', 'PLASTIC SPIDERS', '1.05')
/

INSERT INTO PRODUCTS_TBL VALUES
('119', 'ASSORTED MASKS', '4.95')
/
```

APPENDIX F

Glossary

alias   Another name or term for a table or column.

ANSI   American National Standards Institute.

application   A set of menus, forms, reports, and code that performs a business function using a database.

buffer   An area in memory for editing or execution of SQL.

Cartesian product   The result of not joining tables in the WHERE clause of an SQL statement. When tables in a query are not joined, every row in one table is paired with every row in all other tables.

client   The client is typically a PC, but can be another server that is dependent on another computer for data, services, or processing.

column   A part of a table that has a name and a specific data type.

COMMIT   Makes changes to data permanent.

composite index   An index that is composed of two or more columns.

condition   Search criteria in a query's WHERE clause that evaluates to TRUE or FALSE.

constant   A value that does not change.

constraint   Restrictions on data that are enforced at the data level.

cursor   A work area in memory where the current SQL statement is stored.

data dictionary   Another name for the System Catalog. See *system catalog*.

data type   Defines data as type, such as number, date, or character.

database   A collection of data.

DBA   Database Administrator. An individual who manages a database.

DDL   Data Definition Language.

default   A value used when no specification has been made.

distinct   Unique; used in the SELECT clause to return unique values.

DML   Data Manipulation Language.

domain   An object that is associated with a data type to which constraints may be attached; similar to a user-defined type.

DQL   Data Query Language.

end user   Users whose jobs require them to query or manipulate data in the database. The end user is the individual for which the database exists.

field   Another name for a column in a table. See *column*.

foreign key   One or more columns whose values are based on the primary key column values in another table.

full table scan   The search of a table from a query without the use of an index.

function   An operation that is predefined and can be used in an SQL statement to manipulate data.

GUI   Graphical User Interface.

host   The computer on which a database is located.

index   Pointers to table data that make access to a table more efficient.

join   Combines data from different tables by linking columns. Used in the WHERE clause of an SQL statement.

key   A column or columns that identify rows of a table.

normalization   Designing a database to reduce redundancy by breaking large tables down into smaller, more manageable tables.

NULL value   A value that is unknown.

objects   Elements in a database, such as triggers, tables, views, and procedures.

operator   A reserved word or symbol used to perform an operation, such as addition or subtraction.

optimizer   Part of the database that decides how to execute an SQL statement and return an answer.

parameter   A value or range of values that is used to resolve a part of an SQL statement or program.

primary key   A specified table column that uniquely identifies rows of the table.

privilege   Specific permissions that are granted to users to perform a specific action in the database.

procedure   A set of instructions that are saved for repeated calling and execution.

public   A database user account that represents all database users.

query   An SQL statement that is used to retrieve data from a database.

record   See *row*.

referential integrity   Assures that values from one column depend on the values from another column.

relational database   A database that is organized into tables that consist of rows, which contain the same sets of data items, where tables in the database are related to one another through common keys.

role   A database object that is associated with a group of system and/or object privileges, used to simplify security management.

ROLLBACK   A command that undoes all transactions since the last COMMIT or SAVEPOINT command issued.

row   Sets of records in a table.

savepoint   A specified point in a transaction to which you can roll back or undo changes.

schema   The owner of a set of objects in a database.

F

security   The process of ensuring that data in a database is fully protected at all times.

SQL   Structured Query Language.

stored procedure   SQL code that is stored in a database and ready to execute.

subquery   A SELECT statement embedded within another SQL statement.

synonym   Another name given to a table or view.

syntax for SQL   A set of rules that shows mandatory and optional parts of an SQL statement's construction.

system catalog   Collection of tables or views that contain information about the database.

table   The basic logical storage unit for data in a relational database.

transaction   One or more SQL statements that are executed as a single unit.

trigger   A stored procedure that executes upon specified events in a database, such as before or after an update of a table.

user-defined type   A data type that is defined by a user, which can be used to define table columns.

variable   A value that does not remain constant.

view   A database object that is created from one or more tables and can be used the same as a table. A view is a virtual table that has no storage requirements of its own.

INDEX